Who Owns the Sky?

——————— Who Owns the Sky?

THE STRUGGLE TO CONTROL AIRSPACE

FROM THE WRIGHT BROTHERS ON

Stuart Banner

HARVARD UNIVERSITY PRESS

CAMBRIDGE, MASSACHUSETTS

LONDON, ENGLAND

2008

Library of Congress Cataloging-in-Publication Data

Banner, Stuart, 1963–
    Who owns the sky? : the struggle to control airspace from the Wright
brothers on / Stuart Banner.
        p.   cm.
    Includes bibliographical references and index.
    ISBN 978-0-674-03082-4 (cloth : alk. paper)
    1. Aeronautics—Law and legislation—United States.   2. Airspace
(Law)—United States.   I. Title.
    KF2400.B36 2008
    343.7309'7—dc22   2008012633

CONTENTS

Introduction

An entire book about how the invention of airplanes changed our ideas about who owned the air?

Well, yes and no. That *is* the narrative thread that holds the chapters together, but this book is actually about much more—how lawyers understood the law and its origins, and how that understanding changed over time; why new fields of law form in some areas but not others; how the legal system responds to technological change; and a host of other things besides. The history of aerial trespass may sound like the perfect topic for an absurdly arcane monograph in a comic novel of academic life, and I suppose one could write it that way, but there are many worlds to be seen in this particular grain of sand. I have tried to find them.

It's not what I set out to do. When I started I knew only two relevant events. One was the Wright brothers' first flight in 1903. The other was a 1946 case called *United States v. Causby*, in which the Supreme Court decided that repeated very-low overflights infringed on the property rights of the landowner beneath. It seemed odd to me that the two events were separated by more than forty years. Surely, I thought, the issue had to have come up before 1946. In all that time, someone must have written something about it. I figured I'd do a quick check to see what there was.

I stumbled upon a massive literature. Lots of people had written about aerial trespass, beginning even before the Wright brothers flew, and not ending until well after the Supreme Court decided *Causby*. And they came from all walks of life. Most were lawyers, of course, but the subject was of interest to anyone who cared about airplanes, and almost everyone cared about airplanes. There were arguments over aerial trespass in newspapers, in magazines, in journals for aviation enthusiasts, in books—just about everywhere. Aerial trespass figured in novels, in poetry, and in political philosophy. Whether airplanes were trespassers was, understandably, a question of considerable importance in the early years of flight. The invention of the airplane sparked a debate that lasted for decades, a debate that has been almost completely forgotten today.

As I waded through all this material, it didn't take long to realize that the issue of aerial trespass was connected to much of what was going on in the law generally during the first half of the twentieth century. Airplanes were the Forrest Gump of legal history. They had a small role to play in many of the big stories of the period, from the growing power of Congress over the national economy to the rise of private quasi-lawmaking organizations like the American Law Institute, from the spread of the belief that judges make law rather than find it to the emergence of new kinds of academic expertise, from the changing internal norms of the U.S. Supreme Court to the transition from a multipolar international legal order to the bipolar confrontation of the cold war. This book is, in one sense, an intellectual history of American law in the first half of the twentieth century, told from the perspective of a bit player.

In another sense it is a collection of nutty anecdotes. When aerial trespass was viewed as a genuine problem, people proposed all sorts of solutions, in all seriousness, that sound laughable today. How about requiring airplanes to fly above streets? Or using the government's power of eminent domain to condemn air routes above private land? Or designating the airspace a zone free of national sovereignty, like the ocean, within which aviators of all nations could pass without permission from a government below? Or solving the problem of inconsistent state law with kites, to mark state lines where pilots could see them? A big part of history's charm, at least for me, is the fun of trying to recover a way of thinking in which proposals like these could seem reasonable.

And in a third sense the book is an extended case study of the relationship between technological change and legal change. We all have a vague sense that the law responds to changing technology, and with a little reflection we can all summon examples—in the past industrialization gave rise to new law governing things like accidents and employment, today advances in biotechnology are prompting debates about the ownership and uses of genetic material, and so on. But the questions of how and why technological change leads to legal change are explicitly studied only rarely, and even more rarely with much attention to historical detail. We changed our property law because of the airplane; that much can be stated in a sentence. But how we changed it, and why we changed it—to answer questions like that, you need a whole book.

ONE

A Momentous Problem

As the twentieth century began, every week seemed to bring astonishing news of progress toward human flight. After thousands of years in which men and women looked skyward and dreamed of flying, the conquest of the air seemed imminent. A new era was about to begin. Daring aviators in Europe and North America were risking their lives to claim the honor of being first to fly.

Charles C. Moore was not one of them. Moore was a cautious man. He was a lawyer, an employee of the Edward Thompson Law Book Company of Northport, New York. His job was to write entries for Edward Thompson's legal digests and encyclopedias. These reference works were much more important to the profession in the precomputer era than they are now, but they were also much more tedious to produce. While the Wright brothers were experimenting with gliders on the Outer Banks of North Carolina, Moore sat in his office near the Long Island Sound compiling *The Federal Statutes Annotated,* a listing of every published American court opinion in which a federal statute was mentioned. As European aviators astonished the world with dirigible balloons, Moore was one of a stable of lawyers grinding out *The American and English Encyclopedia of Law,* a thirty-two-volume arrangement of brief summaries of decided cases. Even here, Moore took the safer route. Rather than risking inaccuracy in his entries, he often copied them word for word from the summaries already included in the reports of the cases issued by one of Edward Thompson's competitors, the West Publishing Company.

When Moore finally published a work of his own, he remained in his well-worn groove. Moore's own magnum opus, the only individually authored book of his career, was his two-volume *Treatise on Facts, or, The Weight and Value of Evidence.* The book appeared in 1908, as the Wrights were flying figure eights above France for several minutes at time. For more than sixteen hundred pages Moore followed the convention of the genre in scrupulously abstaining from offering any thoughts of his own. Instead he amassed and classified thousands of judicial opinions lawyers could use in their arguments to support propositions like "Sounds plainly audible are presumed to have been heard" or "Estimates of speed are necessarily inexact." A man who no doubt prided himself on his treatise's lack of creativity or high-flown theory, Moore must have been gratified at its reception among its intended audience of trial lawyers. The treatise became widely known by the no-nonsense nickname "Moore on Facts."

After two decades of this sort of work, Moore left the Edward Thompson Law Book Company, but not because he had wearied of legal encyclopedias. He moved to one of Edward Thompson's competitors, the American Law Book Company in nearby Brooklyn, publishers of the forty-volume *Cyclopedia of Law and Procedure.* Moore retired at sixty-eight after a career of summarizing other people's writing. When he died three years later of pneumonia, Charles Lindbergh had already flown across the Atlantic. Moore merited a short obituary in the *New York Times,* in a position less prominent than that of the president of a Louisville bank but above several others, including a district manager for the Westchester Lighting Company, a veteran of the Spanish-American War, and the founder of a Hackensack shoe store.[1]

But if Charles C. Moore was no aviator, he liked to read about them, and it was his reading—along with his characteristic caution—that gave Moore his modest place in the history of aviation. Moore was the first American lawyer to notice a legal problem that would become a major issue among lawyers in the early years of flight. In the summer of 1900 the New York papers reported the experiments of the retired German general Ferdinand Graf von Zeppelin, who flew a 420-foot hydrogen-filled dirigible for eighteen minutes above Lake Constance. Most readers probably marveled at Zeppelin's feat of engineering or wondered about the future of transportation in an aerial age. Not Charles C. Moore. He was too prudent for that. Where others saw potential, Moore saw a potential problem. He immediately wrote a short essay for *Law Notes,* the lawyers' magazine published by the Edward Thompson Law Book Company.

Moore pointed out that under principles of Anglo-American common law, the owner of land also owned the space above the land, with no height limit. As the ancient maxim put it, *cujus est solum ejus est usque ad coelum*—he who owns the soil owns up to the sky. With virtually all land owned by someone, where could an airship fly? It would be trespassing everywhere it went. Would every landowner along an aerial route be entitled to damages for trespass? Others less careful than Charles C. Moore might thrill to the possibility of aerial navigation, but there was a legal obstacle that had to be surmounted before anyone could fly very far.

In Moore's tone, however, there was a sense of fun at odds with the serious nature of his warning. He found room, within his discussion of the nature of Anglo-American property law, for a joke about the inventor Nikola Tesla. (Not a great joke. About Tesla's view that travel by dirigible was imminent, Moore said: "Mr. Tes-

la's predictions never lack buoyancy.") While observing that flying machines would need parachutes for their passengers just
like steamships needed life jackets, Moore included a parentheti-
cal note about a supposed recent federal regulation requiring "improved breeches buoys specially adapted for use at life-saving stations in rescuing bashful women from stranded ships." (Again,
not a great joke. A breeches buoy was a ring-shaped flotation device with breeches—short trousers—attached. The buoy was at
the end of a long rope and was used to pull survivors from ship-
wrecks. Moore apparently intended to refer humorously to a requirement that the breeches be a certain length.) He repeated a
witticism of the popular late nineteenth-century journalist Bill
Nye, who, when asked about the propriety of boarding or alight-
ing from a moving railroad car, responded "first consult your pas-
tor," advice Moore found funny enough to recommend to airship
passengers of the future.

Moore was an encyclopedia man, not a humorist, and these efforts show why. But he clearly found something amusing in the
relationship of air travel and property law. The mismatch between
his light tone and his serious message suggests he harbored some
ambivalence about the importance of the legal question he had
identified. On one hand, if one took the wording of the standard
legal authorities seriously, aerial trespass would be a genuine problem. The promise of air travel might never be realized, because
pilots would have to pay for the privilege of using the airspace of
all the landowners below. On the other hand, it was hard to imagine such a problem actually stifling the development of air transportation. Lawyers knew better than anyone how malleable the
law could be. If commercial air travel ever became technically feasible, surely it would be possible to overcome the objections of the
people who owned the land beneath.

Or would it? If landowners also owned the airspace, how exactly would pilots get the right to fly through it? To nonlawyers the issue may have seemed trivial, but Charles C. Moore knew it was not. Just as aviators were on the brink of conquering the air, he worried that the law would drag them back to earth.[2]

Over the next several years, some of the lawyers who followed Moore's lead shared his jocular tone, as if they too could not fully bring themselves to believe that the problem of aerial trespass could ever be a serious one. In the spring of 1902, when Francis Baker was appointed to the federal court of appeals, the Chicago Bar Association held a banquet in his honor, at which Baker gave the customary lighthearted after-dinner speech. The French-Brazilian pilot Alberto Santos-Dumont had recently delighted Parisians by circling the Eiffel Tower in a dirigible, earning worldwide fame for walking out onto his ship and making repairs midflight, without a parachute or any other safety gear. Baker mentioned Santos-Dumont, along with another recent inventor whose work promised to transform the world, in a catalog of what he jested were problems of "the uncommon law," to distinguish them from the humdrum common-law issues faced by ordinary lawyers. Baker declared: "Whether or not the use of a right of way a thousand feet above the surface of the earth by Marconi's wireless telegraphy, or Santos-Dumont's transcontinental line of airships, will be an appropriation of land, the title to which exists *usque ad coelum,* is still a problem of the uncommon law." After an evening of drink, the assembled lawyers of Chicago no doubt chuckled in amusement at both notions—that zeppelins would ever fly coast to coast, and that such flights or the transmission of radio waves could ever be considered a trespass.[3]

The New York litigator Arthur F. Gotthold had read about Santos-Dumont's exploits as well. He found it "monstrous to suppose that M. Santos-Dumont must respond in damages for a technical trespass to the owner of every house over which his machine may pass." He knew that landowners were often said to own the space above their land, and he thought it fine that the owner of a house should have the exclusive privilege of mooring an airship to his own flagpole, but not the exclusive right to use the air above. Like Moore and Baker, however, Gotthold was having some fun. His observations on the legal problems associated with the new airships were published in *The Green Bag*, which billed itself as "an entertaining magazine for lawyers." He prefaced them with a jovial remark: "In these days when two out of three practising lawyers write text-books out of office hours, and the third dictates legal monographs before breakfast, it is rare to find a question, the answer to which will not be found in Somebody on Something." After covering the issues airships might raise, he concluded that "a careful study of the lives and works of Aurora, Icarus, Phaeton and Darius Green fail to shed any light on the intricacies of the situation." (In John Townsend Trowbridge's widely anthologized 1869 comic poem *Darius Green and His Flying-Machine,* Green crashes to earth after attempting to fly.) The problem of aerial trespass was serious and funny at the same time. It seemed absurd that a technical property rule about the ownership of the air could ground the incipient aircraft industry. But it seemed possible nonetheless.[4]

It was a St. Louis lawyer named Eugene Angert who most fully exploited this combination of absurdity and gravity. In the later years of his life Angert would enjoy some prominence in St. Louis: he served on the boards of directors of a bank and an insurance company, he was one of the founders of the St. Louis Horticulture Society, and he was a regular speaker at bar meetings. A couple of years before he died from poisoning after having a hair removed from his nose, Angert was the toastmaster at a dinner held for Charles Lindbergh when Lindbergh returned to St. Louis after his transatlantic flight. In 1907, Angert was a young lawyer with a literary bent and an interest in the new flying machines, an interest most likely sparked by the 1904 World's Fair, which had included an aeronautical exhibition that brought most of the world's leading aviators to St. Louis.[5]

Angert wrote a mock retrospective called *A Closed Chapter in Aeritime Law*, a look back from 1975 at how the law of trespass had stifled air transportation. A New York court had held in the 1930s that an airship was a trespasser on the land beneath, Angert explained. The landowner was accordingly entitled to damages—tiny damages, to be sure, but damages nonetheless. That decision unleashed a flood of litigation, as landowners all over the country brought suits against the new airfreight companies. The damages in each case were so small that the landowners themselves had no incentive to file these suits. They were financed instead by the railroads, as a weapon in their battle against the airships for supremacy in freight transportation. Clogging the courts with minute claims for damages proved ineffectual, however, so railroad attorneys turned to a new tactic. They filed suits seeking injunctions on behalf of landowners, court orders that would prevent aircraft from flying over their land.

For a time these suits were successful, and the airships were effectively grounded, but then the lawyers for the aircraft companies fought back. Public opinion was on their side. They were able to persuade the legislatures of all sixty-six states to enact statutes conferring upon airship companies the states' power of eminent domain, which authorized the companies to condemn air routes across private land. The airship companies had to compensate the landowners, of course, but the value of the property right taken was in most cases very small. A single condemnation action was enough to dispose forever of the claims of any given landowner. In 1940 Congress centralized the procedure by providing that when an air company filed a proposed route, the filing would automatically terminate the airspace rights of all landowners beneath. Each landowner would receive one penny in compensation. Angert imagined that a closely divided Supreme Court eventually found this procedure unconstitutional, but by then all the railroads had gone out of business, having lost their competition with the airships. Trespass litigation ground to a halt, because without railroad backing no landowner would go to the expense of litigating. The airlines had won.

Angert's story was both amusing and entirely plausible. The legal details were exactly right, as were the motivations he ascribed to the key players—the landowners, the railroads, and the airship companies. The verisimilitude of the details suggested Angert had a serious purpose in writing his essay, but he made that purpose explicit only in his very last sentence. From the perspective of 1975 his story "was truly a closed chapter of aeritime law," but attending to it was nevertheless important, "because it presents a situation in which the protection of a merely theoretical legal right was resorted to as the means of destroying the practical value of the greatest invention in the history of the world." Laugh all you want to, Angert was saying, but watch out, because if the lawyers weren't careful they might put an end to aviation before it began.[6]

It wasn't long before the question of aerial trespass stopped being funny.

Some had taken the problem seriously from the beginning. In 1903, a month before the Wright brothers' first successful powered flight, the *Youth's Companion* was already warning its enthusiastic readers about trespass. "Before one buys his flying-machine—inventors are promising to put them on the market soon—one should arrange first for a place in which to fly," the magazine explained. "'Free as air' is a common saying, but when one desires to use another man's air he finds that, like many other common sayings, this one is only partly true. It is a principle of law that he who owns the land owns it up to the skies, and may forbid trespass in the air above as well as in the earth beneath."[7]

By the end of the decade many others were treating the problem just as gravely. "What would happen," wondered the authors of a 1910 guide to the construction and operation of flying machines, if realty owners "should prohibit the navigation of the air above their holdings?" A justice of the peace in New Jersey, for example, had placed a large sign on the roof of his house warning aviators not to fly over his land. He had every right to exclude flying machines from his airspace, the authors conceded, because unfortunately "the owner of realty also owns the sky above it without limit as to distance." And this New Jersey judge was not the only one preparing to take action against aerial trespassers. In Massachusetts, a group of florists threatened to go to court for an injunction barring aviators from conducting an exhibition involving flight over their greenhouses, for fear that a crash or even something inadvertently dropped from above might destroy valuable plants. They backed down only when the aviators posted a bond to indemnify them in case of an accident. When a group of lawyers in Rochester, New York, convened a moot court to decide whether an airplane committed trespass by flying over a plaintiff's land, the lawyers unanimously concluded that it did.[8]

Some, to be sure, continued to laugh at the notion of trespass by airplane. When the Georgia lawyer Gus Edwards heard about the sign on the roof of the New Jersey justice of the peace, he thought the story funny enough to include in his compilation of amusing anecdotes for lawyers to tell to juries. "To those who have not studied the extremely interesting range of new possibilities and new problems opened up by the suddenly developing science of flying this may seem far-fetched and rather farcical," *Harper's Weekly* acknowledged in 1909. "But it is the serious, thoughtful opinion of experts and men very learned in the law" that airplanes would be trespassing on the land beneath. One of those learned men was James Watson Gerard, a trial judge in New York (and soon to be ambassador to Germany in the period just before the United States entered World War I). Gerard found it obvious that landowners owned the air above their property and could do just as they pleased with it. They might permit aircraft to use the air, or they might prohibit them. In the United States and England, *Harper's* concluded, "aviators, experimenters, and capitalists who invested in the fascinating new game—comprising a body of thousands of clear-minded men as against hundreds of even a year ago—acknowledge that they have no idea of what their legal rights are." There had not yet been any actual trespass suits against pilots, but that was just a matter of time. Until the issue could be resolved by the courts, "all this is literally 'up in the air.'"[9]

Indeed, by 1910 there was already a considerable body of opinion to the effect that flying machines were trespassers on the land beneath. Alfred Gandy Reeves was a specialist in property law at New York Law School and the author of a two-volume treatise on the subject. "When the lawyer thinks of land," Reeves lectured, "he must immeasurably enlarge upon the ordinary, lay conception of it and make it include everything of which his physical senses might give him knowledge, from the centre of the earth upward into unlimited space." The logical implication was that "he who, without my permission, digs into my soil a thousand feet below the surface, . . . or flies in an air-ship thousands of feet above it, is guilty of trespass." That was simply the nature of land ownership in the United States, agreed the inventor and writer Melvin Severy.[10]

The Cincinnati lawyer George Platt noted that the novelty of flight caused landowners to be indulgent to the occasional aircraft overhead, but that as the novelty wore off and overflights became more frequent, landowners' attitude would surely change. When it did, the pilots would be in trouble. "Having paid the taxes and other charges of the state and observed the building laws, the owner of land is therefore monarch of all he surveys," Platt insisted, "and his land is surrounded by an invisible but ideal legal barrier, extending indefinitely upwards and downwards, beyond which no one may go, unless it be with the owner's consent." He concluded that flight would be legally possible only if—just as Eugene Angert had half-jokingly predicted a few years before— the state were to use its power of eminent domain to condemn air routes, with appropriate compensation paid to the landowners beneath.[11]

In England, meanwhile, the journal *Engineering* paused from its usual technical articles to fret about the law of trespass. "Whether he does damage or not," an unsigned editorial worried, "the aeroplanist might be restrained by injunction from passing over private property." Such an outcome seemed harsh, the editorial explained, but it was necessary, because if a single airplane overhead was not a trespasser, what relief could a landowner have if his skies were infested with them? "Why should they not come until the whole sky is darkened? Take the case of a man who lives near a place where experiments are being tried with these machines. Must he submit to their flying over his land *de die in diem* without being able to raise his voice in protest?"[12]

The English lawyer H. G. Meyer hoped landowners would not file lawsuits against aviators, but he had no doubt they would win if they did. It was a simple exercise in logic. The law was clear that the owner of land also owned the air above and the earth below, without limit. When miners tunneled below the land of another, that was an obvious instance of trespass, and many courts had so labeled it. Why should use of the air be any different? A landowner might not suffer any actual damage when a plane flew overhead, but all lawyers knew that damage was not a prerequisite to an action for trespass. Stepping onto someone else's land without permission might not cause any damage either, but it was still trespass. Meyer came to the reluctant conclusion that pilots would have to rely on the forbearance of landowners if they were to fly over private property.[13]

That thought understandably made aviators uncomfortable. Baden Baden-Powell, a former military balloonist, was the president of the Royal Aeronautical Society and an aeronautical experimenter in his own right. (His older brother Robert was the founder of the Boy Scouts.) The clash between property rights and aviation was "a momentous problem for legislators," Baden-Powell declared. What if a property owner decided to exercise his right to exclude overflights by building wire fences on high poles? There would be some nasty accidents, he predicted, unless the laws were changed quickly.[14]

But high wire fences were hardly necessary—the mere threat of litigation would be enough to ground aircraft, others feared. "At present," the Scottish barrister Roger Wallace explained in 1909, "nobody has the right to fly across occupied land." Wallace was chairman of the Royal Aero Club, so his views presumably carried some weight with British aviators, who were nearly all members. Thus far no one had attempted to put their property rights into action, but Wallace anticipated that the first trespass suits would be coming soon, from people whose land bordered on airfields and who would accordingly suffer the lowest and most frequent overflights. The *Los Angeles Times* imagined a different class of plaintiffs—families accustomed to sunbathing or sleeping on the roof in the hot summer, in privacy. Should pilots have the right to fly over and look down? In only a few years, the question of who owned the air had changed from a joke to a serious problem. "This question, which until recently has been purely academic, is now arising in connection with the probable increased use of appliances for aerial navigation," the *Literary Digest* explained to its large American readership.[15] The air looked boundless to the ordinary observer, but not to lawyers, who knew that Anglo-American law drew invisible property lines in the sky.

Before the airplane, how could there have been law governing the ownership of airspace?

The earliest known English cases, one in 1598 and another in 1610, involved landowners sued, successfully, by their neighbors for building houses that overhung the property line. These aggressive builders were not trespassing on any of their neighbors' ground, but they were liable nevertheless. Accounts of the two cases were published in the reports compiled by Chief Justice Edward Coke, who included a summary of the relevant principle in his widely used early seventeenth-century *Institutes of the Laws of England*. "The earth hath in law a great extent upwards," Coke explained. Land was not just a two-dimensional surface; it included "ayre and all other things even up to heaven; for *cujus est solum ejus est usque ad coelum*." William Blackstone repeated the principle in his *Commentaries on the Laws of England*, the standard reference work for English and American lawyers for more than a century after its initial publication in the 1760s. "Land hath also, in its legal signification, an indefinite extent, upwards as well as downwards," he noted, in words that would echo through judicial opinions on both sides of the Atlantic. "So that the word 'land' includes not only the face of the earth, but every thing under it, or over it."[16]

The nineteenth century saw a proliferation of legal treatises in England and the United States. Many were about property law, and virtually all of them included some version of the *cujus est solum* maxim, typically with a citation to Coke or Blackstone.[17] The three-dimensional nature of land was accordingly common knowledge among lawyers. If a man owned what looked like a circular parcel of land, one American lawyers' magazine explained in the 1860s, his true holding was shaped like a cone, with its apex at the center of the earth and its base at some undefined height. The parcel's apparent circular boundary was merely the intersection of the earth's surface with his conical property.[18]

Builders on both sides of the Atlantic constructed eaves, bay windows, and lopsided houses that leaned over into the neighbors' airspace all through the nineteenth century, acts that resulted in a steady stream of cases in which courts reaffirmed that the air above belonged to the owner of the land below. "The law says the land is his even to the sky, and therefore he has a right to it," declared one Vermont judge in 1888, after the plaintiff's neighbor had projected his roof slightly over the property line, sixteen feet above the plaintiff's land. When Augustus and Caroline Reimer built a bay window out over Broad Street in Philadelphia, or when Robert Woodcock of Grand Rapids, Michigan, refurbished his barn with a cornice that extended over Ada Wilmarth's land, judges ordered the offending structures to be torn down. When L. D. Gulley sold to A. M. Shrago a vacant lot in the business district of Goldsboro, North Carolina, and Shrago discovered that the wall of Gulley's own store next door was not perpendicular to the ground but leaned over Shrago's lot nearly four inches at the top, Shrago was allowed to rescind the purchase on the theory that Gulley did not actually convey what he had promised. As an

English judge put it, "the ordinary rule of law is, that whoever has got the solum—whoever has got the site—is the owner of everything up to the sky."[19]

Trees planted near property lines sometimes grew branches over them, and while so little was at stake in the ensuing disputes that they were rarely litigated long enough to appear in the published case reports, there was nevertheless a jurisprudence of trespassing tree branches as well. By the end of the century it was clear that adjoining landowners had every right to chop them off. "It may be, and probably is, generally a very unneighbourly act to cut down the branches of overhanging trees," cautioned Farrer Herschell, Britain's lord chancellor, when the issue reached the House of Lords. But when branches trespassed in one's airspace, the law allowed what common courtesy did not. "I think it is clear that a man is not bound to permit a neighbour's tree to overhang the surface of his land," agreed Lord Macnaghten. "That, I think, is the good sense of the matter." In Connecticut and New York, hungry neighbors with clever lawyers used the *cujus est solum* maxim to argue for their right to eat fruit growing in their own airspace on branches of their neighbors' trees. If the ownership of land included everything above the surface, they reasoned, didn't that make them owners of the fruit? No, answered the highest courts of both states, following English precedent. Whoever owned the tree owned the fruit as well. When A's dog ran onto B's land, that was a trespass too, but B didn't become the owner of the dog. But if the neighbors couldn't pick the fruit, there was no doubt that they could cut down the branches. Overhanging trees, like overhanging buildings, were aerial trespassers.[20]

Even bullets could be trespassers. In 1878, when a reader of the hunting magazine *Game Bag and Gun* asked about the laws of trespass, another reader—a lawyer in Philadelphia—responded with some advice. If a hunter stands on his own land and fires a shot, he explained, the shot amounts to a trespass against all the property owners whose land the shot crosses, even in the air. The question had not yet arisen in a reported American case, but when it did, the Philadelphia lawyer's advice proved to be sound. As Chief Justice Llewellyn Callaway of the Montana Supreme Court reasoned, a shot fired by a hunter across another's land was "a technical trespass at least," because, according to Blackstone, "whoever owns the land possesses all the space upwards to an indefinite extent." Callaway recognized that "the subject is not without difficulty" and that it would shortly "become one of considerable importance" because of "the rapid approach of the airplane as an instrumentality of commerce." Nevertheless, "it seems to be the consensus of the courts in this country that the airspace, at least near the ground, is almost as inviolable as the soil itself."[21]

By the later part of the century, the *cujus est solum* principle was so ingrained in the thinking of Anglo-American judges that they applied it reflexively to virtually all encroachments into a landowner's airspace. In an English case involving two farms separated by a wire fence, the defendant's horse kicked the plaintiff's mare through the fence. The plaintiff was awarded damages because of the trespass that took place when the horse's foot crossed above the property line. "This may be a very small trespass," Lord Coleridge reasoned, "but it is a trespass in law." In the spring of 1898, a feud between neighboring Iowa families erupted in mild violence, when Anna Hannabalson reached over the fence and George Sessions punched her on the arm. Sessions did no wrong, the Iowa Supreme Court concluded, because he was defending his property against a trespasser. "The mere fact that plaintiff did not step across the boundary line does not make her any less a trespasser," Judge Silas Weaver pointed out. "It is one of the oldest rules of property known to the law that the title of the owner of the soil extends, not only downward to the center of the earth, but upward *usque ad coelum,* although it is, perhaps, doubtful whether owners as quarrelsome as the parties in this case will ever enjoy the usufruct of their property in the latter direction." For lawyers, land was not flat. It was a solid, not a surface, with its boundaries formed not by lines but by vertical planes of infinite height.[22] Trespass in the air was trespass all the same.

A few technological innovations in the nineteenth century gave rise to new uses of the air, but they were easily assimilated to the old rules governing airspace.

Many of the telegraph wires that sprouted all through the century were located above public roads, with the government's permission, so that the telegraph companies would not have to compensate private landowners for the loss of either their airspace or the ground area occupied by poles. When telegraph lines were constructed on private property, it was nearly always along rights of way owned by railroads, who either granted permission to the telegraph companies or had those rights taken from them by the government under the power of eminent domain. The resulting grid of telegraph wires avoided virtually all other privately owned airspace, because it was generally understood that wires could not cross through a landowner's air without his permission (or compensation from the government after an exercise of eminent domain), even wires stretched across a parcel untouched by any pole. "There is no distinction between the occupying land, by passing through a fixed point of space in the air to another fixed point, or by passing in the same manner through land or water," one English judge explained in 1855, in the midst of holding that a telegraph company could be taxed on its property just like any landowner. "Land extends upwards as well as downwards."[23]

When telephone companies began stringing wires overhead toward the end of the century, the same principle applied. In 1903, for example, the Frontier Telephone Company of Buffalo, New York, slanted a thin wire high across a lot belonging to Ernest Butler, from a spot twenty feet above the ground on the west side of Butler's parcel up to thirty feet above the ground on the east side. The New York Court of Appeals had no trouble treating telephone wires just like overhanging eaves. "Was the space occupied by the wire part of the land in the eye of the law?" asked Judge Irving G. Vann. Of course it was. "The plaintiff as the owner of the soil owned upward to an indefinite extent. He owned the space occupied by the wire." Vann reinforced his conclusion with a series of increasingly alarming hypothetical cases. He imagined that the wire had been a huge cable, several inches thick, and just a foot above the ground. Such a trespass would clearly have interfered with Butler's possession of his land. And what if the wire had been a beam supported by posts on the neighbors' parcels? Or a bridge across Butler's yard? And what if the Frontier Telephone Company built a house on the bridge, a house that touched none of Butler's soil? If the thin telephone wire wasn't a dispossession of Butler's airspace, by what principle could a court order the bridge-house torn down? Where could we draw the line? Telephone wires, like telegraph wires, had to be fit into a legal environment in which most of the airspace was already owned by someone.[24]

So did elevated railroads. New York built several, beginning in 1868, and then many cities followed suit, including Chicago in 1892. There were several reasons to locate elevated railways above streets rather than above buildings or vacant lots, one of which was to minimize construction costs. As the New York lawyer Theodore Demarest explained in his review of the legal issues confronting the elevated railroad, had the tracks been built above private property, the cost of compensating the owners would have

Elevated railroads, like telephone and telegraph wires, had to fit into a
legal landscape in which airspace was owned by the owner of the land
beneath. That was one reason to build them above public streets, as in
this view of the Bowery in New York City, photographed in 1900.
LC-USZ62-55950, Prints and Photographs Division, Library of
Congress.

been prohibitive. A Chicago railway company learned this the
hard way, by building four feet of track fourteen feet above an al-
ley belonging to Warren Springer. Springer sued for damages and
was awarded $61,000, or well over $1 million today. The Illinois
Supreme Court had no patience for the railroad's argument that it

had done nothing wrong merely by using Springer's airspace. "A statement of that proposition is a refutation of itself," the Chief Justice sniffed, "and a discussion of why it is not sound is rendered unnecessary."[25]

It was a firmly established legal principle, all through the nineteenth century, that the owner of land owned the airspace above the land. *Cujus est solum ejus est usque ad coelum:* he who owns the soil owns up to the sky. A rule established in cases involving overhanging buildings and trees had been applied without much dissent to new fact patterns created by technological change—to telegraph wires, telephone wires, and elevated trains.

But there *was* one technological change that was giving lawyers some difficulty—balloons.

Joseph and Étienne Montgolfier took the first human balloon flight in 1783, drifting four or five miles across Paris in a hot-air balloon. Ten days later Jacques Charles filled a balloon with hydrogen and flew even farther. Throughout the nineteenth century, balloons of both kinds took to the air for sport, for military purposes, and for scientific investigation. Balloons were never used for commercial transportation because they were at the mercy of the winds—it was a rare traveler who was willing to go wherever the wind was blowing—but there were enough other uses for balloons to ensure that by the century's end many had flown in them, and a great many more had seen them overhead.

The balloon prompted some doubts about the power of landowners to exclude others from the space above their land, doubts that quickly extended to objects other than balloons themselves. In 1815 the English courts considered the case of a man who had nailed to his own house a board that projected over the property line and overhung several inches of his neighbor's garden. The neighbor brought suit for trespass. "This is a clear invasion of the plantiff's possession," his lawyers contended, and they cited the *cujus est solum* maxim to support their argument. "If this be not a trespass, it is easy to conceive that the whole garden may be overshadowed and excluded from the sun and air without a trespass being committed." They must have been confident they would win, as the case seemed just like all the other cases of overhanging buildings.

But Lord Ellenborough, the influential chief justice, had balloons on his mind. "If this board overhanging the plantiff's garden be a trespass," he worried, "it would follow that an aeronaut is liable to an action of trespass . . . at the suit of the occupier of every field over which his balloon passes in the course of his voyage." The notion that balloons were trespassing on the land beneath was too farfetched for Ellenborough to contemplate, and for that reason a board overhanging a garden couldn't be trespassing either. If the board had caused the plaintiff any identifiable harm, Ellenborough concluded, the plaintiff could recover money from the fellow responsible, or perhaps even have the board taken down, but in the absence of any such damage, he had no right to have the board taken down simply because it had invaded his airspace. The invention of the balloon had put a dent in the conventional three-dimensional conception of a landowner's rights.[26]

Ellenborough's view of balloons was often repeated in subsequent years. In the 1830s the English Court of Chancery used balloon overflights to illustrate the principle that the law will not interfere to prevent trivial injuries. "Suppose a person should apply to restrain an aerial wrong, as by sailing through the air over a person's freehold in a balloon," scoffed the vice chancellor; "this surely would be too contemptible to be taken notice of." In the 1860s a British judge in Calcutta reached the same conclusion. "Lord Ellenborough justly ridiculed the notion that travellers in a balloon could be deemed trespassers on the property of those over whose land the balloon might pass," he noted, and it followed that "no man has any absolute property in the open space above his land." After the English case finding trespass where a horse kicked another through a fence, lawyers' magazines in Britain and the United States questioned the decision because of its implication for balloons. "The doctrine leads to some strange conclusions," they pointed out; "take the case of a balloon passing over land at a height of three miles." By the later part of the century, some lawyers accordingly concluded that balloons were trespassing only when they landed—also a matter of concern to balloonists, who often could not control where that would be but not while they were aloft.[27]

Ellenborough's conclusion—that the invasion of airspace did not entitle the landowner to have the offending object removed without some showing of injury—was also a frequent topic of discussion in subsequent years. For the rest of the century, lawyers argued over whether the landowner could file an action for *trespass* in the strict legal sense of the word, a kind of lawsuit entitling him to the remedy of *ejectment,* a court order restoring the landowner's possession of the airspace, or whether the landowner instead had to bring an action for *nuisance,* a claim that the invasion had caused him some harm. Either type of suit could force the defendant to remove the offending structure. The difference was in the proof required of the landowner. Ejectment required no showing of harm to the landowner. The fact that his airspace was occupied by another was enough. But an action for nuisance required a showing of harm.

American courts occasionally followed Ellenborough in refusing to order the removal of protruding objects without proof of harm. In 1863, for example, a New York court considered one of the cases involving overhanging eaves and gutters. The overhang "was undoubtedly a violation of the rights of the plaintiffs,"

the court recognized, "but we think ejectment, or an action to recover the possession of real estate, was not the appropriate remedy." The plaintiff was entitled to have the eaves and gutters removed, in the court's view, only if they constituted a nuisance.
But most courts continued to find that the simple occupation of
the airspace, without a showing of harm, was enough to entitle a
landowner to have the offending structure removed. The space
above land was part of the land itself, the Pennsylvania judge
George Sharswood reasoned, so if a landowner was entitled to
ejectment for the occupation of his land, he should also be entitled to it for the occupation of his airspace.[28] The issue was still
being debated at the end of the century. It would take on a new
life with the invention of the airplane.

Nor did everyone agree with Lord Ellenborough's comments
about whether aeronauts in balloons were trespassing on the land
beneath. By the end of the century the contrary view was probably at least as widely held. The earliest and most influential critic
of Ellenborough was the English judge Colin Blackburn. In an
1865 prosecution of a hunter for trespassing, Blackburn referred
parenthetically to Ellenborough's doubt that a balloon in the air
above private property was trespassing. "I understand the good
sense of that doubt," Blackburn explained, "though not the legal
reason of it." It may have seemed silly that a balloon could be trespassing, but such was the law. Blackburn's opinion soon became
as widely quoted as Ellenborough's had been a half century earlier.
When advertisers began placing signs on balloons tethered to the
ground, English and American lawyers' magazines, citing Blackburn, concluded that the balloons would be trespassing on the
neighbor's airspace if they were blown sideways across the property line. Lawyers sometimes hedged their discussions of the issue
with adjectives suggesting that landowners suffered no real injury
from overflying balloons and were quite unlikely to sue. Articles

on both sides of the Atlantic referred to the "technical" trespass committed by a balloon in the air, as distinct from the "actual" trespass the balloon would commit when it landed. In his treatise on Anglo-American law, the law professor Henry Terry similarly supposed that it would be a "theoretical" trespass to fly in a balloon over land owned by another.[29] Calling the trespass technical or theoretical was an indirect way of saying that in such cases the law was out of step with the expectations of the parties, in that neither landowners nor balloonists thought there was anything wrong with overflights. But those expectations didn't take overflights out of the category of trespasses. Balloonists might not think to avoid flying over private property, and landowners might not think to complain, but the balloons were trespassing all the same.

The most thorough discussion of the issue was undertaken by the Oxford law professor Frederick Pollock, who concluded that in the dispute between Ellenborough and Blackburn, Blackburn was the winner. It was clear, Pollock noted, that a person could commit trespass at any depth beneath the earth's surface, most obviously by mining someone else's land. Such cases were very common. If entry below the surface was a trespass, Pollock could find no reason why entry above the surface wasn't a trespass as well. "The improbability of actual damage may be an excellent practical reason for not suing a man who sails over one's land in a balloon," he explained, "but this appears irrelevant to the pure legal theory." Every day people committed equally harmless trespasses by walking briefly on land owned by others. No one sued over such trivial matters, but everyone agreed that they were still trespasses. The same was thus true of trespass in the air. Ellenborough's position led to a conundrum, Pollock added. No one could doubt that it would be a trespass to park a balloon permanently above a man's land. But if it wasn't a trespass to have the balloon

Balloons often flew over private property, often inadvertently, as in this scene of a crash in France in 1868. Balloons raised the first doubts as to whether landowners owned the airspace above their land. Drawing by Albert Tissandier. LC-DIG-ppmsca-02481, Prints and Photographs Division, Library of Congress.

there at all, how could a continuing trespass be committed by keeping it there?[30]

Whether balloons were trespassing while in the air was a question that never got definitively resolved, because neither English nor American landowners ever sued balloonists for aerial trespass. There *were* occasional suits against balloonists for the damage they caused upon landing. One of them, the 1822 New York case of *Guille v. Swan,* became famous, both as a source of law and a source of amusement. When Guille's balloon landed in Swan's garden, hundreds of people broke through Swan's fences, some to help Guille and others curious for a closer view of what was still a novelty. Swan's flowers and radishes were destroyed, some by the balloon but much more by the crowd. Guille was found liable for both sorts of damage, on the theory that he should have expected that his descent would draw a crowd. For almost a century the case would be cited for the legal rule that a wrongdoer is responsible for all the damage he ought to have foreseen. Lawyers would make jokes about it for nearly as long. "Navigation of the air will remain an unsolved problem," one New York lawyer declared in the 1870s, "if garden shoots are to be preferred to parachutes." In 1889 the case was still remembered well enough for the lawyer-humorist Irving Browne to publish a lengthy poem about it. The poem ended:

> For parachutes the courts care little,
>   Balloonatics no rights enjoy;
> But they will not abate a tittle
>   'Gainst those who garden-shoots destroy.

Maybe this was funny at the time. But if it was clear that balloonatics enjoyed no rights against landowners when they hit the ground, their rights in the air were uncertain, for want of litigated cases. Learned judges and lawyers had weighed in on both sides, but there was no final answer.[31]

American and English lawyers and judges had little trouble finding trespass in cases involving overhanging buildings and tree branches, overflying bullets, hooves and fists projecting over property lines, telegraph and telephone wires, and elevated railroads. Balloons, on the other hand, presented a much harder problem. The many writers who expressed opinions on the subject never articulated exactly what it was about balloons that seemed to place them in a different category, but it isn't hard to make a few guesses. The other methods of aerial trespass all took place at a relatively low elevation, sometimes just a few feet off the ground. Balloons flew much higher, sometimes thousands of feet up. They were accordingly a far smaller intrusion on any interest one might impute to an owner of land—privacy, the ability to use the airspace, or simply the desire to avoid annoyances. Balloons, moreover, occupied the airspace only temporarily. Most of the other instruments of aerial trespass were permanent fixtures. Again, this distinction counseled in favor of treating balloons more leniently. Finally, there was a good policy reason for not treating balloons as trespassers, one that did not exist for the other methods of trespass. Balloons were useful for science and the military, but balloons could scarcely avoid flying over private property. There was no analogous reason to protect overhanging buildings or tree branches. The telegraph, the telephone, and the elevated railway could all be confined to narrow routes above public or railroad land, so there was no need to allow them to be located elsewhere.

By the first decade of the twentieth century, when controversy erupted over whether the new flying machines were trespassers, there was thus already a large body of law governing the ownership of airspace. Nearly all of it was in the landowners' favor. If the aviators and their lawyers had any glimmer of hope, it lay in the uncertainty introduced by the balloon cases. Dirigibles and airplanes could fly even faster than balloons, and perhaps one day even higher. They promised to be even more useful. Shouldn't the law, aviators must have wondered, be even more careful to protect them?

Aviators and lawyers were, of course, the primary participants in the trespass debate, but they weren't the only ones. The ownership of space was of interest to all sorts of people for all sorts of reasons, whether or not they intended to take to the air themselves.

One such person was the social reformer Henry George. George spent much of his career advocating measures, especially a tax on land, to counteract what he saw as the harmful consequences of the private ownership of land. The prospect of flight gave him one more ground for his argument: the fear that owners of land might also monopolize the air. When the English social theorist Herbert Spencer claimed the existence of a natural right of access to air—"air cannot be monopolized," Spencer asserted, far too loosely—George took the opportunity to set him straight. Air *is* monopolized, George insisted, by the owner of the land beneath. Whenever land was bought and sold, the exclusive right to air was bought and sold as well. "And were the air-ship perfected," George continued, a landowner "would have the same legal right to forbid trespass on *his* light and air, and to demand payment for any use made of it or any passage through it, thousands of feet above the surface, as he now has to forbid trespass on his ground." Advances in mining technology had already allowed the owners of land to claim exclusive rights to minerals deep underground; one day advances in aviation would allow them to do the same for the space high above. Whether 35 feet over the ground, or 3,500, or 35,000, the legal principle was the same, "for the ownership which attaches to land under our laws is not to be really measured by linear feet and inches, but by parallels of latitude and meridians of longitude, starting from the centre of the earth and indefinitely extendible." George himself thought this a bad thing, but he also thought Spencer foolish for claiming otherwise. Citing Blackstone, George declared: "The land-owner is, in law as well as in fact, not just a surface owner, but a universe owner."[32]

If Henry George had reasons of his own for thinking about the air, so did Boyd Henry Bode, a professor of philosophy at the University of Illinois and later Ohio State. Bode would become best known in the 1920s and 1930s as a proponent of progressive education, much like John Dewey, but he began his career as a logician. In his 1910 textbook *An Outline of Logic*, Bode used the debate over airspace as an example of how apparently clear words can be ambiguous when new factual situations arise. A decade earlier, the word *trespass* had seemed precise enough. But did a flying machine trespass on the land beneath? No one could be sure. The word itself hadn't changed; it was change in the surrounding circumstances that had pumped ambiguity into it. "It is evident," Bode concluded, "that the connotation of the word 'trespass' must be made more explicit to meet the emergency."[33]

George and Bode had intellectual interests in the air, but there were others with large sums of money at stake. New buildings were going up, structures that reached such astonishing heights that contemporaries found a new word to describe them. Very tall ship masts and sails had once been called *skyscrapers,* as had very tall men and horses, but beginning in the late nineteenth century the word was largely reserved for the steel-frame office buildings that blotted out the downtown sky. Joseph Pulitzer's New York World Building, completed in 1890, was the first to pass three hundred feet. A rush of even taller structures followed, including the six-hundred-foot Singer Building in 1908 and the seven-hundred-foot Metropolitan Life Building in 1909, both in New York. Similar, if shorter, buildings went up in other major cities as well.

The very existence of these buildings depended on the landowner's legal right to use the airspace above his land, sometimes far above. The new flying machines could not have a right to use that same airspace without imposing a corresponding limit on the height of buildings, so real estate lawyers quickly recognized that the two issues were connected. Airplanes and skyscrapers both represented progress, but could they coexist?[34]

The question was drawn even more sharply when owners of land in a few of the largest cities began selling off "air rights" to others. When the New York Central Railroad converted from steam to electricity, it was able to cover the train tracks and sell the rights to build above them. In Chicago, the Illinois Central sold its air rights to the Chicago Daily News. As the Daily News's lawyer explained, the News purchased "the entire interest in the property in question, *excepting* therefrom the space below a designated plane, and *excepting from the exception* the right to run columns and foundations through the excepted space." Similar transactions took place in Philadelphia, Boston, Baltimore, and Cleveland. But what exactly had the purchaser of air rights acquired? How far up did air rights extend? To the heavens? Did landowners even have air rights at all? The Chicago real estate lawyer Nathan MacChesney declared that he had "never heard any doubt expressed" about the landowner's rights above the land "until recently in connection with the rights of aviators above private property." There would be no doubt as to the landowner's right to sell the airspace, he recognized, "were it not for the fear in the minds of certain writers and persons interested in the development of aviation that such a theory would retard the development of aviation by inviting action for trespass." MacChesney did not wish to ground the airplanes. The problem, he acknowledged, was to find a rule that would accommodate aviators and landowners alike.[35]

As the novelty of flight captured the imagination of writers around the world, the aerial trespass question even made an appearance in literature. Tom Swift was the hero of a series of novels for children, most of which were published in the 1910s and 1920s. Airships figured prominently in many of these books, including *Tom Swift and His Airship* (1910), *Tom Swift in the Caves of Ice: The Wreck of the Airship* (1911), and *Tom Swift in Captiv-*

ity: A Daring Escape by Airship (1912). Tom flew yet again in
Tom Swift and His Great Searchlight (1912), in which he spies on
Andy, his rival, by flying over Andy's house and watching him at
work, on his roof, building an airship of his own. Tom must be
flying extremely slowly, because as he sails by, accompanied by his
friend Ned, he has time for an extended conversation with Andy
about the nature of property rights in airspace.

> "Hello Andy!," called Tom, as he swept slowly overhead.
> Andy looked up, but only scowled.
> "Nice day, isn't it?" put in Ned.
> "You get on away from here!" burst out the bully. "You are tres-
> passing, by flying over my house, and I could have you arrested
> for it. Keep away."
> "All right," agreed Tom with a laugh. "Don't trespass by flying
> over our ship, Andy."

On one interpretation of this passage, Tom was a better pilot than
lawyer. He may have been trespassing by flying above Andy's land,
but Andy could not commit trespass by flying above Tom's airship. The debate was over whether the owners of land owned up
to the heavens, not whether the owners of personal property—
items other than land—did as well. But one could also understand Tom's joke as a derisive reference to Andy's assertion of
property rights in the air. He may have been implying that a landowner could not exclude aviators from the space above his land
any more than one aviator could exclude another from flying
above his airship. Either way, the fact that this passage was published at all, especially in a book for children, suggests that all
sorts of people were aware of the issue of aerial trespass.[36]
    The most extended fictional treatment of aerial trespass took
place in *Virginia of the Air Lanes,* a novel published in 1909 by

the Iowa lawyer Herbert Quick. Quick had a varied career: he was a prosecutor, the mayor of Sioux City, and an official of the Federal Farm Loan Bureau during World War I. He was also a prolific writer of novels, short stories, and nonfiction books. In *Virginia of the Air Lanes,* a mysterious enterprise called the Universal Nitrates and Air Products Company is found to have been quietly purchasing the air above farms, streets, and waterways all over the world, creating a plaid pattern made up of long strips of air ownership. "These seemingly worthless rights," the breathless narrator explains, "were like a huge spider's web spun as a net over the world—Europe and Asia, as well as America. Some one with great resources was up to something big. Something was to be caught in the net. But what?"

Before long, the company begins filing trespass lawsuits against the owner of every airship in the United States. In New York, for example, the suit alleges

> that the plaintiff was the owner of all rights of navigation in the air in certain described belts or bands surrounding the City of New York, dividing it into portions, and gridironing the continent; that the defendants had in the past habitually trespassed on these by flying over them in air-ships; that the passage to or from the City of New York over the sea, the river, or other route was impossible save by such trespass; and therefore injunction was asked prohibiting the defendants, their servants and all other persons from departing from or coming to the said City of New York through the air owned by the plaintiff, or from navigating any aërial craft across, over or through the real property of the plaintiff wheresoever situated.

The Universal Nitrates and Air Products Company had succeeded in controlling the right to fly. Some laugh at the lawsuit, but more thoughtful observers recognize that "two perfectly well-known legal principles were here united in an audacious attempt to monopolize the air: the rights attaching to ownership of land, and that of injunction to prevent trespass."

After a spirited hearing in court, the requested injunction is granted. All existing airships are grounded. The Universal Nitrates and Air Products Company licenses the right to fly in its airspace to a single manufacturer, the Carson-Craighead Aeronef Company, which, as the sole lawful producer of flying machines, earns a fortune. (*Aeronef* was a then-current French word for aircraft.) As the book ends, Virginia, the heroine, marries one of the owners of Carson-Craighead.[37]

Permeating the story is Herbert Quick's amusement that familiar legal principles could yield such an absurd result. One senses his delight at sharing this discovery with his readers, and his assumption that nonlawyers would be just as interested in it as he was. Here again, the aerial trespass issue was presented to an audience far wider than lawyers and aviators.

In England, meanwhile, Arthur Empson wrote an extraordinarily complex will in 1909, a will that divided his land among his descendants in a series of life estates that would last for two hundred years. Empson expected that the land's primary benefit would be the coal deposits beneath it, so he was especially careful to specify how these should be exploited. Empson's fourth son, William, was only nine when his father died. He would grow up to be a famous poet and literary critic. William Empson was well aware that his family's well-being depended in large part on the rule that the owner of land also owns above and below the surface. One of his earliest and best-known poems, written when he was a student at Cambridge, reflected on the absurd implications of the rule, both above and below. The poem was called "Legal Fiction."

Law makes long spokes of the short stakes of men.
Your well fenced out real estate of mind
No high flat of the nomad citizen
Looks over, or train leaves behind.
Your rights extend under and above your claim
Without bound; you own land in Heaven and Hell;
Your part of earth's surface and mass the same,
Of all cosmos' volume, and all stars as well.
Your rights reach down where all owners meet, in Hell's
Pointed exclusive conclave, at earth's centre
(Your spun farm's root still on that axis dwells):
And up, through galaxies, a growing sector.
You are nomad yet; the lighthouse beam you own
Flashes, like Lucifer, through the firmament.
Earth's axis varies; your dark central cone
Wavers, a candle's shadow, at the end.[38]

Empson was a student of English and mathematics, not a lawyer,
but he knew that land, as a legal matter, was not flat. It was shaped
like a lighthouse beam emanating from the center of the earth
and broadening as it reached the stars. The *cujus est solum* maxim
seems to have been widely known in the early twentieth century.

But of course the aerial trespass debate was conducted mostly by
lawyers. "When we watch an aviator in his white-winged aeroplane making a daring flight and soaring over the earth," the Denver lawyer Wayne Williams recognized, "we do not think of him
as a violator of the law, yet, technically, that is what he is; for,
throughout all of his journey, unless he be over the water, he flies
over the land of others, and this is a trespass upon the land of
those where the air craft has flown." Flight was still such a novelty

that no one would think of suing an aviator for trespass, but when the thrill wore off and overflights became more frequent, landowners were certain to grow more litigious.[39]

In the years around 1910, as aviators achieved greater distances aloft, commercial air travel began to look like a realistic possibility. Lawyers increasingly turned their attention to the problem of trespass. "In view of the successful experiments with the 'dirigible war-balloon' made recently at Farnborough," the English *Solicitor's Journal* observed in 1907, "it is extremely possible that airships will soon be constructed for the purpose of conveying passengers from place to place above the surface of the ground. When this happens, a great many legal problems will have to be solved," the foremost of which, in the *Journal*'s view, was that of trespass. The early aircraft flew so low, for reasons of safety, that the *Journal* expected trespass suits to be imminent. "The question, when it comes up for decision, will certainly be raised in an acute form, for an airship plying for profit will endeavour to keep as near the ground as practicable—say, between fifty and 100 feet under ordinary circumstances." Landowners could not be expected to tolerate such overflights for long. "It is an abominable nuisance," agreed an American lawyers' magazine, "when an airship or dirigible, propelled by an ill-smelling motor circles over a man's garden or house at a slight altitude from the earth."[40] Aerial trespass litigation was on its way.

Lawyers began to prepare for it. "To what extent aerial voyagers may cruise in the ocean of atmosphere resting on private property," the *Maine Law Review* declared in 1910, "is a matter demanding careful thought and close study." At the Dickinson Law School in Pennsylvania, students in the moot court competition for 1909 argued a fictional case in which an aviator was sued for trespass after flying his airplane five hundred feet above the plaintiff's house. The law journal *Case and Comment* devoted an entire

Orville Wright and Frank Lahm set a record in 1909 by flying for fifty miles above Fort Myer, Virginia, at a speed of forty miles per hour. In the years around 1910, as planes began to fly far enough and fast enough to raise the possibility of commercial air travel, lawyers turned their attention to the problem of aerial trespass. LC-USZ62-89971, Prints and Photographs Division, Library of Congress.

special issue to the incipient "Law of the Air." A lawyer in Little Rock, Arkansas, identified no fewer than thirty-five novel legal questions thrown up by the possibility of flying above privately owned land, ranging from how a landowner could ascertain the exact location of a flying machine to whether towns should impose property taxes on air. Most, however, were variants of one big question: Who owned the airspace?[41]

These early discussions suggested considerable unease among the profession, created by a sense that the world was changing but the law was lagging behind. American property law was "utterly inadequate" to the task before it, one lawyers' magazine insisted. "Either the old legal principles must forsake their solid foundations and take unto themselves wings, or else we must develop new principles, by statute or otherwise, to meet situations hitherto utterly unknown." In the new "aerial age," another writer agreed, there was an urgent need to attend to the legal questions that were soon to arise. "Suppose an airship flies across your domain. Can you object? Legally, your ownership reaches down to the center of the earth. How high up does it reach?" With the prospect of "some mechanical device for air-transportation" operating overhead, one Canadian lawyer wondered, "would the individual poised in balloon or aeroplane over the messuage of a neighbour, be a trespasser, pure and simple?"[42]

Simeon Baldwin, the chief justice of the Connecticut Supreme Court, was well aware that legal change needed to accompany technological change. "The lawyers in every country have been kept busy during the last century in developing a special body of law, first for the railroad, then for the telegraph, and then for the telephone," he reasoned. Baldwin himself had been one of those lawyers, as counsel to several rail lines in the 1870s and 1880s. Now he saw a new challenge ahead. Lawyers "must soon address themselves to a new task of the same nature. The air-ship has at last been brought to a state of efficiency which, while far short of perfection, takes it out of the field of mere experiment and seems to assure its speedy employment in the transportation for hire of passengers and goods." But where could these new airships go? "Is there, let us first ask, a right to navigate the air?" Or did the owner of the land beneath have "such a right in the air above his property that . . . he could complain of legal injury from the use of it for an air-ship voyage?"[43]

Did he? The lawyers had their work cut out for them.

TWO

An Aerial Territory

The invention of the airplane, meanwhile, was giving rise to a second legal problem just as important as the first. Did a nation have the right to exclude foreign airships from the airspace above its territory? Or was the atmosphere like the ocean, a zone through which anyone could pass, regardless of nationality? Did the sovereign power of the nation-state extend upward, or was it confined to the surface of the earth?

In one sense, as many commentators recognized in the first decade of the twentieth century, this issue was the analogue, in international law, of the domestic legal question of whether the owners of land owned the airspace above. The domestic question was one of property rights within each national legal system, while the international question was one of sovereign rights within a mostly inchoate system of world order, but functionally they were the same. When a person or a nation controlled the ground, what rights did that person or nation have in the air above?

In another sense, however, answering the question of airspace rights at the national level was a prerequisite to answering that question at the individual level. That is, if a country *didn't* have sovereign power to govern the airspace above its land, how could it establish property rights in the air? By what authority could a nation allocate the use of the air, whether to landowners or to aviators? The issue of aerial sovereignty was thus simultaneously analogous to and more fundamental than the issue of aerial property rights.

This question was much more important in Europe than in the United States. In the early years of flight, an American pilot would have had to begin a voyage very close to the Canadian or Mexican border in order to have any hope of crossing an international boundary. In Europe, by contrast, flights beginning in one nation could easily enter the airspace above another. The frequency of such international flights, everyone realized, was likely to increase over time. But how should they fit into the legal system? "States have a terrestrial territory and maritime territory. Do they also have an aerial territory?" asked the French lawyer Paul Fauchille in 1901. "Does the column of air above their lands and waters come under their domination?" Before the Wright brothers flew, just as European aviators were experimenting with the first successful dirigibles, Fauchille recognized that the airships of the future would pose some thorny problems of state power. If nations "have neither property nor sovereignty in the air," he wondered, "don't they at least have certain rights in it? And if they have rights, on what are they based?"[1]

Whether a nation could exclude foreign aircraft was just one of several international legal issues produced by the invention of the airplane. The range of conceivable problems was limited only by lawyers' imaginations. The English barrister Norman Bentwich brooded over how flying machines miles above the earth would be treated under the international rules governing espionage. The German lawyer Alexander Meyer worried about the citizenship of babies born aboard airships above foreign countries. The American lawyer Denys Myers even imagined the perfect crime, committed by an American with "a pet enemy, who is an Italian, and both are in France. The American suavely invites the Italian aboard his airship and takes him up into the air beyond all limits claimed by anybody to be under the control of the subjacent territory." High enough to evade the jurisdiction of any nation, "the American pilots the craft above Swiss territory, knocks off the Italian, who lands in Bern and in the yard of the residence of the Russian minister, a portion of Swiss soil which is acknowledged to be Russian by reason of its diplomatic use. The American continues his aerial voyage, landing in Germany." Under existing rules, Myers concluded, there was no way to tell which nation had the right to prosecute the American murderer, and it was entirely possible that no nation would.[2]

But if the nation's uncertain right to exclude foreign aircraft was not the only problem of international law introduced by the airplane, it was the most important. By the start of World War I there was an enormous literature on the topic, in several languages. The leading participants in the debate were lawyers and law professors, mostly in western Europe but also in the United States, who thought of themselves as members of the new discipline of international law, an effort to tame national self-interest with liberal, humanistic principles untethered to existing treaties or legislation. International law, in this view, was not simply a record of what states had done or agreed to do. It was rather a statement of what they *should* do, according to norms that expressed the progressive development of civilized conscience, norms that scholars believed they could identify by a combination of introspection and the study of past writers. "So many acute minds have attacked the subject from its various points of view," remarked the University of Chicago's Blewett Lee in 1913, "that nothing short of genius could accomplish originality in discussing it."[3] Of course, that didn't stop Lee or anyone else from trying.

No legal issue is entirely new. Lawyers, accustomed to reasoning by analogy, can always find a precursor that is similar in some respects. Just as the question of whether airplanes were trespassing brought to mind earlier disputes about overhanging buildings and tree branches, the question of aerial sovereignty summoned memories of previous debates over governmental power.

Balloons had been put to military use almost from the moment they were invented in the late eighteenth century. The French army used balloons to scout enemy troops in the fighting of the 1790s that followed the French Revolution. In the American Civil War, the North likewise used balloons for reconnaissance. The balloon would never become a military staple, like the airplane would, because it was at the mercy of the winds. The fear that bombs or other weapons might be dropped from balloons was nevertheless real enough to prompt two international treaties banning the practice, one in 1899 and another in 1907. "The launching of projectiles from balloons belongs in the same class of undertakings as the proposition to subject coast cities to ransom at the demand of a powerful fleet," explained George B. Davis, the U.S. Army's judge advocate general, shortly after the 1907 treaty. "That is, both have been proposed, but neither has been seriously considered by a responsible belligerent; indeed, neither practice has any existence in fact, but both have been regarded as constituting a sufficiently serious menace to humanity to warrant an international conference in formulating prohibitory declarations with a view to prevent their occurrence."[4] Balloons continued to be used in wartime, however, to gain information about the other side.

Because of the attention given to military ballooning in the nineteenth and early twentieth centuries, it was clear that any resolution of the aerial sovereignty question would not allow aerial bombing. It was generally accepted at an early date that war in the air required special rules of its own.[5] (Of course, when war came, many of those rules would be disregarded.) But a ban on bombing did not answer the question whether, in peacetime or in war, a nation had the right to cordon off its airspace. Was national defense to be paramount? Or should the interests of commerce and travel prevail?

This question was a new one with respect to the air, but it had been the subject of a famous debate three centuries earlier with respect to the ocean, which was, to the seventeenth century, something like the atmosphere was to the twentieth—a vast resource newly opened up for exploitation. On one side of the seventeenth-century debate was the Dutch lawyer Hugo Grotius, who argued in his *Mare Liberum* that no nation could claim exclusive rights to the ocean. Rather, Grotius contended, the ocean was common to all, and all had the right to navigate wherever they wished. On the other side was the English lawyer John Selden, who responded in a book he pointedly called *Mare Clausum* to signify his opposition to Grotius. Selden argued that nations could exercise control over water just like they did over land. Both *Mare Liberum* and *Mare Clausum* became fundamental texts of international law. Both were familiar to lawyers of the early twentieth century. The debate over aerial sovereignty thus drew heavily from the arguments made by Grotius and Selden.

The Grotius-Selden debate, as deployed by lawyers trying to resolve the question of aerial sovereignty, was inevitably a simplified version of the seventeenth-century controversy. Grotius and Selden were hardly the first authors to express opinions as to whether the sea could be monopolized by a single sovereign; indeed, both drew extensively on ancient sources addressing the same subject. Nor were they the only prominent disputants in the seventeenth century, a period when the dramatic expansion of trade and colonization made oceanic sovereignty an important political question throughout Europe. Finally, twentieth-century lawyers tended to abstract the views of Grotius and Selden away from their immediate political contexts. Both were, in effect, lawyers representing clients. Grotius was asserting the right of the Dutch republic to trade in the East Indies, in opposition to the monopoly over trade claimed by Portugal. Selden was defending the English effort to prevent unlicensed foreigners (particularly the Dutch) from fishing in the waters around England.[6] With details like these stripped away, twentieth-century lawyers depicted a stylized theoretical argument between Grotius, as a proponent of absolute freedom of navigation, and Selden, as an advocate of exclusive national control.

Grotius was understood as relying primarily on the intuition that the very nature of the ocean rendered it incapable of being exclusively possessed. Unlike land, which could be bounded and marked as property, the ocean was too big and too fluid to be owned by individuals. "That which cannot be occupied, or which never has been occupied, cannot be the property of any one, because all property has arisen from occupation," Grotius claimed. "Therefore the sea can in no way become the private property of any one, because nature not only allows but enjoins its common use." And occupation was a prerequisite to national sovereignty just as it was to private property. "Public territory arises out of the occupation of nations, just as private property arises out of the occupation of individuals," he reasoned. "It has therefore been demonstrated that neither a nation nor an individual can establish any right of private ownership over the sea itself." The ocean "can neither be seized nor inclosed"; indeed, the ocean "rather possesses the earth than is by it possessed."[7]

In this stylized debate, Selden stood for the opposite intuition: that the ocean in fact *could* be possessed. "The Seas are, by all manner of Law, every way capable of private Dominion, as is the Land," Selden insisted. There was nothing in the nature of water that rendered it incapable of being possessed, as was demonstrated by the common and undisputed possession of lakes and rivers. "The Sea it self (as to its fluid Constitution) is no other than a River, Fen, or Lake, differing only in bigness from the rest." And if individuals could possess bodies of water as their property, then nations could exercise sovereignty over those same bodies of water.[8]

Grotius, as things turned out, was on the winning side. International law would come to allow nations to exercise sovereignty only in the immediate vicinity of their coasts. The rest of the ocean, the vast majority of it, was open to all.[9] But what did that mean for the atmosphere? Did airplanes have the same freedom of navigation in the air that ships had in the ocean?

Paul Fauchille thought so. Fauchille was one of the era's leading scholars of international law, despite never holding a teaching position. Founder and editor of the *Révue Générale de Droit International Public,* a journal that still exists today, he would become best known for his four-volume treatise on international law, which was published shortly before he died in 1926.[10] Fauchille's nearly book-length article on "le domaine aérien," which appeared in the *Révue Générale* in 1901, was the first systematic effort to address the question of aerial sovereignty posed by the new flying machines. Because of Fauchille's timing and his thoroughness, his views received wide circulation outside of France, and set the terms of the debate for the next decade and a half. Whether one agreed with him or not, anyone writing about aerial sovereignty had to take Fauchille's opinion into account.

Fauchille analyzed the problem of the air much like Grotius had analyzed the problem of the ocean three centuries earlier. "A thing is not susceptible of ownership, private or public, unless it lends itself to a certain appropriation," he began. "In order to be the owner of any surface, one must be able to occupy it in a real and continuous manner." Land could be occupied, but could the air? Fauchille thought not. "By its immensity and its fluidity, the atmospheric layer resists all possession. It is, materially and physically, impossible for a people, even with all the forces of the world at its disposition, to exercise over the air an effective grasp, to mark it with the seal of its authority. The only way to occupy it is to launch balloons into it; but could such an occupation really give rise to possession?" Fauchille was writing just before the invention of the airplane, when the balloon was the only means of rising into the air, but his point would have been the same even afterward. Flying a balloon or an airplane *through* the air was not a method of *occupying* the air.

Even in the future, when Fauchille expected that there would be airships capable of hovering in a single location, he insisted that they would not be capable of marking out a portion of the air. "Appropriation by this method, if it were possible, would only give the State a confined possession, limited to the volume of the airship," he reasoned. "In truth, possession does not extend beyond the thing apprehended." Land could be enclosed, and possessed in its entirety, but the atmosphere could not. Fauchille concluded that air was simply not capable of being possessed.

But not all the air. The part of the air closest to the ground could be possessed by constructing buildings in it, and buildings of course occupied the space they filled. The tallest building then in existence was the Eiffel Tower, which was approximately three hundred meters high. Fauchille used this fact to deduce a pair of complementary principles. "First, above 300 meters, the air is not and cannot be an object of possession. Second, up to 300 meters, the air is only reduced to possession to the extent that it is actually occupied: air that is transformed by neither construction nor planting remains entirely free."[11]

Thus far Fauchille had addressed only the question of property in the air, not the issue of national sovereignty over it. Like Grotius, however, he believed that the two issues were related. Sovereignty, like property, had to be established by acts of possession, and Fauchille had already demonstrated that the air was not capable of being possessed. "By its very nature, it rebels from all material possession," he declared. "No doubt the balloons that pass in space occupy the part of the atmosphere that they traverse; but this occupation is hardly an appropriation: necessarily ephemeral, it is not enough to produce sovereignty."[12] Fauchille accordingly concluded that the air, above the height of buildings, was open to aviators of all nations, just like the ocean, beyond the territorial waters of individual nations, was open to all navigators.

Several later writers followed Fauchille in comparing the air to the ocean. "Has the subject of one State a right to fly across the territory of another?" asked the Cambridge law professor H. Brougham Leech. "There is one clear and useful analogy—that of the sea. In spite of certain differences, it is so close that it will suggest not only many rules for the aerial code, but also the principles upon which these regulations will be founded." From this analogy, Leech concluded, like Fauchille, that "foreign aircraft have the right to traverse the atmosphere which the territory of any State subtends, and that the Governments of the territories so traversed have a right to take all steps necessary for self-protection."

The right of self-protection was limited to the lower parts of the airspace, however, just like the nation's sovereignty was limited to the parts of the ocean closest to the shore. "This right can only be exercised within such a limited space as is capable of control from below—*i.e.,* it will be measured, as in the case of the sea, by the range of the guns which are now being constructed for this purpose. We thus arrive at a zone or belt of atmosphere, corresponding to the belt of territorial waters, and an upper region of the air—the supraterritorial atmosphere corresponding with the open sea, in which the passage of aircraft is as free as that of ships upon the ocean."[13]

The analogy between the ocean and the atmosphere appealed to those, like Leech, who viewed consistency and logical structure as desirable characteristics in the law. The analogy was nothing new: it had often been made, in the opposite direction, by earlier writers seeking to explain why the ocean was free to all navigators. For instance, in Henry Wheaton's widely read treatise on international law, a volume published in many editions from the 1830s through the 1880s, Wheaton remarked that "the sea is an element which belongs equally to all men like the air. No nation, then, has the right to appropriate it." Grotius himself had made the analogy, and indeed he acknowledged that so had Ovid, for the same purpose. (According to Grotius's account of Ovid, "nature has made neither sun nor air nor waves private property; they are public gifts.") Ovid and Grotius knew nothing of flying machines, of course, and nineteenth-century lawyers like Wheaton knew only balloons, but the antiquity of the analogy only made it more compelling to theorists of a natural-law bent. If the air and the ocean shared certain attributes, it was hardly surprising that perceptive observers would have noticed the analogy for thousands of years.[14]

Proponents of the free navigability of the atmosphere were not limited to making analogies to the ocean or evaluating the true nature of air. They also had some instrumental arguments on their side. Allowing a nation to shut its airspace could be a crippling blow to commerce and travel, worried the French lawyer Édouard d'Hooghe; "it would render all navigators victims of formalism, intransigence, and government stupidity." Aerial sovereignty would be especially dangerous to landlocked countries like Switzerland or Serbia, who could be deprived of access to the rest of the world. Trade via the ocean had so enriched the world by the early twentieth century that it was hard to imagine life without it. The air promised to be another ocean, another realm within which people and goods could move from one nation to another, for the benefit of all. The airplane, many hoped, might even promote international harmony by bringing people of different lands closer together.[15] What good could come from giving national governments the power to close off the air?

The other side of the debate focused on the same issues that had been introduced by Paul Fauchille. Was the air truly incapable of being possessed? Was it really analogous to the ocean? And were the consequences of allowing governments to exclude foreign aircraft any worse than the consequences of *not* allowing them that power?

By 1910 many were arguing that the air in fact *was* capable of being possessed. States *did* control the air, insisted the New York lawyer Arthur Kuhn, who would later be one of the founders of the American branch of the International Law Association. "It is true that their control may not be complete," he conceded, but their control of the land was not complete either, and that did not prevent them from exercising sovereignty over the land. In any event, "as soon as the art [of aviation] has . . . been regularly established, states will be able to execute their will upon the zone abutting them from above." The English lawyer G. D. Valentine agreed that technological change, in both aviation and weaponry, meant that "powers in possession of the subjacent land will, in fact, be able to exclude vessels at will from the whole zone of the atmosphere suitable for aerial navigation." That was enough, in his view, to be "such effective occupation as to give rise to the full right of sovereignty."[16] Aviation had undergone enormous change since Fauchille began the debate in 1901, and similar change was likely in the future. As the range of things that could be done in the air expanded, so too did conceptions of aerial sovereignty.

Others pointed out that even if the air could not be possessed in the same manner as the earth, nations were nevertheless long accustomed to exercising sovereign power over it. They passed laws regarding air pollution, for example, and there was little doubt of their authority to do so. As Oliver Wendell Holmes suggested in 1907 in upholding Georgia's authority to forbid copper-mining companies from releasing poisonous gas into the atmosphere, "it is a fair and reasonable demand on the part of a sovereign that the air over its territory should not be polluted." National governments had recently begun entering into international agreements to govern the new technology of wireless telegraphy, agreements that likewise assumed that nations had power over their air. The hunting of birds was regulated in almost every nation, and some birds flew very high above the earth, much higher than any building. The Cambridge law professor Harold Hazeltine noted that the very existence of the *cujus est solum* maxim implied a recognition that the state had the sovereign authority to allocate property rights in the air. After reviewing all these examples of state regulation of the atmosphere, the Harvard political scientist George Grafton Wilson concluded that it made little difference whether or not the air could be possessed. Either way, "states assume that they have jurisdiction in the air space above their territory."[17]

The New York lawyer Arthur Kuhn, one of the first American specialists in international law, was an early proponent of the view that nations
had sovereignty over the airspace above their territory. LC-DIG-ggbain-
39145, Prints and Photographs Division, Library of Congress.

As flight grew more common, and the dangers it posed became
more conspicuous, many began to speak of aviation regulation as
an inevitable response to those dangers, one that required sovereign power over the air. "If any accident occur to the machinery
which enables an aeroplane to support itself in the air, and experi-

ence shows that this is not of infrequent occurrence, the aeroplane must descend on State territory," reasoned H. Erle Richards, a professor of international law at Oxford. "So long as the law of gravity prevails, a State must have unfettered control over air vessels passing above its territories, in order to protect itself." And governments had more to protect against than accidents. If the air, like the ocean, were free to all navigators, Valentine worried, "foreign navies would have the power to hover over the country, nay to engage in warfare above it." If the air were free, others added, governments would have considerable trouble collecting customs duties, enforcing quarantines, and preventing crimes like smuggling. "Either Customs must be entirely done away with," Baden Baden-Powell predicted, or else nations would have to devise some way to secure their borders against aerial trespassers.[18] Without the ability to control the air, the nation might be left defenseless against a set of foreseeable perils.

In the years around 1910 it accordingly became common to argue that the analogy between the atmosphere and the ocean was a poor one. Events far out in the ocean might not affect occupants of the land, Arthur Kuhn pointed out at a meeting of the American Political Science Association, but the same could not be said of the air. "There is a direct interest on the part of the state in the abutting airspace," he suggested, "if for no other reason than the law of gravity." A faulty ship could cause harm only to its sailors and its cargo, agreed Denys Myers, but a faulty airplane had to come to rest somewhere on the land below. "This difference," he concluded, "is of sufficient fundamental importance to be the deciding factor" in permitting nations to exclude aircraft from the skies. The analogy between the ocean and the air, joked one English lawyer, "might be correct if the bottom of the sea were inhabited." Even Paul Fauchille had to concede by 1910 that "the situation is not the same in the two cases: in the case of the sea, there is, besides the high sea, the territorial sea where the coastal

State has the power to guarantee its self-preservation; in space, things are very different: an aviator at any height can throw contaminated objects or contraband to the ground."[19]

Proponents of the freedom of navigation in the air were anxious that a nation with the power to exclude foreign aircraft might one day exercise that power, to the detriment of world commerce. But proponents of aerial sovereignty had a response. The possibility that a nation might shut its skies was but "a visionary danger," Valentine contended. It was far more likely, he predicted, that nations would join together in an international convention, permitting each other's nationals to fly above each country, under a system of more or less uniform regulation.[20] If so, the instrumental arguments in favor of free navigation would evaporate. Aviators would be able to fly everywhere, without compromising the ability of the nations below to protect themselves.

There were thus two ways of understanding "the aerial ocean," as the French lawyer André Blachère elegantly put it. "On one side is the sovereignty of the State—integral and egotistical—on the other the still imprecise rights of the international community. And the problem oscillates between these two invisible poles."[21]

The participants in this debate tended to divide by nationality. Most of the partisans of free navigation were French, while most of its opponents were not. "The French jurists preach a doctrine which must touch the freedom-loving nature of mankind sympathetically," needled the German law professor Hans Sperl. "They say that the air is free from all control of law, a No Man's Land to which no state can lay claim. . . . This view must be condemned by every practical person." Denys Myers agreed that France was "where aerial freedom has its only serious advocates."[22] But this division between the French writers and the others was surely more attributable to chronology than national character. The French writers had, by and large, written first, before much was known about the practical details of flight. By 1910 they had even begun publishing a monthly journal, the *Revue Juridique Internationale de la Locomotion Aérienne,* devoted to articles on air regulation, at a time when the subject was only just becoming prominent in other countries. Their work had necessarily been more theoretical than pragmatic. Writers in English and German, often working several years later, had the benefit of practical experience.

In any event, after a decade of debate the two sides had come closer together. Even the most vociferous partisans of free navigation acknowledged that aviation could not be *completely* free, because states needed to prevent accidents and defend themselves against enemies. Advocates of national sovereignty, meanwhile, recognized that states *should* and probably *would* permit most foreign aircraft to fly through their airspace, even if they were not required to. By 1911 the most perceptive analysts of the debate, in France and elsewhere, were noticing that virtually every author's proposed mode of regulation would yield similar results, whether expressed as a regime of free navigation with exceptions for national self-protection or as a regime of state sovereignty in which states would allow overflights that posed no harm to state security. "The real question will not be: must the state have authority in the air, but: how much authority and to what height?" recognized the Dutch scholar Johanna Lycklama à Nijeholt. "We have therefore not before us a pure repetition of the 'mare liberum' and 'mare clausum' of bygone centuries, for the important part of aerial navigation will take place in those lower regions where nearly all recognise the right of control of the groundstate and do not demand a state of liberty like the liberty of the open sea."[23]

Perhaps the answer would lie somewhere between the polar positions of free navigation and complete national sovereignty over the air.

One obvious possibility was to slice the airspace horizontally, into a territorial zone below a certain height and an international zone above. "The State has a right of sovereignty only over the domain of the air that can be made the object of a property right to the profit of its subjects," the French scholar Paul Loubeyre reasoned. In the upper air, beyond the reach of the people below, aviators could fly free from sovereign power. This scheme had the benefit of being congruent with the regulation of the ocean, which was likewise divided into a territorial zone near the land and an international zone beyond. But it also had some serious defects. For one, how could a government official on the ground determine how high a plane was flying? "Any one who has observed aeroplanes at a height of a thousand feet or more realizes the force of this objection," declared the American lawyer Berkeley Davids. For another, the location of the dividing line would be arbitrary and constantly changing. "Is the highest structure in each country to be the measure for that country alone, the Eiffel Tower for France, the spire of Salisbury Cathedral for England, the high skyscrapers of New York for America?" Harold Hazeltine wondered. "Or, shall the height of the world's highest structure—at present the Eiffel Tower—be taken as the measure for the zones of all states? And, suppose a new and higher structure be erected somewhere upon the habitable globe, or suppose the Eiffel Tower itself falls to the ground, is the sovereignty zone of all states to be raised or to be lowered in consequence?" And what about future developments in weaponry? "If Krupp invents a gun that will hurl projectiles 20,000 metres instead of 11,500 metres as at present, is the air zone of sovereignty to be at once raised all over the world?" And what about the fact that some parts of the world were flat and others mountainous? Should the division between the lower and upper air be a straight line or should it follow the contours of the earth? Drawing a line in the air would be far more difficult than drawing a line in the water.[24]

An even bigger problem with the concept of a two-zone atmosphere was the fact that unlike in the ocean, the peril associated with an accident in the air did not decrease with the plane's distance from the land. "The danger does not only not diminish at a greater height, but actually increases," warned one reviewer of such a proposal.[25] Crashes that might cause minor injuries at fifty feet would be fatal at five thousand, not just to the aviator but to those on the ground as well. Once again, the ocean was proving to be a poor analogy to the air.

Where, then, would be the middle ground between free navigation and complete national sovereignty over the air? The French law professor Alexandre Mérignhac declared that nations exercised "sovereignty but sovereignty attenuated, diminished, reduced to the need to protect certain important interests," interests like the health and safety of their citizens. The Italian law professor Enrico Catellani labored to distinguish between two sorts of circumstances. "The State will be able to prohibit at any height, in the space over its territory, all that endangers its security or limits its sovereignty or compromises in any manner the use of its territory," he declared. "On the other hand, the airspace must remain completely free from all dependence with respect to the subjacent State so far as usage, and especially passage, in all cases in which this usage or passage would not give rise to such consequences."[26] Few could have objected in principle to such distinctions, but they were at such a level of abstraction that they could hardly have been implemented in practice, because they raised more questions than they answered. Which flights endangered health and safety? Which ones limited state sovereignty? And who should have the power to decide?

In the years before World War I, internationally minded lawyers held a few international conferences to discuss these questions. Lawyers and professors from all over Europe gathered in Verona in 1910 for an event they called the International Juridical Congress for the Regulation of Aerial Locomotion. They resolved that "the atmosphere above the territory and territorial waters is to be considered territorial atmosphere subject to the sovereignty of the State," but also that "in territorial space, the passage and circulation of airships should be free, except for regulations necessary to protect public and private interests, and except for the juridical regime inherent in the nationality of the airships."[27] There was so much tension between the first and second of these provisions, and so much ambiguity in the two exceptions to the general rule of free passage, that the resolution could have meant anything to anyone. The work of the Verona congress had little or no influence.

Some of the same people attended a meeting in Madrid the following year sponsored by the Institute of International Law. The Institute was, and indeed still is, a Belgium-based organization of distinguished lawyers and professors. Formed in 1873, by 1911 the Institute had reached some prominence, particularly after it won the 1904 Nobel Peace Prize for its work in promoting the use of arbitration to decide disputes between countries. If there was any private organization capable of bringing order to the question of aerial sovereignty, it was the Institute of International Law. But the outcome of the Madrid session was a short statement no more useful than the one produced the year before in Verona. "International aerial circulation is free," the Institute declared, "except for the right of the subjacent States to take certain measures to be determined, in view of their own security and that of the persons and property of their inhabitants." Again, the language was so abstract that few could object, but that same abstraction meant that those who voted in favor of the resolution need not have agreed on very much. Similar gatherings of a self-styled International Juridical Committee on Aviation, in Paris in 1911, Geneva in 1912, and Frankfurt in 1913, yielded similar results.[28]

The delegates at these meetings were not representing their countries' governments; they spoke and voted as individuals. Without any real responsibility or authority, they found it more useful to reach agreement on generalities than to argue over the details. Everyone recognized that nations had to have *some* power to govern the air, and everyone hoped for a future of safe international commercial aviation, without the hindrance of international boundaries. Nations would have to reach some understanding, somewhere short of the utopian ideal of an unbounded atmosphere, but there was no consensus as to exactly how much power, or what kind of power, should belong to national governments.

National governments, meanwhile, were gradually moving toward asserting complete sovereignty over their airspace. In 1910, representatives of nearly every country in Europe, including all of the most powerful, met in Paris to work out principles governing aviation. The French proposed a rule similar to the one promulgated by the nongovernmental conferences, in which the air would be free, except to the extent necessary for states to protect the safety and property of their residents. But Germany and Britain insisted on full control of the air, without any concession of a freedom of navigation. Under the German proposal, states would have the power to allow or not allow foreign aircraft to fly overhead, so long as the restrictions were applied equally to domestic aviators. Britain would not even go that far. The British favored a regime in which each nation regulated its airspace as it saw fit, without any obligation to treat foreign and domestic aircraft equally. The conference ended in an impasse, without any agreement. All nations agreed that they needed some control over their airspace, but they disagreed as to how much.[29]

In the absence of international agreement, nations began acting for themselves. Britain enacted regulations in 1913 prohibiting foreign aircraft from flying over the country without advance permission. Russia soon did likewise. That same year, France and Germany reached an agreement in which each allowed nonmilitary overflights by the other, subject to some detailed restrictions. Other nations banned flight by foreign aircraft over certain portions of their territory. The very existence of these measures presumed a background norm of complete state sovereignty over the atmosphere. "The regulations issued by the great powers under the pretext of national defense amount to a prohibition of passage from one State to another," complained one of the French advocates of limited sovereignty. In a period when the European powers were all building up their militaries, in fear of the war that we know with hindsight was soon to come, there was little room for free navigation of the air. By 1914 European governments had effectively settled on an answer to the question Paul Fauchille had posed back in 1901. States *did* have an aerial territory above their land, and they controlled it just as firmly as the land itself.[30]

World War I only confirmed this pattern. The idea of using airplanes in battle was much older than the airplane itself. Tennyson had foreseen aerial combat in his 1842 poem "Locksley Hall," the relevant couplets of which were often quoted in the early years of aviation:

For I dipt into the future, far as human eye could see,
Saw the Vision of the world, and all the wonder that would be;
Saw the heavens fill with commerce, argosies of magic sails,
Pilots of the purple twilight dropping down with costly bales;
Heard the heavens fill with shouting, and there rained a ghastly dew
From the nations' airy navies grappling in the central blue.

More recently, in 1908, H. G. Wells had published his novel *The War in the Air,* which predicted a catastrophic worldwide war triggered by a German airship attack. The book was so popular that within two years translations were published in French, German, Russian, and Dutch. Similar novels of air combat were published in other countries around the same time, including Rudolf Martin's *Berlin-Bagdad* in Germany (1907) and Emile Driant's *L'Aviateur du Pacifique* in France (1909). Such authors took the premises of their plots from the headlines. The European arms race leading up to 1914 included airplanes and dirigibles, particularly in France and Germany but also in Britain, Austria-Hungary, Russia, and Italy.[31] The extensive use of the air in World War I was no surprise.

The war removed all doubt that nations would need to exercise complete sovereignty over their territories. "The moment war came," recalled the English lawyer J. M. Spaight, "the air frontiers closed with a Janus-like clang." Most nations shut their borders to foreign aircraft. The neo-Grotian claim, that air by its nature could not be possessed, virtually disappeared. As the nations of Europe battled for the control of airspace, it was clear that air not only *could* be possessed but that it had to be possessed if a country hoped to defend itself against attack. "Before the World War partial freedom of the air seemed at least probable, if remotely so," *Aviation* magazine explained to its readers after the war ended. Because of the war, however, "all freedom theories have been

World War I put an end to the idea of airspace as a zone free of national sovereignty. In this German poster from 1918, British planes bomb a German factory, under the caption "What England Wants!" Poster by Egon Tschirch, LC-USZC4-12309, Prints and Photographs Division, Library of Congress.

swept aside for the centuries-old doctrine of full state sovereignty." At the war's end Spaight concluded, "Right or wrong, the principle has been established that States control the atmosphere over their territories, and, in legislating for the air, we must start from that principle."[32]

International aviation was one of the subjects taken up at the Paris Peace Conference when the war was over. The resulting Convention Relating to International Air Navigation indeed proceeded from the principle that the air, just like the land, was part of a nation's territory, and that nations had the right to keep foreigners out. The very first article of the Convention declared that "every Power has complete and exclusive sovereignty over the air space above its territory." Freedom of the air, commentators recognized, had suffered its final, fatal blow.[33] In times of peace, a state adhering to the Convention pledged "to accord freedom of innocent passage above its territory . . . to the aircraft of the other contracting States," provided that several conditions were met. Nations had to certify the airworthiness of aircraft and the competency of pilots, for example. They had to register aircraft and exchange registers monthly. If these prerequisites were satisfied, nonmilitary planes would be allowed to cross through the airspace of another nation, within routes fixed by the government below. They were not allowed to land, unless the host government permitted. Military planes were not allowed to cross through another nation's airspace at all, without special authorization.

The Convention Relating to International Air Navigation was drafted at the same conference that produced better-known postwar institutions like the League of Nations and the Permanent Court of International Justice, and it was part of the same framework. International aviation was to be governed by a new organization called the International Commission for Air Navigation that would be a component of the League of Nations. Disputes regarding the interpretation of the Convention would be resolved by the Permanent Court of International Justice. Although territorial sovereignty had won out over freedom of navigation, the Convention was idealistic in its own, more modest way, in that its drafters, no less than the proponents of free navigation, envisioned a smoothly functioning system of international aviation. "Even if the Convention plays havoc with excellent juristic theories," Blewett Lee concluded, "we must be prepared to sacrifice logic for the peace of the world, and to accept that which can be made better, rather than stand out for an impossible perfection." If nations did not *have* to allow foreigners to fly overhead, perhaps they would recognize that opening their skies to foreign aircraft was in their mutual self-interest.[34]

Most of the nations of Europe ratified the Convention within a few years. Although American delegates had played a large role in drafting the Convention, the United States never ratified it. There was no objection in the United States to the principle of sovereignty over the air. Rather, because the Convention was part of the postwar package dominated by the League of Nations, the failure of the League to gain American support doomed the Convention as well. American nonparticipation would be an annoyance to American pilots for some time to come, because the Convention prohibited signatories from entering into air travel treaties with nonsignatories, which meant that Canada, a signatory, could not agree to air traffic rules with the United States. "Imagine, for instance, a passenger in an air liner flying from New York to Montreal through clouds," complained Godfrey Lowell Cabot, the president of the National Aeronautic Association, in 1925. "He would feel much safer if he knew that no one but air liners proceeding north were allowed to fly between 5,500 and 6,500 feet altitude and saw by the altimeter that his plane was at 6,000." Cabot was a wealthy Boston industrialist and philanthropist who had taken up flying as a naval officer in World War I, while in his fifties. He knew all too well that international air travel was being hindered by American isolationism. Indeed, the only reason American pilots could fly into Canada at all was that the Canadian government granted permission as a matter of courtesy, in a series of short-term grants throughout the decade. Every six or twelve months the United States had to request permission yet again, in what the federal government's National Advisory Committee for Aeronautics deplored as "the annual recurrence of diplomatic negotiations with Canada on this subject."[35]

International air travel was still much less important in the United States than in Europe. No European country except Russia was big enough to operate a purely internal system of air travel. Most flights originating in the United States, by contrast, never crossed an international border. With only two neighbors, the United States could get all the access it needed through bilateral agreements. That would change. In the late 1920s, when technological progress caused American commercial airlines to develop an interest in flying beyond North America, the United States would participate in the Havana Convention, an agreement among twenty-one nations of the Western Hemisphere with terms very similar to those of the Paris Convention. In the 1940s, when transoceanic flight became a commercial possibility, the United States would become a leader in the establishment and ongoing governance of the worldwide regime that would replace the Paris and Havana Conventions.[36]

By the end of World War I, then, the world had settled on an aerial trespass rule at the national level. A nation had the right to exclude foreign aircraft from the airspace above its territory. Most of the countries with airplanes had agreed to waive that right under specific circumstances, in exchange for similar waivers from other countries, but underlying the system of international air travel was the fundamental principle that a nation had complete control over its own airspace. Whether a plane could enter any particular part of the air depended entirely on the wishes of the national government below. Sovereignty extended upward to the sky. This principle would be the basis for occasional incidents of international conflict throughout the twentieth century, in which nations would shoot down foreign aircraft that entered their airspace without permission.[37]

But what about individual property owners? Did they have a right to exclude aircraft from their airspace analogous to the right possessed by their governments? That question still remained open.

THREE

The Peculiar Beauties of the Common Law

All through the 1910s and 1920s, lawyers and others would debate the aerial trespass question. Nearly everyone who participated in this discussion had the same goal; they all wanted airplanes to be free to fly without hindrance from landowners beneath. There *were* occasional dissenters. "The theory of a fee simple title is that the holder owns up to the sky and down to the center of the earth," insisted Judson West, a justice of the Kansas Supreme Court, in his 1921 introduction to the law for nonlawyers. "What right has an aviator to make a racket and scare my family just over the top of my roof any more than on the ground?"[1] But West was unusual. Virtually the entire debate was not over ends but over means. How could flight be reconciled with the landowners' control of their airspace? What was the best way to ensure that aviators would not be hemmed in by lines drawn on the ground?

Some early commentators recognized that even if airplanes were trespassing on the land beneath, in practice there was little an aggrieved landowner could do. If he brought suit for damages against an aviator, he could recover an amount equivalent to the loss he suffered by the flight, but in most cases that loss would be so small, if it existed at all, that it would not justify the cost of bringing the suit in the first place. He could ask the court instead for an injunction barring future overflights, but an injunction was also likely to cost more than it was worth, for even if the land-owner could obtain one, how could he enforce it? "What signs shall mark or designate his holdings, so that a flyer 1,000 to 2,000 feet in the air can recognize them and fly elsewhere?" wondered the Washington, D.C., lawyer Henry Randall Webb. Warning aviators off one's land would be impossible. To make matters worse, Webb added, "an injunction only applies to those against whom it is issued; and court orders can not be taken against all known and unknown flyers at once." Even if a landowner could identify all who flew over his land, he would have to go to court each time he found someone new—he would "become a very busy man and what is called a chronic litigant."[2] When one con-sidered the difficulty of enforcing an injunction barring aerial trespass, together with the fact that the damages suffered by the landowner from each overflight were likely to be nominal, courts might not even be willing to grant such injunctions in the first place. The landowner's legal remedies against trespassing aviators thus looked more theoretical than real.

In ordinary trespass cases, where the trespasser was on the ground, landowners in the early twentieth century also had the right to eject trespassers themselves, so long as they used only rea-sonable force. But it was hard to imagine how a landowner could prevent overflights within the confines of this rule. It would be impossible to build a fence high enough to keep a plane from fly-ing overhead. The landowner might conceivably fire shots at the plane, in the hope of scaring the pilot away. He might take to the skies in a plane of his own and fly very close to the offending plane, again with the goal of scaring off the pilot. But either of these strategies was so dangerous that it would almost certainly be unlawful, as an exercise of unreasonable force. Indeed, the land-owner would likely be committing a felony even if he did not hit the plane, and if he hit it, and the pilot died, the landowner would be guilty of manslaughter. "From whatever point the question is approached," one English lawyer reluctantly concluded, "it seems clear that the owner would not be able to enforce his right of ejectment."[3]

If the landowner could neither physically eject nor successfully sue a trespassing aviator, from the perspective of the legal system perhaps the problem would disappear. On paper the law would forbid aircraft from flying over land without the landowner's per-mission, but in practice such flights would be routine, because pilots would know they had no reason to fear litigation or vio-lence from landowners. "The result is that the law will frown upon the aviator," one Harvard law student suggested, "but un-less he causes actual damage it will connive at the formal wrong." Considering the analogous question of whether wireless messages were trespassing on the land beneath, the dean of the University of Memphis Law School proposed the same outcome—tolerating widespread lawbreaking in the interest of technological progress.[4] Maybe the solution was simply to rest content with a formal property law at variance with the actual state of the world.

But this was hardly a satisfying answer. That every right had a remedy had long been an axiom of the Anglo-American legal sys-tem. The New York lawyer Lyttleton Fox pointed this out to non-lawyers in the pages of the widely read *North American Review*. "Frequent and universal trespass on a large scale, theoretically banned by the law while in effect protected by it," Fox explained, was an outcome in such flagrant violation of the normal relation-ship between rights and remedies that courts would be unlikely to approve of it. Nor would landowners submit quietly. Fox predicted that they would continue to file trespass claims, even fruitless ones, in part because of their fears of heavy objects dropped from flying machines, and in part because they hoped to exact money from aviators who preferred a settlement to litigation. "If trespass is committed," Fox concluded, "it will not continue for lack of active and interested persons to invoke the aid of the courts against it." If commercial aviation ever became feasible, the profits would be too attractive a target for litigious landowners and their lawyers. "With indulgent philanthropy we may watch aircraft in their experimental stages pass over our houses and lands," remarked the Chicago lawyer Carl Zollman. "But our feelings will change when we learn that great companies have been formed and are making profit by passing over our farms and city lots."[5]

The idea of doing nothing, and relying instead on the landowner's lack of an effective remedy, thus never caught on. Among writers on the subject there was something close to a consensus that *something* had to be done in order to free aircraft to fly over land without trespassing.

There was a precedent of sorts for this problem. Telegraph and telephone wires had been retrofitted onto the patchwork of privately owned land by running them along public highways, so as to avoid trespassing on the land beneath. Thomas Russell, a charter member of the Aero Club of Illinois, proposed that the same could be done for airplanes. If the government established air routes above roads and confined aviators to those routes, Russell suggested, the problem of trespass would be solved. Of course, the resulting network of air routes would create a new problem—the danger of crashes—but Russell believed that a few rules of the

The English aviator Claude Grahame White flies above Executive Avenue, between the White House and the Old Executive Office Building, in 1910. Some suggested solving the trespass problem by establishing air routes above roads and other public rights of way, but the idea proved impractical. LC-USZ62-10900, Prints and Photographs Division, Library of Congress.

road would permit safe flying. Planes would have to keep to the right when passing. At night, or in fog, they would carry a green light on the right, a red light on the left, and a white headlight in front. Maybe they could be equipped with horns, or whistles, or bells, to signal their presence to other aircraft. By these means, planes could safely avoid flying over private property.[6]

"Well-defined aerial highways are imperative," agreed the New York lawyer John Eubank. If the space above roads was too narrow, he advised, the solution would be to acquire wider aerial strips through the government's power of eminent domain. "At any rate," he concluded, "the cost of acquiring the airspace right of way would be small and would soon be returned to the public treasury in the form of increased taxes through the enhancement in value of the property along and subjacent to the aerial highways."[7]

But proposals like these never caught on either. In the early years of flight, aeronauts navigated by watching the ground below, so they might have been able to see the roads, but a strong wind could be enough to blow them off course. In later years, when they flew higher, the difficulty grew greater, because even with navigational instruments they often had no way of knowing exactly where they were. "If a lane be laid out, how may the aviator be confined to it?" asked the Louisville attorney Edmund Trabue, at the annual meeting of the Kentucky State Bar Association. "He soars so high that he could know his whereabouts only through the compass, and he is often the sport of the storm, and he is confronted by clouds and fog which may lead him astray." To make matters worse, expert fliers had informed Trabue that "even the compass is an imperfect guide because of motor and magneto proximity, and that when the aircraft moves with the wind, there is no way of defining the drift and direction of the gale."[8] If aviators were too high to see the highways, and often could not stay above them even when they could see them, requiring planes to fly over highways was tantamount to prohibiting flight.

Airplanes were not like telegraph wires. They did not stay still. The solution that had been worked out for wires would not work for airplanes. If planes were to fly over private property, something would have to be done about the landowner's rights to the space above his land.

The *cujus est solum* maxim was a product of the common law. Neither England nor the United States nor any individual state had ever enacted a *statute* providing that owners of land also owned the airspace above the land. The rule had been declared by English and American judges, in the course of deciding disputes between neighbors. In the first three decades of the twentieth century, many lawyers on both sides of the Atlantic accordingly argued that judges should now change the rule, in response to the invention of the airplane. "If balloons or airships are to be the vogue," the Pennsylvania lawyer Archibald McClean maintained as early as 1904, "then it is time to see what the law is going to do and say on the subject. Law is so elastic that it can adjust itself to all new conditions." The common law's elasticity soon became a standard theme in discussions of the sort. "It is one of the peculiar beauties of the common law," proclaimed a Virginia lawyers' magazine, in its brief treatment of the law governing the new airships, "that it adapts itself to the rights of the parties under every change of circumstances, so as to keep step with the march of progress." The common law always responded to scientific advances, explained Edwin Albertsworth, a law professor at Cleveland's Western Reserve University. He provided several examples from recent years—the X-ray, the telephone, even the rise of eugenics, which at the time seemed to many to be a technological change at least as exciting as the others. All had required the common law to adapt. And now the airplane, the latest step in the march of progress, would likewise produce "a modification of the inherited legal view with reference to torts of trespass to realty."[9]

How one thought about this argument depended on how one

thought about the common law generally. What exactly were the sources of the common law? And how did it change?

One source of the common law, probably the one that lawyers had considered most important a century earlier, was custom. When William Blackstone's ubiquitous *Commentaries on the Laws of England* referred to "that antient collection of unwritten maxims and customs, which is called the common law," he was describing the understanding of generations of English lawyers. Thomas Wood, the author of a popular legal treatise of the 1720s, explained that one of the categories of English law included "several *General Customs;* these Customs are properly called the *Common Law.*" John Cowell similarly divided the law of England into two types: statutes enacted by Parliament and "Ancient Customes confirmed by the consent of the People."[10] The common law was not something *created* by judges, on this view. Rather, judges were discerning and applying rules that had an existence independent of the judges, rules that received their force from their long use among the people as a whole.

This understanding of the common law as founded on custom crossed the Atlantic and persisted in the United States after the American Revolution. James Wilson was one of the initial justices of the United States Supreme Court and one of the new country's first law professors. The *evidence* of the common law, he explained to his audience at the College of Philadelphia, could be found in the published reports of the opinions of judges. But "its *authority* rests not, on those written monuments. Its authority rests on reception, approbation, custom, long and established." James Sullivan, the attorney general of Massachusetts, relied on this same understanding to allay Americans' concerns about the common law, which was, after all, the law of a country against which they had only recently fought a long and bloody war of independence. The common law was not "a coercive institution, imposed by the authority of another nation," Sullivan counseled. "It is the will of the community, in its collective quality." As Joel Bishop declared in his legal textbook of the 1860s, "the common law is but custom, sanctioned by judicial decision."[11]

If the common law rested on custom, it followed that as custom changed, so should the common law. This was a prominent theme in the years following the Revolution, as lawyers and judges adapted English law to suit conditions in the United States. "It is characteristick of a system of common law, that it be accommodated to the circumstances, the exigencies, and the conveniences of the people, by whom it is appointed," James Wilson lectured. "Now, as these circumstances, and exigencies and conveniences insensibly change; a proportioned change, in time and in degree, must take place in the accommodated system." The New York judge James Kent, whose *Commentaries on American Law* would serve as an American version of Blackstone for much of the nineteenth century, was of the same view. "Considering the influence of manners upon law, and the force of opinion, which is silently and almost insensibly controlling the business and the practice of the courts," Kent suggested, "it is impossible that the fabric of our jurisprudence should not exhibit deep traces of the progress of society."[12]

Indeed, when the new American states enacted statutes incorporating the common law of England, they expressly adopted only so much of the common law as suited local circumstances, a transplant that explicitly required American judges to take into account differences between English and American ways in discerning the common law. That the common law changed to suit the changing times thus became even more a truism in the United States than it had been in England. The common law "adapts itself to all the changes and vicissitudes of individual or national condition, expanding or contracting as exigencies require," law students learned from the midcentury guidebook written by the New York lawyer John Anthon. The South Carolina lawyer James Walker began his treatise on the common law by insisting that "no custom can prevail in a nation which is repugnant to its sentiments or sense of justice."[13] The common law was no more static than the customs from which it was built.

The idea that the common law rested on custom was one that waned over time, but it never completely disappeared. "Undoubtedly the creative energy of custom in the development of common law is less today than it was in bygone times," Benjamin Cardozo admitted in 1921. Cardozo was then a judge on the New York Court of Appeals and one of the leading jurisprudential writers of the era. He would later join the U.S. Supreme Court. By the twentieth century, Cardozo noted, legislatures sat more frequently than before and enacted statutes much more often, so judges had less need to welcome new customs into the law. "But the power is not lost because it is exercised with caution," he observed. "In the memory of men yet living, the great inventions that embodied the power of steam and electricity, the railroad and the steamship, the telegraph and the telephone, have built up new customs and new law." And now, in Cardozo's view, custom was on the verge of producing a new common law governing airplanes. "Already there is a body of legal literature that deals with the legal problems of the air."[14]

If the common law of aerial trespass were to take its shape from custom, it was clear to some that airplanes would have the right to fly over private property. "The question of the ownership of the air, while never finally adjudicated in this country, seems to be obvious, from common usage," insisted L. D. Gardner, the publisher of *Aviation* magazine. For centuries, landowners had never complained about the use of their airspace by birds, bees, or carrier pigeons belonging to others. Now radio waves traveled above others' land, again without drawing any protest from the land's owners. Surely the custom was to allow planes to do the same. The Washington lawyer Berkeley Davids provided more examples. No one had ever contended that the smoke from A's chimney trespassed when it crossed over B's land. And more to the point, "in the century and a quarter that man has been able to navigate the air, first by balloons and lately by aeroplanes, there has been no contestation of the right of aeronauts to pass over private land." At aviation exhibitions, pilots had flown repeatedly over land without first asking permission of the owners, and no one had filed suit yet. There was thus a custom of acquiescence to overflights.[15]

William MacCracken was even able to quantify this custom. MacCracken, a flight instructor during World War I, would become the most important American government official in the field of aviation in 1926, when he would be appointed as the first assistant secretary of commerce for aeronautics. In the early 1920s, as a member of the board of governors of the National Aeronautic Association, he was one of the leading American promoters of aviation. In that capacity, he urged that the common law should allow overflights of private land, because that was what the public already expected. "During the years 1920 and 1921," MacCracken pointed out, "air craft travelled approximately 12,000,000 miles in the United States without any single property owner presenting a claim for aerial trespass."[16] By custom, aviators already had the right to fly over private property. If the common law was simply congealed custom, aviators would not be liable for trespass.

By the time the airplane came into use, however, the idea that custom was a motor of the common law had long been in decline, as Cardozo recognized. Judges back in Blackstone's period had tried to ascertain the existence of customs, law professor Edgar Kinkead taught his students at Ohio State, but judges in the twentieth century no longer did. William Pattee, the dean at the University of Minnesota Law School, agreed that "in ancient days customs had the force and effect of law," but not any more. The Harvard law professor John Chipman Gray was even skeptical about whether custom had *ever* been as important as Blackstone and others had claimed. "Not only does custom play a small part, at the present day," Gray noted, "but it is doubtful if it ever did, doubtful whether, at all stages of legal history, rules laid down by judges have not generated custom, rather than custom generated the rules."[17] The elaboration of common law was not a backward-looking exercise in spotting existing customs, many lawyers believed by the turn of the twentieth century. Rather, it was a process both backward- and forward-looking in which judges identified the proper rule by using their powers of *reason*.

There was nothing new about the notion that the common law rested on reason. Edward Coke, the leading English legal commentator of the seventeenth century (and the judge who put the *cujus est solum* maxim into wide circulation in Britain), had famously said that "the common law itselfe is nothing else but reason"—not the sort of reason available to the untutored, but "an artificiall perfection of reason, gotten by long study, observation, and experience." Many later English writers agreed. "The Common Law is Grounded upon Reason," affirmed the lawyer Giles Jacob in his treatise for students. "Our lawyers are with justice so copious in their encomiums on the reason of the common law," Blackstone recognized, "that they tell us, that the law is the perfection of reason, that it always intends to conform thereto, and that what is not reason is not law."[18]

English lawyers of the seventeenth and eighteenth centuries

perceived no tension in relying simultaneously on custom and reason as sources of the common law. Customs did not speak up for themselves. It was the judge's reason that allowed him to discern whether a relevant custom existed, what that custom was, and how it applied to the dispute before him. "But here a very natural, and very material, question arises," explained Blackstone, just after discussing the role of customs and maxims in forming the common law. "How are these customs or maxims to be known, and by whom is their validity to be determined? The answer is, by the judges in the several courts of justice. . . . Their knowledge of that law is derived from experience and study."[19] And customs themselves were virtually always consistent with reason—that was why they became customs in the first place. One could hardly imagine an unreasonable custom. Custom and reason could coexist peacefully as sources of the common law, because they were extraordinarily unlikely to yield different outcomes.

In the United States, by contrast, where judges had been instructed by state legislatures to apply only so much of the English common law as suited local conditions, custom and reason were more likely to conflict. A custom widely followed in Britain might be unreasonable in America. In such cases, American lawyers agreed, it was reason that should prevail. Deference to past practice "might, perhaps, be well eno' in England," jeered the Vermont judge Nathaniel Chipman, in one of the very first published collections of American court opinions. But not in the United States. "If no reason can be assigned, in support of rules," Chipman concluded, then "to adopt such rules, is certainly contrary to the principles of our government, and the spirit of our laws." In Connecticut, agreed Congressman Zephaniah Swift, the common law had force only "as far as it is warranted by reason."[20]

There was still room, of course, for substantial overlap between a custom-based and a reason-based understanding of the common law. As times changed, customs would change, but so too would the conventional view of which rules were most reasonable, and both changes would proceed in the same direction. Over time, meanwhile, the corpus of published judicial opinions grew exponentially, so judges found themselves drawing more on written legal precedents and less on unwritten sources of law, whether found in reason or in custom. In any given case there might be no practical difference between relying on custom and relying on reason, because the outcome would be the same either way.

Nevertheless, by the second half of the nineteenth century the habit of testing customs and precedents for consistency with reason produced a new understanding of the common law. The traditional view had been that the common law had an existence independent of the views of the judges who expounded it. Judges did not make the law; they *found* it. "The *decision* of a court is but *evidence* of what the law is," declared the Pennsylvania judge Hugh Henry Brackenridge; it was not the law itself. This view remained current well into the twentieth century, although it is impossible to know how widely it was held. The more one believed in custom as source of the common law, the more one was likely to believe that judges found the law rather than making it. "Substantially the whole private law which governs the larger part of human conduct has arisen from and still stands upon custom," the New York lawyer James Coolidge Carter insisted. Carter accordingly concluded that judges did not make law at all. Even in a novel case, one presenting facts with no precedent, the judge's job was to find "the true legal character" of the new facts, and then to find its appropriate preexisting category of cases. When a judge performed this task, Carter maintained, "he would correctly declare the law, but he would not make it."[21]

But this view began to come under considerable pressure in the late nineteenth century. If the common law was not based on custom, from what sources did judges derive it? Or to put the question the other way round, if the common law was the product of reason alone, to what materials did judges apply their reason? If judges formed the common law by choosing the rule that seemed most sensible to them, they scarcely differed from legislators, who did the same thing. Indeed, one could view them as nothing but interstitial legislators, making new law in the gaps where the legislature had neglected to act.

More and more American lawyers accordingly came to believe that judges made law. "Both courts and parliaments legislate," the law professor John Norton Pomeroy declared in the 1860s. "It is an entire misconception of the functions of the judicial tribunals, to describe them as wanting the legislative power, but as possessing only the capacity to declare the law to exist, as though from time immemorial a legal principle or rule had lain hidden and unnoticed, awaiting a discoverer, until an adventurous judge had brought it to light." Judges differed from legislators only in their unwillingness to face up to the true nature of their decisions, argued a young Boston lawyer named Oliver Wendell Holmes in one of his first published articles. Asserted Holmes, "Every important principle which is developed by litigation is in fact and at bottom the result of more or less definitely understood views of public policy; most generally, to be sure, under our practices and traditions, the unconscious result of instinctive preferences and inarticulate convictions, but none the less traceable to public policy in the last analysis." Proponents of the view that judges were lawmakers loved to poke fun at the conundrums that resulted from assuming that judges found preexisting law. "What was the Law in the time of Richard Coeur de Lion on the liability of a telegraph company to the persons to whom a message is sent?" sneered John Chipman Gray. The Berkeley law professor William

Carey Jones was similarly amused by a recent English case in which a rule established in the seventeenth century was treated as having been in force in the fourteenth.[22] These puzzles disappeared when one abandoned the belief that the common law was something judges found rather than something judges made.

Even as lawyers began to think of the common law as something made by judges for policy reasons, however, the profession's official discourse did not change. Virtually all judges continued to write opinions as if they were finding the law rather than making it, even if their genuine beliefs about the common law were different. Lawyers, tasked with persuading judges to rule for their clients, continued to construct arguments that likewise assumed judges found a preexisting common law, even if, in their private moments, they knew that judges were making the law. This divergence between how lawyers talk about the law and what they actually think about it has been with us ever since. ("I am not so naive," Justice Scalia has written, "as to be unaware that judges in a real sense 'make' law. But they make it as judges make it, which is to say as though they were 'finding' it.")[23] This incongruity between private thought and public discourse may spring from the discomfort many lawyers feel with the notion that judges are lawmakers. But whatever the cause, the rise of the conception of judges as makers, rather than finders, of the common law did not produce a corresponding change in the writing style of official documents. Lawyers and judges continued to pretend that judges were finding a preexisting common law.

The aerial trespass debate took place midway through this process. The new way of thinking about the common law, as something made by judges, was in the ascendant, but the old way was still vibrant, both as the genuine belief of many lawyers and as the surface discourse of nearly all of them. People who wanted to modify the common law to accommodate the airplane could thus draw on two distinct styles of argument. If the common law was something judges *found,* proponents of change had to contend that the common law had *never* deemed overflight to be a trespass. The *cujus est solum* maxim was simply incorrect. If the common law was something judges *made,* on the other hand, proponents of change had less need to scrutinize the past. Whatever the law was in the preflight era, they could argue, the law now should be different.

The prospect of aerial trespass suits prompted many writers to look at the *cujus est solum* maxim more closely than anyone ever had before. What exactly did the maxim mean? Was it really true that the owner of land owned up to the heavens?

The first scholars to examine these questions in any serious sense were in Europe, where the tradition of studying law as an academic subject was stronger than in Britain or the United States. The French legal historian Jean Brissaud pointed out at the turn of the twentieth century that the *cujus est solum* maxim was hardly consistent with European historical practice, in which mines and treasures located underground were owned by monarchs rather than the owners of the land above. Luigi Miraglia, professor of the philosophy of law at the University of Naples, traced the maxim to Gino da Pistoia, the fourteenth-century Italian commentator on Roman law, but contended that the maxim in fact had no basis in Roman law. Under Roman law, according to Miraglia, the owner of land could not necessarily control the space above or below the surface. Justinian, for example, had held that the owner of a building could not build so as to prevent the wind from reaching his neighbor's threshing-floor. Copper mines belonged to the finder, not the landowner. Constantine recognized a free right to quarry marble, provided the quarrier gave a tenth of the proceeds to the landowner. "Rights for the Roman jurisconsults extended only so far as they were useful," Miraglia concluded; "when the utility was lacking the right ended." In France, the early years of flight prompted law students to write dissertations on the roots of the law governing aviation, and they too found *cujus est solum* absent from Roman law.[24] If its truth depended on the accuracy of its ostensible Roman origin, maybe the maxim was incorrect.

Other students of Roman law, however, thought that Roman landowners *did* own their airspace. In the English-speaking world, the first serious investigation of the maxim's origin was undertaken by Henry Goudy, the Oxford historian of Roman law. Goudy thought the maxim originated with one of the glossators, the late medieval commentators on Roman law. Like Miraglia and the French historians, Goudy found the maxim absent from Roman legal texts, but unlike them, he thought it "would not have sounded strange to the classical jurisconsults." In fact, while Goudy acknowledged that there was no way to know for sure what the Romans would have thought about balloons and airplanes, he ventured to guess that they would have allowed landowners to prevent air transit above their land. He based his conclusion on the distinction he found that Roman jurists made between *aër* and *coelum*. *Aër* was air, the gas that flowed over the earth's surface. Under Roman law, air was *res communis,* a thing incapable of appropriation. But *coelum* meant something closer to airspace, the area through which the air flowed. *Coelum* was capable of private ownership. "The common user [that is, use] of *aër* is indeed asserted by many passages in the Digest," Goudy concluded, "but private ownership of the *coelum* is also asserted. There is no inconsistency."[25] Maybe the maxim was correct after all.

But then Goudy's view had critics as well. One was James E. G.

de Montmorency, professor of comparative law at the University of London, who concluded from his review of the Roman sources that the private ownership of airspace reached only to a height of fifteen feet above the ground. Everything above that, he determined, belonged not to the landowner but to the state, so that the government had the power to set the rules for airships. The French lawyer Eugène Sauze thought the maxim was a piece of "juridical nonsense" with its origin in an error by the early thirteenth-century Italian glossator Accursius.[26] Roman law was no clearer than English law.

The debate went on for decades without ever being resolved. There was no more actual information to be added, so later writers were content to repeat whichever view of Roman law they preferred. When the Cambridge law professor Harold Hazeltine, for example, glibly asserted that *cujus est solum* was a maxim of Roman law, the former Yale law professor Simeon Baldwin, by then the governor of Connecticut, replied just as breezily that it was not.[27] Among genuine historians of the civil law, it was understandably not an attractive project to imagine how Roman or medieval jurists might have treated airplanes.

Lawyers were trained to test the limits of a rule by the fact situations to which the rule had been applied. Judges might have *said* that a landowner owns up to the heavens, lawyers were quick to point out, but if one looked at the actual outcomes of these cases, one could infer a much more modest rule. "All of truth there seems to be in the maxim of ownership to the sky," insisted one American lawyers' magazine, was that landowners could use their own airspace—not that others were barred from using it as well. The landowner's use was "interfered with only when enjoyment of the soil is diminished"—that is, an overflight was unlawful only when it amounted to a nuisance. Under English law, anyone had the right to fly over land, agreed the young barrister Norman Bentwich, who had recently returned from a trip to New York, where he had glimpsed Wilbur Wright skimming a few hundred feet above the Hudson River. The *cujus est solum* maxim, Bentwich concluded, was only an injunction against flying so low or so loud as to interfere with the owner below.[28]

Another way to line up the past cases was to emphasize the height of the intruding objects. The cases had all involved trespassers very low to the ground—things like overhanging buildings and trees. "No actual decision of the courts," affirmed a law student in St. Louis, "does more than give a landlord a proprietary right in the lower stratum of the air." The higher reaches of airspace thus remained open for travel. The maxim was obviously formulated in an era before flight was possible, many reasoned, so it could not have been intended to bar overflights. The American lawyer Henry Spurr concluded that it was just "a rule to ensure the owner the beneficial use of his land against encroachment by his neighbors, as far up or as far down as he might wish to go. It could not have meant anything more."[29]

Indeed, if one took a scientific point of view, *cujus est solum* couldn't really mean what it said, in either direction, insisted one English lawyer. Below the earth's surface, a landowner could never actually own all the way down. "Scientists tell us that the centre of the earth is mere molten matter," the lawyer explained, "and that after breaking through the earth's crust—only a matter of some miles—there would be nothing but molten substance for the owner to exercise his ownership over." Above the earth's surface, the decided cases rendered a passing airplane a trespasser only if it flew so low that "the branches or leaves of the trees growing on the land or the chimney-pots of the houses standing on the land are hit by the machine." In short, "the 'up' theory has much less truth in it than the 'down' theory, and even the 'down' theory, as we have intimated, is mere theory." The Chicago lawyer Carl Zollman pressed the point even more forcefully. If the maxim were taken literally, he observed, "the exact center of the earth would become the most disputed territory imaginable," because "every landowner everywhere would have a claim to it." Going up, meanwhile, "it would follow that the ownership of a farm might carry with it legal rights in planets billions of miles away." From the absurdity of both propositions Zollman inferred that the maxim's authors could not have intended it literally, or that if they had, they were wrong.[30]

Arguments like these were attempts to weaken the maxim by discrediting its history. If the common law was something judges *found,* not something they made, then mistakes committed by past judges might be grounds to reject their opinions as to what the law required. Maybe the maxim originated in an initial erroneous interpretation of Roman law that came to be taken for the truth after it had been parroted enough times. Maybe the maxim came to life when English judges and treatise writers reached too strong an inference from a handful of decided cases. Either way, if the common law existed prior to, and independently of, its declaration by judges, then the fact that the maxim had been handed down for centuries was not, in itself, enough to establish its truth. Of course, the fact that the maxim had been repeated so often by so many judges was reason to think twice, or even more than twice, before casting it aside. The more writers who subscribed to a rule, the less likely it was that *all* of them could have been wrong. Moreover, the principle of *stare decisis*—that past cases should be treated as precedent—was an expression of the idea that stability in the law was a value in its own right. Even if the law was something judges found, a maxim as old as *cujus est solum* could not be lightly disregarded. Nevertheless, if its original expositors had been wrong, then so were all of the subsequent writers who repeated it.

Then again, if judges *made* the common law, the circumstance that the maxim originated in error was of no significance at all, because by the early twentieth century judges had stated the maxim countless times, each of which was itself a statement of the common law. The Des Moines lawyer Stuart Ball was no fan of the maxim, but he had no patience for historical investigators who thought their work would promote aviation. "The antiquity and the origin of the phrases, while of importance and interest to the legal historian, are entirely beside the point in an argument over whether the law of today allows ownership over the airspace or not," Ball insisted. "If their implications have been adopted by our law, the discovery of the meanest sort of an origin for them would not affect the result." Ball's younger brother George would go on to some renown decades later as undersecretary of state during the Kennedy and Johnson administrations, but Stuart Ball was primarily interested in legal theory, and, like more and more lawyers in the early part of the century, he was certain that a judicial statement of the law was the law itself. "It is probable that at the time these maxims were first formulated, their full application was not conceived, however conceivable; nor were they accurate statements of then existing rules of law," Ball conceded. But none of that made the slightest bit of difference, because "it is indisputable that such phrases have had great influence in the development of our legal ideas. Few phrases have been more quoted." Or as the English lawyer G. D. Valentine put it, the maxim's "origin is medieval and obscure, but it has been adopted by all our modern writers."[31] If the common law had no existence independent of the declarations of judges, then the maxim was clearly part of the common law, because it had been declared by judges so many times.

Those who believed that judges *found* the common law (and those who spoke as if they believed it) were not limited to casting doubt on the maxim's origins. There was much more to the common law than the *cujus est solum* maxim. The common law gave rights to landowners, but it also gave rights to travelers, rights that in some circumstances allowed passage through private property. Could aviators take advantage of them?

R. Floyd Clarke was a New York lawyer who, as one 1909 admirer put it, "has given much study to the to-be aerial jurisprudence." Clarke pointed out that seas and navigable waterways, even waterways that flowed through privately owned land, were, under the common law, open for travel. A ship that sailed through private property on a river, for example, was not committing trespass. The owner of the adjoining land—even the owner of land on both banks—was not allowed to block navigation by extending an obstacle across the river. Where water was concerned, the needs of commerce had trumped the interests of private landowners. And what was the atmosphere but another navigable passageway? Airplanes were like ships, and the airspace was like the water. Just as ships had a public right of water passage over private property, airplanes had a public right of air passage. "Thus by a simple application of a fundamental common-law principle to the new combination of facts, without in the least changing the doctrines of the common law, but only properly fitting one of the two old principles to the new common combination of facts," Clarke concluded, "the matter is covered conveniently and equitably."[32] The landowner might indeed own the airspace up to the heavens, but aviators would nevertheless have the right to fly in it. All the materials for a satisfying solution to the problem were already contained in the common law.

Other commentators stretched for other analogies. In the southern and western United States, cattle and horses were allowed to roam at large over privately owned land. Maybe aircraft were like cattle. If a cow who actually stepped on another's land was not a trespasser, then how could a plane, which flew over the land at a great height, be one? In certain extreme circumstances, travelers had a right to enter private property—for instance, when the road was blocked by snow, or when a ship in distress reached a privately owned dock. If necessity justified such entries, couldn't it also justify overflights? After all, flying over private land was necessary if there was to be commercial aviation at all. In the United States, batted baseballs sometimes flew over privately owned land adjoining the field, but if the land's owner "should bring an action," one lawyer speculated, the suit "would not be looked upon with benevolent eyes by an American jury of baseball fans." Wasn't an airship even more harmless than a baseball? If one looked back even further into the common law's past, one might discern a murky right of public passage on highways over private land. And wasn't the air a highway of sorts?[33] Lawyers ransacked the common law for doctrines that might be updated for the benefit of aviators.

But it was the analogy between navigable waterways and navigable airways that was most frequently repeated, because it seemed the closest. "Is there a right to navigate the air," Simeon Baldwin wondered, "corresponding to the right to navigate the sea?" Some were certain there was. "The air, for purposes of navigation, must be as free as the sea and the waters of navigable rivers," insisted one American lawyer. "No musty common-law maxim can be allowed to stand in the way of progress in aviation."[34] The beauty of the analogy was that it bypassed the musty maxim altogether.

One could admit the truth of *cujus est solum* and concede the landowner's control of his airspace, while still finding room for aviators passing through. One could retain the older picture of the judge as a finder, not a maker, of common law, by providing judges with ancient and legally sanctioned practices to follow.

More strategies were available to those who believed that judges were law *makers*, not law finders. The times had obviously changed. The *cujus est solum* maxim had been devised in an era before flight was possible. Now that circumstances were different, one could argue, judges should modify the common law to keep up. *Cujus est solum* "no longer applies," as one London lawyers' magazine declared, "owing largely to the advent of airships and aeroplanes." Aviators were trespassers under current law, the *Literary Digest* explained, but "the situation is not as bad as would at first blush seem." That was because the landowner's right to possess the sky was established "by the common law only. The common law is a wonderful, mutable system . . . to be stretched and distended by the provident hands of courts," who would no doubt change the law to say "that the ownership of the air lies in the people, not in the individual, and that the ancient doctrines and the former precedents no longer control."[35]

One change often suggested was that judges should place an upper limit on the landowner's rights to airspace. Ownership to the heavens "seemed reasonable and satisfactory to all for centuries," the American lawyer Richard Mollica conceded. "No one questioned its soundness, for with what rights was it inconsistent?" But now everything was different. "Flying machines have been developed to such an extent that aviation is already beginning to take its place as a means of transportation. There is nothing perhaps which is more essential to economic and social progress than transportation." Indeed, he anticipated, aviation would produce such great economic benefit that its value to landowners would far exceed whatever injury they suffered from overflights. The common law was not static, so it could adapt along with the new conditions. Mollica accordingly concluded that allowing overflights above a certain height would not infringe any common-law rights of landowners. The rights they once held, in the preflight era, no longer existed.[36]

By the 1920s the idea that judges were *sub rosa* lawmakers was a commonplace among the law professors who became known as legal realists. One was Leon Green, then beginning his career at the University of Texas. In Green's view, aviation was likely to cause a change in the law of trespass, by causing judges to begin denying landowners the right to exclude others from their airspace, a right Green recognized "has been by common consent accorded a landowner throughout the history of the common law." He predicted that judges would adopt a new rule, one that "would relieve the aviator from being a trespasser while flying above the owner's land so long as he respected the owner's zone of operations." Setting that boundary might present some difficult factual questions, others realized.[37] It would depend on how the landowner was using his land, what sort of neighborhood was involved, and so on. But such complications did not prevent lawyers from arguing that judges should modify the common law and allow aviators to fly above a certain height without being liable for trespass.

The other common proposal for judge-led change was to abandon trespass altogether, in favor of holding aviators liable only for nuisance. "Now that the airship has come into such common use," one Virginia lawyer remarked in 1912, "the courts cannot much longer dodge an adjudication upon the status of the common-law rule of real property, that the proprietor owns ab solo usque ad coelum. We predict, however, that the court will hold this maxim to be obsolete." The lawyer suggested that American judges were likely to reach a result similar to that reached in a recent case in Paris, in which a court had held an aviator liable to landowners for overflights—not for trespassing, but for disturbing the landowners and frightening their horses with loud engine noise. "Before the days of aerial navigation there was little occasion to question the soundness of the old maxim of our law, *Cujus est solum ejus est usque ad coelum*," another lawyer agreed. With airplanes, however, he recommended the substitution of a nuisance rule for a trespass rule.[38]

Like Leon Green, advocates of change often couched their proposals as predictions of what judges *would* do, not what they *should* do, but it was clear enough that these writers favored the course they foresaw judges taking. "The law of trespass will undoubtedly be greatly modified in the next few years by the rapid advancement of the science of aviation," one St. Louis law student asserted in 1919. He acknowledged that the *cujus est solum* maxim was still in force as the common law of Missouri. But he was certain that courts in Missouri and other states "will act upon the question when it arises with an eye to substantial justice between the parties" rather than blindly following precedent. "So if a man flies over my land so high as not to interfere with my enjoyment thereof, then I am entitled to no substantial compensation; but the instant he injures me then his trespass *per se* in so flying relieves me of the necessity of showing negligence on his part."[39] This proposed rule was stated a bit differently than the law of nuisance, but it would have yielded identical results in virtually all cases—liability only where the aviator caused some kind of damage to the landowner below. Like many writers on the subject, moreover, the student was slipping back and forth, apparently without noticing, between a prediction of what courts

In its early years the airplane posed some serious risks for landowners
beneath. Planes flew low enough that noise and dust were recurring
complaints, pilots sometimes dropped things from open cockpits, and
of course there was always the danger of a crash. Many lawyers argued
that these forms of damage could be redressed through the law of
nuisance rather than trespass, a move that would clear the skies for
flying. LC-USZ62-73870, Prints and Photographs Division, Library
of Congress.

would do and his own opinion about what was right. A conception of judges as lawmakers allowed precisely that.

Why did lawyers interested in promoting aviation pay so much
attention to the common law? Everyone knew that judges were
not the only ones with the power to change the common law.
Legislatures could trump the common law in this area, as they did
in so many others, simply by enacting statutes. Why not just en-

courage legislators to modify the *cujus est solum* doctrine, either by limiting it to a certain height or by converting it to a rule of nuisance?

Many did urge legislative change. Charles Evans Hughes, the governor of New York (and soon to become a justice of the U.S. Supreme Court) spoke out in 1910 in favor of a statute defining the right of aircraft to fly over private property. "It is evident that flying man has no absolute right to pass over the property of another," insisted the lawyer Denys Myers. "The subject is one for statutory regulation." Legislation of the sort was "imperative and inevitable," one law student declared.[40] Such calls for statutory change were common.

Some of these proposals were quite elaborate. Lord Montagu of Beaulieu, an early promoter of the automobile and the airplane, suggested dividing the air into five levels. Up to 2,000 feet flight would be prohibited; the *cujus est solum* doctrine would in effect be capped at that height. The zone between 2,000 and 4,000 feet would be reserved for ordinary commercial flights. High-speed commercial flights would occupy the stratum between 4,000 and 6,000 feet. Next would be military airspace, from 6,000 to 10,000 feet, and then finally the level above 10,000 feet would be open to anyone. Other proposals for regulation were much simpler. The Denver lawyer Wayne Williams, for example, hoped for a statute creating a "zone of innocent passage" for aircraft, at a height that would vary by locality.[41]

In the United States, however, there was a serious obstacle to such proposals. Lurking behind all these suggested statutes, and no doubt inhibiting many more, was the worry that any legislative incursion on the landowner's right to his airspace would be unconstitutional. If the airspace was the landowner's property, there was a plausible argument that a statute taking that property away from the landowner required compensation. The lawyer

Thomas Marshall favored legislation allowing aircraft to fly over private property, but he feared that "it is questionable whether the states have the power to confer the right of flight over another's land upon any member of the public by statute, without compensating the landowners." When the American Bar Association established a committee on the law of aviation, the committee was tentative, for the same reason, about recommending any legislation at all.[42]

One way around this obstacle, as Marshall suggested, would have been for the government to compensate landowners for their losses. Some, considering the price justified by the gains to commerce, urged states to exercise their power of eminent domain and condemn the airspace above a certain height. The New York lawyer Lyttleton Fox acknowledged that simply declaring the air free for travel "would hardly seem practicable in this country, as constituting a taking of property without due compensation." But he thought that the "project of condemning the air, while in a sense novel, would be perfectly feasible." It would not be a complete solution, he recognized, "because as matters stand at present the aeroplanist, in order to make a landing, must arise and descend on a slanting course, and should this continue to be necessary trespasses would be committed while passing between the earth level and the upper air."[43] But it would be a start, and it would be the only way of circumventing the Constitution.

William Lamb, the chief lawyer for the U.S. Department of Commerce in the early 1920s, even proposed that Congress condemn all of the airspace over privately owned land throughout the entire United States. He expected his proposal to be costless to the government, because he did not anticipate that any landowner would be able to prove that he or she had suffered any actual loss.[44]

Condemning the airspace, however, would have been an enormous administrative burden. R. Floyd Clarke shuddered at the prospect of "the description in a petition of condemnation of all the parcels of real estate throughout the State and notice to all the owners, mortgagees, etc." Just notifying the landowners, Clarke despaired, would be "a stupendous and almost impossible undertaking."[45] And even if that hurdle could have been mounted, condemnation might well have required separate hearings, and possibly even jury trials, for each individual landowner, at which each would have the opportunity to establish the amount of loss that he or she would individually suffer from overflights. For anyone who gave thought to the time and expense that would be involved in condemning enough airspace to allow commercial air travel, the use of the state or federal government's eminent domain power was not an attractive option. Promoters of aviation were back to the constitutional problem. A statute abrogating the *cujus est solum* maxim, by allowing aviators to fly over private land, ran a considerable risk of being held unconstitutional.

This was why lawyers in the 1910s and 1920s paid so much attention to the common law. Because of the fiction that judges did not make the law but found it, a judicial determination that aviators could fly over private property was not susceptible to constitutional challenge. If a judge, rather than a legislature, were to modify the *cujus est solum* maxim, the surface discourse of the legal system would not deem him to be changing the law at all. He would instead be understood to be discerning what the law had always been. "A judicial determination along this line will, under our form of government, be far better than any attempt to settle the matter by legislative action," Carl Zollman explained, in an unusually frank admission. "A judicial determination that the existing law allows aerial navigation over private property will be far more satisfactory than any legislative attempt to so change the law as to make flying legally possible. The most carefully worded statute on this subject would probably be subject to the objection that it is taking property without due process of law, and therefore is unconstitutional."[46] Legislatures and courts could both change the law, most lawyers doubtless recognized in private, but in public only legislatures could do so. One of the peculiar beauties of the common law was its ability to change in full view without anyone admitting to the change. If a judge abrogated the *cujus est solum* maxim, landowners would not be *losing* any rights to airspace. Rather, they would be newly viewed as never having enjoyed those rights at all.

This debate over whether and how the common law should be changed to accommodate airplanes went on for decades, from the dawn of flight at the turn of the century through the 1930s. In one sense the debate was timeless. Some of the arguments scarcely changed between the first decade of the century and the fourth. They involved questions fundamental to the legal system. What was the nature of land? What was the source of common law? Lawyers might reasonably have expected that the answers to questions like these would not change over time, or at least not change very quickly or very often. That intuition, no doubt, accounts for the static quality of much of the debate over aerial trespass.

The absence of change was also due in part to the lack of decided cases. As we will see in the next chapter, there would be no American court decisions concerning aerial trespass until the 1920s, and even then the early decisions didn't fully address the question of whether aircraft were trespassing on the land beneath. The common law of aerial trespass changed very little, if at all, between 1900 and 1930, so the materials at the disposal of lawyers in the construction of arguments did not change either. Thirty years after *cujus est solum* was recognized as a serious prob-

lem, lawyers were still trotting out Coke and Blackstone, Ellenborough and Blackburn, overhanging eaves and tree branches.

But of course some aspects of the world were changing very
quickly, in ways that were quite relevant to the debate. In 1909
Louis Blériot startled the world when he became the first to fly
over the English Channel at its narrowest point, a trip of twenty
miles. No plane "will ever fly from New York to Paris," Wilbur
Wright affirmed the same year. "That seems to me to be impossible. What limits the flight is the motor. No known motor can
run at the requisite speed for four days without stopping." A decade later two British pilots crossed the Atlantic nonstop in sixteen hours. Early aviators were nervous about exceeding one hundred feet in altitude. By 1913 a few pilots had reached twenty
thousand feet, and by 1929 the record was over forty thousand
feet. Commercial passenger flights were a far-off dream in 1910,
but by the 1920s there were several passenger airlines in operation. The U.S. Postal Service began delivering mail by airplane in
1918. By 1922 it was already operating seventy planes, which in
that year alone carried more than sixty million letters. Mail posted
in New York before ten in the morning, the postmaster proudly
announced, was delivered in San Francisco before the close of the
following business day.[47] By the time the debate over aerial trespass petered out, the aviation industry looked nothing like it had
at the start.

Meanwhile parts of the legal background were changing as
well. The growing power of the incipient aviation industry was
prompting new statutes, in the United States and abroad. Changing attitudes about the relationship between private property and
government regulation were on the verge of transforming American constitutional law. The pace of events would accordingly ac-
celerate in the 1920s.

FOUR

A Uniform Law

One obvious fact about airplanes was that they crossed jurisdictional boundaries. A flight could easily begin in one nation or one state and end in another. As the speed and the range of planes increased, a single flight could subject the aviator to the laws of multiple jurisdictions. What would happen if those laws were inconsistent with one another?

This was recognized as a looming problem before anyone could fly very far. "It will certainly be difficult for the aeronaut, sailing above the clouds, to know whether he is in New York or Pennsylvania, and whether he may go two hundred miles an hour or only twenty," remarked one lawyer in 1909. But all he could suggest was a joke: "Perhaps kites will solve the problem, and along the borders of each state we shall see a great number of these hitherto not very useful playthings bearing such signs as this: 'PENNSYLVANIA LINE: SLOW DOWN TO TWENTY MILES.'"[1] Each state had the power to enact its own idiosyncratic aviation laws. In each, state legislators had to be responsive to local conditions if they hoped to stay in office. Americans were accustomed to different laws in different states, and in many areas those differences mattered little, because it was not hard to adjust one's conduct upon entering a new state. But aviation was different. In the air, it was far more important that state law be uniform.

The aerial trespass question played an important role in this desire for uniformity, because it was not hard to foresee trouble from inconsistent state trespass laws. If some states allowed over-flights of private land but others did not, or if they imposed different height requirements to avoid liability for trespass, what was an aviator to do? How would he know when he was entering a new state? Even if he did know, how could he keep track of the divergent laws of each state? "No aeroplane would venture to fly without a lawyer," complained the president of the American Flying Club, "should all the forty-eight states take a hand at governing flights over their territory."[2] A flight that was perfectly legal at one moment might turn into a trespass at the next, without any warning.

The problem was just as intractable from the state's perspective. Under the Constitution, state governments had less power to regulate interstate activities than those conducted entirely within the state's boundaries. But how was a state official to know whether the airplane overhead was on an interstate or intrastate voyage? "Will it be necessary for the airship to descend at every State boundary, though such boundary may run through a mass of jagged mountain peaks?" wondered one lawyer. "Will the development of aerial navigation thus be crippled by requiring frequent and sometimes dangerous and utterly purposeless landings?"[3] No matter how one looked at it, the prospect of differing state aviation laws was something to avoid.

One possible solution was to have the federal government, not the states, control aviation with standard nationwide rules. This possibility was debated at great length, because for the first three decades of the twentieth century the scope of the federal government's constitutional authority to regulate aviation was not at all clear. But federal control was not the only way to harmonize inconsistent state laws. A second way, and one pursued with greater enthusiasm in the early years of flight, was to persuade the states to do the harmonizing themselves. If the states would enact identical statutes, the problems of inconsistency would vanish, without any need to press against the limits of federal power.

Aviation was hardly the only field in which consistency was desirable but federal authority was uncertain. The early years of flight also happened to be the early years of a movement among lawyers to create uniform state laws regulating a wide range of subjects. The issue of aerial trespass intersected with this movement in the 1920s to produce the first efforts at solving the trespass problem by statute.

Uniformity in the law was already a very old ideal by the turn of the twentieth century, one with roots both intellectual and practical. American legal intellectuals had long been dissatisfied with what seemed to be the law's hodgepodge character. Law, they argued, was not an assemblage of unrelated doctrines that might vary irregularly from one place to the next. It was instead a *science.* "When we say that a branch of human knowledge is a science," explained one American lawyer in the 1830s, "we mean, in general, that it is founded on principles inherent in the subjects to which it relates. We mean also that those principles serve as a basis whereon we may classify the subjects of that particular branch of knowledge." The apparent multiplicity of legal doctrines, on this view, concealed their underlying dependence on a small number of fundamental principles from which the doctrines were derived. The law formed a logical, coherent whole, like geometry or zoology. The law, considered as a science, was based on "axioms as self-evident as those of mathematics," from which the skilled lawyer could derive "postulates as admissible." It followed that if two judges came to opposite conclusions, one must have been mistaken. Mathematicians and physicians sometimes disagreed as well, but that did not render mathematics or medicine any less of a science capable of yielding correct answers.[4]

The rise of the American law school in the late nineteenth century was both a product of this conception of law as a science and a boost to its prevalence. The Harvard dean Christopher Langdell, who did more than anyone else to create the modern law school in the United States, based much of Harvard's curriculum on the idea that students could be trained to derive correct answers to legal problems from an appreciation of the law's inherent logical structure. "Law, considered as a science, consists of certain principles or doctrines," he declared. "If those doctrines could be so classified and arranged that each should be found in its proper place, and nowhere else, they would cease to be formidable from their number." The law library, where the case reports were shelved, "is to us all that the laboratories of the university are to the chemists and physicists, the museum of natural history to the zoologists, the botanical garden to the botanist."[5] It was the repository of the raw material from which a legal scientist could induce laws just as regular, and just as true, as those discovered by natural scientists.

This idea of law, as consisting of doctrines logically derivable from a small number of basic principles, was thriving (at least in the most highly regarded law schools) in the early twentieth century. It was also under vigorous attack, even at its peak. Oliver Wendell Holmes intended his famous assertion that "the life of the law has not been logic: it has been experience" as a direct response to claims like Langdell's. "The law embodies the story of a nation's development through centuries," Holmes scoffed, "and it cannot be dealt with as if it contained only the axioms and corollaries of a book of mathematics."[6] But if not everyone agreed that the law had an underlying coherent structure, the concept was prevalent enough, at least as an ideal, to contribute something to the movement for uniform state law.

Probably more important, however, were the practical sources of the uniform law movement. For many practicing lawyers and their clients, inconsistent state law was simply a pain in the neck. This was particularly true in the commercial world, where a single transaction might be governed by the laws of more than one state. "Under the present system," complained the Cincinnati lawyer Francis James, there was no way to predict the validity of commercial paper as it moved from state to state. "If the instrument be issued in New Jersey and a lawyer be consulted, he may say that by the decisions in Massachusetts the transaction is invalid, by those of New York it is valid, and he does not know which view, if either, the Courts of New Jersey will adopt." The law professor Joseph Beale provided an even more complex example. "A builder of locomotives in Rhode Island sells a locomotive to a railroad in Connecticut," Beale imagined, "retaining title as security for payment, and records the transaction in Rhode Island as the law requires, and the locomotive starts on its travels; through New York and Connecticut, Massachusetts, Vermont, New Hampshire, and Maine, leading the railroad's creditors on to a race of diligence. May they reach the locomotive by an attachment, in spite of the recorded lien of the seller?" asked Beale. The answer depended on the law of the state where the locomotive happened to be, but that law was different in each one. "The wise creditor will try it on in each state. He may be sure that in some states he will have his costs for his pains; but in one of the six he is pretty sure to get relief, and no human power can tell him which one it will be."[7] One did not need a high-flown jurisprudential theory to want uniform state laws.

The more reflective among the lawyers pushing for uniformity recognized that technological change had created the problem they sought to address. "A hundred years ago," the Pennsylvania lawyer Ovid Johnson remarked, people and goods crossed state lines much less frequently, and so "any want of harmony in the legislation of the states touching matters of the general welfare was seldom felt, and therefore gave rise to little inconvenience." Now, however, the railway and the telegraph had transformed communication, travel, and commerce. The automobile and the airplane promised even more change to come. When states had divergent laws, "friction is apt to begin as soon as a mere artificial line is crossed and an adjacent jurisdiction is entered." Making those laws uniform would produce "unshackled trade between the states," predicted the Connecticut lawyer Lyman Brewster, as well as "greater certainty in inter-state contracts," and "less uncertainty and delay in inter-state litigation."[8]

Advocates for uniformity conceived of the movement as genuinely public-spirited. Who, after all, could object to making the law simpler and more consistent? Uniformity would not just reduce the costs associated with interstate transactions, however; it was also likely to increase the flow of business to lawyers in major cities, many of whom were leaders of the movement for uniformity, at the expense of lawyers in smaller towns. Lawyers in places like New York and Chicago often retained local counsel to give advice on idiosyncratic state law, but that function would disappear along with state idiosyncrasies. Uniformity "would make the law a trust administered solely in the large cities," complained the Arkansas lawyer George Rose. "Then the lawyer in New York or Chicago would have no need for his colleague in Iowa or Nebraska. Being at the great centers of commercial and financial activity, he would control all the business of importance, leaving to his less fortunate brother little more than the resources of the scavenger." Where big-city lawyers saw efficiency, Rose, and perhaps the members of the Arkansas Bar Association who sat in his audience, saw only monopoly and the homogenizing corporatism of modern life. "The lawyers in the large cities would be benefited by a uniformity that would make their practice universal, and enable them to monopolize legal business; but where would be the benefit to the community at large?" Rose asked. "In these days the trusts are crushing the individual, the great department stores are ruining the commercial life of our cities, and the adoption of uniform State laws would reduce the Bar to the same condition."[9]

Such complaints did little to slow the move toward uniform state laws. At its inception in 1878, the American Bar Association adopted uniformity as one of its objectives, and to that end it created in 1892 the organization that would become the National Conference of Commissioners on Uniform State Laws, an institution that still exists today. The Conference's first annual meeting included representatives from only seven states, but before long most states began sending delegates. The organization's task was to draft proposed uniform state laws, which members would then seek to have introduced into their home state legislatures.[10]

The Conference began with statutes to harmonize state commercial law. Its first product was a Uniform Negotiable Instruments Act, published in 1896. In less than a decade, it became the law of twenty-five states.[11] By 1916 it had been enacted by forty-four of the forty-eight states. Next came a Uniform Sales Act and a Uniform Warehouse Receipts Act, which were also widely adopted. As the Conference established itself, it began to wander on occasion from commercial topics. It drafted a Uniform Divorce Act in 1907, a Uniform Child Labor Law in 1911, and even a Uniform Flag Law in 1915 to regulate desecration of the flag. These noncommercial ventures were never as successful as the Conference's commercial acts. The advocates of uniformity had been right to emphasize mercantile considerations all along.

Urban lawyers were not the only constituency for standardization. Their large commercial clients favored it too, in the hope that complying with one uniform law would be less costly than complying with a variety of laws in different states. The American Bankers Association, for example, had its own committee on uniform laws that worked toward the same goal as the National Conference. The Bankers Association was so enamored of the Uniform Negotiable Instruments Act that it paid to have copies printed and distributed to state legislators all over the country. It did not take long for national trade associations and large businesses to begin participating in the National Conference's meetings, in order to influence the wording of the uniform acts. When the Conference's committee on commercial law met in New York in 1909, for example, they were joined by representatives of the American Bankers Association, the American Warehousemen's Association, the National Board of Trade, the Merchants Association of New York City, the Richmond Chamber of Commerce, the National Industrial Traffic League, the National Manufacturers' Association, the Erie Railroad, the Pennsylvania Railroad, and the New York, New Haven and Hartford Railroad.[12] Uniformity of state law allowed organizations operating on a multistate scale to focus their lobbying at a single point.

Uniformity accordingly threatened a tilting of the playing field toward large urban enterprises that paralleled the centralization of legal work. Some of the uniform acts were viewed with suspicion in rural states for this reason. One state legislature reportedly refused to enact the Uniform Negotiable Instruments Act after learning that it was favored by the American Bankers Association, on the theory that if it was good for urban bankers, it must be bad for state residents. One of the state commissioners from New England attributed this attitude to the "lamentable phase of American politics," but this sort of nervousness about uniform state law may instead have been produced by a rational assessment of the interests of small businesses in rural states.[13] Whatever the cause, it did not slow the movement toward uniformity, particularly in commercial matters. The movement would reach its peak in the 1950s, with the drafting of the National Conference's best-known product, an all-encompassing Uniform Commercial Code.

Aviation was a commercial topic, and one as to which interstate uniformity was particularly desirable. "The art of aviation has now been sufficiently developed to warrant" legislation, Simeon Baldwin urged in 1910. "It would be easier now to secure a uniform law in all the states than it might be later. The subject is one that might well be taken up by the Conference of Commissioners on Uniform State Legislation."[14] But the Conference had other areas of law to handle that seemed more important than aviation. The industry was still so new that there were not yet many inconsistencies between the laws of different states; indeed, there was not yet much state law on aviation at all. The problems of banks and other large interstate enterprises loomed much larger in the consciousness of an urban lawyer than the problems of aviators, most of whom were individuals or very small businesses. Aviation would have to grow before it could claim a place on the agenda of uniformity.

While the uncertain status of the landowner's property rights in the air inhibited American legislation, European countries began enacting statutes authorizing aviators to fly over privately owned land. These countries all began, before the invention of the airplane, in the same position as Britain and the United States, in that some version of the *cujus est solum* maxim was ensconced in the law as a verbal formula, although of course the rule had never been tested by the new possibilities of flight. The influential French Civil Code, for example, declared that "the ownership of the soil carries the ownership of whatsoever is above and beneath it." Similar formulations existed throughout Continental Europe and in Japan. "In almost every country," explained the Dutch scholar Johanna Lycklama à Nijeholt, "the extent of land-property is ruled by the old adage 'Cujus est solum ejus est usque ad coelum.'" In her 1910 book on air law, one of the very first legal treatises in the world written by a woman, Lycklama à Nijeholt found functionally identical phrases everywhere from Portugal to Turkey.[15]

With the prospect of flight, the maxim became just as controversial in Continental Europe as it was in Britain and the United States. "Aviators make fun of it," reported the French lawyer Henri Guibé. "They pass above like birds, and laugh at the complaints and the menacing gestures of the people below." The questions that preoccupied Continental lawyers were the same ones current in the English-speaking world. What exactly did it mean to own the space above the soil? How far up did the landowner's rights extend? Did they allow the landowner to exclude aircraft, even when overflights caused no harm? "It is this question," the French court clerk Gaston Bonnefoy declared in 1909, "that has preoccupied our jurists the most."[16] In Europe these issues arose within a legal climate less resistant to the legislative modification of property rights. Continental European countries were thus quicker than Britain or the United States to adjust their property law in response to the development of aviation.

The first to change was Germany. The German Civil Code of 1900 included the standard statement that "the right of an owner of a piece of land extends to the space above the surface and to the substance of the earth beneath the surface." That much was familiar ground. But new in 1900 was a second sentence: "The owner may not, however, forbid interference which takes place at such a height or depth that he has no interest in its prevention."

With this addition the problem of overflights was solved, just as the first dirigibles were staying aloft for minutes at a time. It was generally understood that the new airships would not be trespassers, so long as they stayed high enough to avoid disturbing landowners below. As early as 1907 the Munich-educated London barrister Ernest Schuster was confident that while telegraph wires obstructing the German sky would infringe the landowner's rights, "aerial navigation at a considerable altitude comes within the statutory qualification" depriving the landowner of any power to interfere.[17]

Switzerland followed suit seven years later. The Swiss Civil Code of 1907 provided that "the ownership of the soil implies the ownership of all that is above and below the surface," but only "to such a height and depth respectively as the owner may require." As in Germany, overflights became clearly lawful, so long as they did not interfere with the landowner's use of the land. "As for aerial navigation," explained a pair of Swiss law professors in their treatise explicating the new civil code, "it certainly escapes from the rights of the owner of the soil, because it exceeds his sphere of interest."[18]

The German and Swiss statutes received rave reviews in the United States and Britain. Simeon Baldwin, the governor of Connecticut, thought them "quite in accordance with the spirit of our times," times in which "modern government tends, at all points, to push the public good farther and farther into what was formerly thought the inviolable domain of private right." The English lawyer G. D. Valentine found them "agreeable to general sentiment" in Britain, where "we regard the water, the air and the light as open to all." From Boston, Denys Myers admired Germany and Switzerland for passing laws "specially intended to affect aëronautics," and predicted that other countries would do the same.[19]

They soon did. In 1911, France enacted a statute specifying that aircraft were free to fly above the nation's territory. The French minister of public works explained that "the aim of the government was, while protecting the public, not to injure in any way a new national industry." The statute did not preclude courts from requiring compensation to landowners for damage to their property, and in subsequent cases courts did just that. The statute had been in effect for less than a year when a group of farmers whose land abutted the Buc aerodrome near Paris complained that while taking off and landing, planes flew over their farms at very low altitudes—only five to fifteen meters, according to the farmers—which frightened both animal and human laborers in the fields. The farmers asked for compensation, as well as an injunction barring future overflights at less than two hundred meters. The court refused to grant the injunction; "it is not the function of the Court," the judges declared, "to fix the height at which aviators must fly." But it did award compensation for the farmers' losses. In a similar case decided a year later, another court reached the identical result. It held that "the freedom of the air is complete and the *circulation aerienne* is in the present state of the law free from all restraint," but nevertheless awarded damages to the farmers because the flights at issue had been at insufficient altitude.[20]

France thus joined Germany and Switzerland in clarifying that airplanes were not trespassing on the land beneath simply by flying over it. Landowners had no right to exclude temporary occupants of their airspace, one French treatise explained. "For example, the landowner could not prevent the passage of balloons or aeroplanes in the part of the sky above his property." American lawyers once again wished for something similar. The news from France "not only accords with common sense," one American lawyers' magazine remarked, "but, in view of the modern developments of aviation, appears to be compelled *ex necessitate*."[21]

Yet the American constitutional tradition of insulating property rights from adverse legislation continued to prevent any of the American states from making the same move.

Britain shared some of that tradition, with an unwritten constitution that, like American written constitutions, provided an ambiguous degree of protection to property rights. It was thus a marker of how thought was changing in the English-speaking world when in 1911 the Home Office prepared a bill that would have provided that "the flight of an aircraft over any land in the British Islands shall not in itself be deemed a trespass." The bill went nowhere at the time, but a few years later, as World War I drew to a close, the government's Civil Aerial Transport Committee endorsed the principle of explicitly authorizing aircraft to fly over private land. The bill's language went too far, the committee concluded, but the underlying principle was sound. "This clause is very important to private landowners," the committee explained. "It proposes to deprive the landowner of his frequently asserted right to the air space over his land *usque ad coelum*. To retain this doctrine in its entirety would be fatal to civil aeronautics. On the other hand, to allow unrestricted flying over private property at all altitudes would interfere with the reasonable rights of landowners." The committee accordingly recommended adding clauses preserving the ability of landowners to sue aviators for trespass and nuisance where they suffered damage from overflights.[22]

The Air Navigation Act of 1920 embodied this compromise between the interests of landowners and those of aviators. It provided that "no action shall lie in respect of trespass or in respect of nuisance, by reason only of the flight of aircraft over any property at a height above the ground, which, having regard to wind, weather, and all the circumstances of the case is reasonable." Aviators who kept at a reasonable altitude would be safe from lawsuits.

The act continued: "but where material damage or loss is caused by an aircraft in flight, taking-off, or landing, . . . to any person or property on land or water, damages shall be recoverable . . . without proof of negligence." When aviators caused damage by flying too low, or by dropping objects from their planes, they would have to compensate landowners regardless of how careful they had been.[23]

By 1920 much of western Europe had attained uniformity on the question of aerial trespass. Law professors continued to work toward worldwide consistency. When the International Law Association's Aviation Committee met at the Hague in 1921, for example, it resolved "that the aerial laws as to damage, trespass, nuisance, etc., should be uniform in all States," and provided a template it urged nations to follow. The very first of its model provisions was closely patterned on Britain's Air Navigation Act: "No action shall lie for trespass or nuisance by reason purely and solely of the flight of any aircraft over any property at a reasonable height."[24] This was an issue of domestic national law untouched by the 1919 Convention Relating to International Air Navigation. The Convention required signatory states to allow aircraft of other signatory states to pass through the airspace, but it said nothing about whether or under what circumstances airplanes would be trespassing on the land beneath. Yet even without much pushing from outside, European nations were moving toward uniformity.

While these European nations were protecting aviators from trespass suits, American states were legislating as well, but the fear of overstepping constitutional boundaries inhibited states from doing anything inconsistent with the *cujus est solum* maxim. Connecticut was the first state to regulate aircraft by statute, in part because of Governor Simeon Baldwin's personal interest in the issue.[25] Connecticut's act of 1911 included detailed provisions about the registration of aircraft, the markers aircraft would have to display, a licensing requirement for pilots, the operation of aircraft by nonresidents of the state, the fees that would be charged for various government actions, the liability of aviators for injuries caused by flights—in short, provisions about everything related to airplanes except whether they were trespassing by flying over private property. On that question the statute was studiously silent. The same was true of the law passed two years later by Massachusetts, which skated as close to abrogating *cujus est solum* as possible without actually doing so. The Massachusetts statute established minimum flight altitudes of three thousand feet above cities, one thousand feet above towns with more than five thousand inhabitants, and five hundred feet above other towns. It also required aviators to "fly at such altitude as will best conduce to the safety of those below" when flying over buildings. These provisions seemed to imply that planes were allowed to occupy the airspace above privately owned land, but they were carefully worded to avoid any explicit authorization of overflights.[26]

Many other states likewise began regulating aviation by statute over the next decade, but these statutes, like those of Connecticut and Massachusetts, said nothing about aerial trespass. No state would address the issue for several years to come. It was not for lack of interest in the question. Whether aviators were trespassing on the land beneath was just as important in the United States as in Europe, but American legislators were hemmed in by contemporary understandings of the Constitution. "If the space is owned absolutely by the surface owner," reasoned the Cornell law professor George Bogert, legislation would be unconstitutional if it purported to open that space up to aircraft. "There can be no development of aerial transportation without a constitutional

Simeon Baldwin was one of the leaders of the American bar in the late nineteenth and early twentieth centuries. As a lawyer, he authored some of the earliest articles on aviation law and drafted the first proposal for a federal statute to regulate aviation. As governor of Connecticut, he was primarily responsible for the country's first state aviation statute, enacted in 1911. LC-DIG-ggbain-05137, Prints and Photographs Division, Library of Congress.

amendment by which the people of the states give up their property rights in space to some extent and allow an easement of passage. Otherwise the expense of acquiring rights of way and defending trespass and injunction suits would bankrupt all aerial transportation companies." Elza Johnson, the legal advisor to the U.S. Army Air Service, the precursor to today's U.S. Air Force, recommended such a constitutional amendment, without which, he feared, any regulation of the airspace would be impossible.[27] Where European legislators were pressing against one legal doctrine, *cujus est solum,* American legislators were pressing against two. They had to grapple with a second and even stronger restraint, a constitutional protection for property rights that did not exist in Europe.

That constitutional protection, however, was only as strong as the property rights it enforced. There were already many lawyers prepared to assert that *cujus est solum* was not an accurate statement of the common law, and that landowners had no right to exclude aircraft from their airspace. As this view came to be more widely held, the constitutional obstacle to legislation would evaporate proportionally. If *cujus est solum* had never been the law, after all, then landowners would lose nothing from statutes giving pilots the right to fly over private land.

The first reported American judicial decision on whether airplanes were trespassers was not written until 1922, nearly two decades after the Wright brothers' first flight. By then the airplane was no longer a novelty. Americans were producing several hundred planes per year. (In 1918 that figure spiked to fourteen thousand, virtually all of which were for the military.) The postal service was operating regular airmail routes. Private airlines were flying passengers on scheduled flights. Earl Findley, a captain in the Army Air Service, calculated in early 1921 that more than forty million dollars was currently invested in nongovernmental aviation, and that over the past twenty months private aircraft firms had carried more than three hundred thousand passengers more than fourteen million miles.[28] Lawyers had been offering dire predictions of trespass suits for years, yet in all that time no court had published an opinion on who should win.

There had been occasional disputes between landowners and aviators all along. In 1920, for example, when a flight over a farm in Barre, Vermont, allegedly caused the farmer's high-strung horse to bolt straight into a barbed-wire fence, the farmer sued the aviator for trespass, according to an account in a contemporary magazine. The case may have settled before trial, or the farmer may have dropped the suit, because the case does not appear to have been litigated to a conclusion. In the same year another aviator flew very low over a golf course along the Hudson River, for the pure sport of annoying the golfers, before landing on the fairway. The country club was reported to be considering litigation. No doubt there were other landowners who were angry about the airplanes they increasingly saw overhead.[29] But very few proceeded to court.

One who did seems to have won a trespass case in 1921. According to a short newspaper account, a trial judge in Cleveland agreed with the landowner that his property rights extended upward without limit, and that overflights at any height were therefore trespasses. "If a person can go over one's land with impunity at a height of a mile," the judge asked, "what is to prevent him from going over at 25 feet?" The judge predicted that aviation companies "would have to obtain rights of way in the air similar to those which railroad companies must acquire on the surface."[30] This decision was never published, and indeed from the newspaper story one cannot even tell whether the judge made his remarks orally or in writing. Like virtually all unpublished court decisions, no one except the parties involved seems to have noticed it. It had no effect on the debate over aerial trespass.

For the vast majority of landowners, a trespass suit was simply not worth the cost, in time and money, of filing. A landowner had to suffer considerable annoyance from overflights to make a suit worthwhile. One might suppose that people living next to airports would have fallen within that category, but until 1922 none pursued a trespass case long enough for a court to reach an outcome. Indeed, it appears that none of them pursued a nuisance case either. Regardless of the law of trespass, a landowner who suffered actual damage from frequent low, noisy overflights would have had a plausible claim for nuisance, yet there were no reported cases before 1922. The law waited for a particularly irritable landowner to be the first to file a lawsuit that would yield a published opinion.

That person turned out to be Oscar P. Grube, a farmer in Bell Township, Pennsylvania, a small town near Punxsutawney in the western part of the state. The adjoining farm was owned by a man named Bargerstock, who leased part of his land to aviators for use as an airstrip. Harold Nevin, one of the aviators, operated one of the early airlines; he flew passengers in his single small plane, sometimes for short distances, and sometimes around in circles just for fun. One summer day in 1922, Nevin had a passenger aboard for one of his circular flights. He took off from Bargerstock's airstrip. By the time he crossed above the property line separating Bargerstock's land from Grube's, he was about fifty feet off the ground. Nevin's plane continued to climb as it traversed the airspace above Grube's farm, until it left Grube's airspace at an altitude of about 350 feet. Nevin then circled around and landed back at Bargerstock's airstrip, without crossing a second time above Grube's land.

Nevin's flight was harmless enough, but for Grube it must have been the last straw, because he went straight to a justice of the peace and filed a criminal trespass charge against Nevin. Perhaps Grube and Nevin had argued about Nevin's flights in the past. Maybe Nevin had ignored Grube's repeated requests to stop flying over his farm. Whatever the reason for Grube's anger, an ordinary civil trespass suit was not enough for him. He had to file a criminal charge, and that was his undoing. Trespass is both a civil wrong and a crime, but not all civil trespasses are also criminal. Under Pennsylvania's criminal trespass statute, trespass was a crime only where the alleged trespasser had first been warned, by printed notices posted upon the land, that his presence amounted to trespassing. The justice of the peace found Nevin guilty and fined him one dollar plus the cost of prosecution, but his conviction was reversed within a day or two by a county judge, who held that the state legislature could not have intended to include overflights within the criminal trespass statute. An aviator could hardly be expected to see printed notices posted upon land while he was flying by. Nor could an aviator be required to descend, alight from his plane, and examine the landscape for "No Trespassing" signs every time he crossed over a property line. The statute had been enacted in 1905, when air travel was extraordinarily rare. The judge accordingly concluded that Pennsylvania's criminal trespass statute applied only to conventional trespasses committed on the ground, not to overflights by airplane.[31]

"Aerial Trespassers Exonerated" proclaimed the headline in *Aviation* magazine, and the popular press reported that flights over private property had been held not to constitute trespass, but this was something of an overstatement. Nevin had been exonerated of criminal trespass, but the ruling of the county judge had said nothing about ordinary civil trespass, the kind of lawsuit lawyers had been worrying about for two decades. Whether aviators were trespassing in the civil sense remained an open question, even in Pennsylvania. Oscar Grube was left to pay his lawyer's bill plus $100 in court costs. Grube's lawyer, W. B. Adams, furnished the press with the unlikely explanation that Grube had started the proceedings not for his own benefit but "purely to ascertain the law in the case and the rights of landowners in relation to airplanes." If so, he had paid a high price, and because Adams filed a criminal rather than a civil suit, the rights of landowners were no clearer than before.[32]

A year later, an accident in Minnesota provided the occasion for the first American court decision on whether airplanes were trespassers in the ordinary civil sense. After a plane crashed on his lawn in the summer of 1923, a St. Paul resident named Johnson brought suit against the firm that owned it, the Curtiss Northwest Airplane Company. Johnson asked for damages, of course, but he also asked for an injunction ordering the company to refrain from flying any aircraft over his land, at any altitude. The case came before John C. Michael, a trial judge in St. Paul, who thus became the first American judge to write an opinion on the subject that had agitated American lawyers for two decades.[33]

Michael began with the *cujus est solum* maxim. He acknowledged that if the maxim were taken literally, he would have to grant the injunction, because the Curtiss Northwest Airplane Company would be committing trespass every time it flew into Johnson's airspace. But Michael, like many American lawyers by 1923, did not think well of the maxim. It "was adopted in an age of primitive industrial development by the courts of England, long prior to the American revolution," he scoffed, "when any practical use of the upper air was not considered or thought possible, and when such aerial trespasses as did occur were relatively near to the surface." Now everything was different, because of the airplane. "We are passing through an age of marvelous achievements in the way of useful mechanical inventions," Michael declared, "with the result that practical air navigation is now an accomplished fact. Its possibility of great public usefulness in rapid communication and transportation seems already to be well demonstrated."

So far Michael had said nothing with which anyone could disagree. There was no doubt that the *cujus est solum* maxim had been devised at a time when aerial trespasses were close to the ground, or that airplanes were very useful. The question was what to do with these facts. On one view, the common-law property rights of the landowner required that he be compensated before planes could cross his territory. On a second, the maxim was an inaccurate statement of the common law, because it exaggerated the outcomes of the actual cases on which it was based. On a third view, the maxim *was* an accurate account of the law, but the law itself had to change to accommodate the aerial age, and judges were fully empowered to change it. Michael took this last view. "Common law rules are sufficiently flexible to adapt themselves to new conditions arising out of modern progress, and it is within the legitimate province of the courts to so construe and apply them," he insisted. He then proceeded to do just that. As applied to overflights, he held, the *cujus est solum* maxim "is only a legal fiction, devoid of substantial merit." Minnesota already had a statute, enacted just two years before, prohibiting aviators from flying above large cities like St. Paul at less than two thousand feet. So long as they remained that high, Michael reasoned, they could not be trespassing on the land beneath. "The upper air is a natural heritage common to all of the people, and its reasonable use ought not to be hampered by an ancient artificial maxim of law," he concluded. "Modern progress and great public interests should not be blocked by unnecessary legal refinements."

Michael's opinion, like most state trial court opinions, was never published in the official case reports, but it quickly became widely known, especially after the lawyers for the airplane company sent a copy to the *American Law Review,* which published the full text a few months later. *Aviation* magazine published it as well, and applauded it as "a very important decision" establishing "the freedom of the air."[34] In a narrow legal sense this was an exaggeration: the opinion established the law in a single county in Minnesota, and judges elsewhere remained free to disagree. But in a broader sense it was no exaggeration at all. For years lawyers had filled the pages of their professional journals with worries about what would happen when the growing aviation industry collided with the ancient property rights of the owners of land. They had come up with all sorts of arguments for why aviation should win. But those arguments had never been put to the test. Finally, after twenty years of nervous commentary, a judge had decided that airplanes were not trespassers.

Aviators and their financial backers could celebrate Judge Michael's opinion both as indicator of the changing legal climate and as a motor of that change. On the one hand, Michael's decision was proof that the view of *cujus est solum* as an outdated principle was within the mainstream of legal thought. It was one thing for a handful of lawyers connected with the industry to say so, but to have a judge, even a state trial judge, express the same opinion gave it a stamp of legitimacy that no speech or journal article could match. On the other hand, lawyers knew that in the process of common-law change it was the first hurdle that was the highest. Judges were instinctively conservative. Few wanted to be the first to change the law. Now that one judge had done so, however, other judges could cite his opinion as precedent. They could comfortably depict themselves as followers rather than initiators of a trend. Lawyers hoping to clear *cujus est solum* from the skies might reasonably have expected that now, with one battle behind them, the others would be much easier to win.

Johnson v. Curtiss Northwest Airplane Company was the first decided aviation trespass case in the United States, and it would be the last for several years. Courts in several other states would decide similar cases in the 1930s, but by then the legal landscape would look very different.

In 1920, before either *Nevin* or *Johnson* had been decided, the National Conference of Commissioners on Uniform State Laws appointed a committee to discuss the feasibility of a uniform state law to govern aviation. The emergence of aviation on the Conference's agenda, which had previously included familiar commercial staples like negotiable instruments and warehouse receipts, was a marker of how much the industry had grown. "The whole world has come to a realization of the fact that Aviation is practical and not a mere art or fad," explained the committee that recommended the adoption of a uniform aviation law. "Many states in the Union now have scores of aviators constantly flying from state to state carrying commerce between the states, which aviation needs regulation."[35] The Conference's usual function was to harmonize already existing state laws, but here was an opportunity for a preemptive strike. If the Conference moved quickly enough, its uniform law would be the first statute governing aviation in many states. In every state it would be the first to establish a rule for aerial trespass.

George Gleason Bogert, the dean of Cornell Law School and an active member of the National Conference, drafted a proposed uniform act in early 1921. Bogert may well have known more about aviation regulation worldwide than anyone in the country: his discussion of "Problems in Aviation Law," published while he was at work on the draft uniform act, was a thorough account of the subject in both Europe and the United States.[36] After several rounds of revision, the National Conference approved the Uniform State Law for Aeronautics at its annual meeting in the summer of 1922.

The law covered a wide range of subjects, including the liability of the owners of aircraft for injuries to people or property on the ground and for collisions with other planes, and the jurisdiction of state courts over contracts and torts relating to flights. It prohibited dangerous stunts over thickly inhabited areas. It even banned hunting while in flight. (In a footnote to his explanation of the law, Bogert deplored "the inhuman and unsportsmanlike conduct involved in shooting game from an aircraft.") The Uniform State Law for Aeronautics deliberately avoided establishing licensing requirements for pilots or planes. "The theory of the State Act," NCCUSL explained in a promotional pamphlet, was that such matters "should be left for federal regulation, on account of the almost universal interstate nature of flight. . . . To have state licensing and registration would be a source of annoyance and expense."[37] The idea was to plug the holes in federal law before any federal law even existed, by dealing with the hodge-podge of state law issues that were understood to be outside the authority of the federal government.

The most important parts of the law were sections 3 and 4, which addressed the question of trespass. These sections were modeled on Britain's Air Navigation Act of 1920, which was but a year old when Bogert began his work.[38] Section 3 reaffirmed the landowner's rights to airspace. "The ownership of the space above the lands and waters of this State," the law declared, was "vested in the several owners of the surface beneath." This ownership, however, was "subject to the right of flight described in section 4." Most of what section 3 gave to landowners was then taken away by section 4. It provided: "Flight in aircraft over the lands and waters of this State is lawful, unless at such a low altitude as to interfere with the then existing use to which the land or water, or the space over the land or water, is put by the owner." Aviators would have a right to fly over private property, so long as they stayed high enough to avoid disturbing landowners below.

Bogert characterized this right of flight as an *easement*, the right to use property owned by another. Like many of his contemporaries, he analogized it to the easement of navigation the common law allowed over privately owned navigable waterways. "If this easement does not exist," he acknowledged, "the development of aeronautics is impossible and flight over the lands of another is a trespass,—two conclusions which seem neither reasonable nor desirable. To require a license by every land owner for flight over his land and to compel condemnation proceedings for aircraft routes, would place a perpetual bar in the way of the development of aeronautics." The uniform aeronautics law thus incorporated many of the arguments lawyers had raised over the previous decades. It declared a *preexisting* right of flight—not a new one, because a new right of flight would require compensating landowners for what they lost. The right was based on an analogy to the ancient easement for navigation over water, so the law could be *found*, not made. The recognition of landowners as owners of their airspace allowed judges and legislators to say that they were doing nothing inconsistent with the *cujus est solum* maxim. Landowners still owned up to the heavens; they just had to allow aircraft to fly through what they owned, whenever such flights did not interfere with their use of the airspace. Henry Hotchkiss, a lawyer in New York and the author of one of the earliest treatises on aviation law, acknowledged a few years later that "the rule stated in the Uniform Act is valid only in so far as it correctly expresses the pre-existing law. If the common law as expressed by the maxim is properly interpreted as having wider scope," he cautioned, "then the change of interpretation, modifying as it must a property right, would be open to constitutional objections." The Iowa lawyer Stuart Ball put it more frankly. The easement declared by the uniform aeronautics law, he admitted, was "at best a more or less awkward concession to necessity," a way of allowing overflights without having to pay landowners for changing the law.[39]

Some of the people behind the uniform aeronautics law were the same sort of civic-minded urban lawyers and academics who drafted and approved the other uniform acts. George Bogert, the principal draftsman, would soon leave Cornell to become a professor at the University of Chicago, where he would become a well-known expert on the law of trusts. Nathan MacChesney, the president of the National Conference of Commissioners on Uniform State Laws at the time, was a Chicago lawyer and a longtime advocate for standardizing state law, which he believed to be—as he titled two of his many speeches on the topic—"a means to efficiency consistent with democracy" and "a needed protection to and stimulus of interstate investment." He was a past president of the Illinois State Bar Association; later he would become a trustee of Northwestern University and an enthusiastic campaigner for Herbert Hoover. Two of the other members of Bogert's committee were lawyers from Washington, D.C., and Providence, Rhode Island. But the committee also included lawyers from Laramie, Wyoming; Wilmington, Ohio; Okolona, Mississippi; and Montpelier, Vermont; so non-urban interests were certainly well represented.[40] There was no urban–rural divide over aviation, as there was in some other commercial matters. Rural aviators and aircraft companies had nothing to lose from the uniform aeronautics law.

The law spread very quickly. MacChesney proudly reported at the Conference's next annual meeting that in its first year the aeronautics law had already been enacted by seven states and the territory of Hawaii.[41] These adoptions all took place in 1923, just after the Pennsylvania trespass case, and just before the one in Minnesota. It is possible, although there appears to be no evidence for it, that the judges in those cases were aware of the aeronautics law, and the reverse is also possible—the legislators in the eight jurisdictions that enacted the aeronautics law may have known of the two cases. (Neither Pennsylvania nor Minnesota was one of the eight.) We can say at the very least that the trend of thought among American lawyers in 1923 was that airplanes were not trespassing on the land beneath, because they had a preexisting right to fly over at a sufficient altitude.

The uniform law continued to spread in later years. By 1925 it had been adopted in ten states and it was under consideration in others. It was enacted in two more states in 1927, and then in nine more in 1929. In 1933, Georgia became the twenty-second state or territory to adopt it.[42] In all these states, flying over privately owned land received official blessing.

The uniform law attracted its share of opponents along the way, in part because of the easement for overflights. When the aeronautics committees of the American Bar Association and NCCUSL met at the Willard Hotel in Washington in early 1922 to discuss Bogert's draft, some of the participants were adamantly opposed to it on the ground that a statute allowing overflights would unconstitutionally infringe the property rights of the landowners below. "There are insuperable constitutional objections to a bill of this kind," James Nelson Frierson insisted. If the government were to build roads over private land, he reasoned, the government would have to condemn the land and compensate the landowner, "and if it is above the land they have to condemn and take it there [too], it seems to me." Frierson was the dean at the University of South Carolina Law School and a conservative interpreter of the Constitution. "Unless the courts and the lawyers to assist them are willing to warp the Constitution from its bases," he declared, there was no way to allow airplanes to fly over private property without paying for it. Elza Johnson, the legal advisor to the Army Air Service, felt the same way. Title to every parcel of land in the country originated with the government, he explained. When the land's first private owner received his grant, rights to the airspace were not excluded. Therefore, he concluded, the airspace passed along with the ground, and the ground's current owner owned the airspace, too.[43]

But by the 1920s this was clearly a minority view, both at the Willard Hotel and in the wider legal community. "I do not think anybody is going to fear an aviator is going to be held liable for trespass," advised Chester Cuthell, general counsel to the Curtiss Aeroplane and Motor Corporation, the largest American airplane manufacturer during and after World War I. "If he got into the courts I think the courts would throw it out immediately." T. C. Powell, the president of the Chicago and Eastern Illinois Railway, joked that only two decades earlier people had believed that property rights extended "from the surface outwardly to the center of the universe, a point so far distant that astronomers have just decided that this center is somewhere in the Milky Way at a distance of about fifty-two thousand light years from the sun." By the 1920s, however, "these former impressions as to ownership of any such air rights had faded away." All that was left, in Powell's view, was "the hope that airplanes may be restrained from coming so close to the ground as to be a definite menace to those who are compelled to stay on the ground."[44] As the uniform law worked its way through bar committees and state legislatures, few lawyers had any criticism of the right to fly over private land.

The main opposition to the uniform law, before its adoption, had nothing to do with its substance. The objection was that a state law, even a uniform one, would only delay the enactment of federal regulation, which the industry deemed more important. "I have in the last week or so had a great many letters," George Bogert reported in early 1922, "and the principal thought in those letters has been: Let us have no State legislation on the subject of aeronautics; let us confine the legislation entirely to Federal legislation." One of the participants in the meeting at the Willard Hotel was Fiorello La Guardia, the future mayor of New York, who was then between stints in Congress. La Guardia had flown in the army in World War I. After the war, as president of the New York Board of Aldermen, he had acquired a practical knowledge of local politics. "I think it is very splendid," he said of Bogert's draft of the uniform law, "but the motion which I would make would be to strike out everything after the enacting clause." If states were given the chance to enact aviation laws, he feared, each state would soon have "your commissioner of aviation and your inspectors of equipment and inspectors of pilots, and examiners, then you are going to build up in every state a machine that will oppose" federal regulation in order to preserve their jobs. Chester Cuthell was worried that the states, having once enacted uniform legislation, would keep on legislating in nonuniform ways. "And I tell you when I see forty-eight sovereign states preparing to inflict a few more handicaps on us," he said, "I begin to shudder."[45] These were disagreements over means rather than ends. All parties involved wanted uniform national regulation; their only difference was over how best to get there.

After the uniform law had been adopted, a new objection came from the New York City Bar Association, some of whose members thought the "so-called uniform aeronautic law" did not go far enough in restricting the rights of the landowner. They (or more likely their clients in the emerging business of radio) were unhappy with section 3's affirmation that airspace was owned by the owner of the land beneath. They were worried that an explicit statement that landowners owned their airspace, without including an easement for the propagation of radio waves analogous to the one for overflights, might be interpreted by courts to imply that radio waves were trespassers. "If the owner of the surface is declared to be vested with ownership of the space above the surface, subject only to the right of flight, may it not be possible that such owner sometimes may prevent the use of such space in radio transmission?" they asked. "Some day some apparatus may perhaps be invented by which radio transmission may be stopped, interfered with, or even destroyed. Section 4, as now phrased, would prevent the surface owner from interfering with the right of flight in the space above his land but would not prevent him from interfering with the right of radio transmission." They feared that radio broadcasters (who were almost certainly the real interests behind the lawyers' objections) would one day have to pay off landowners in the form of royalties or airspace rentals, to ensure that broadcasts could go through. The prominent New York lawyer Charles Boston, who chaired the American Bar Association's own committee on the law of aviation (and who would become the ABA's president a few years later), acknowledged that the uniform law was intended "very properly to save the right of flight." Nevertheless, he agreed, "the effect is to make a universal legislative grant which will impede other proper uses of the upper air."[46]

The complaint from New York was enough to convince the newest member of George Bogert's committee. Ernst Freund was a well-known progressive law professor and political scientist at the University of Chicago, the author of some of the era's leading works on the regulatory power of legislatures. He had not been a member of the committee when it was drafting the uniform law. Freund had no particular knowledge of aviation or radio. His area of expertise concerned the constitutional limits on state authority. Freund pointed out that as a logical matter there was no need for the uniform law to say anything at all about the landowner's rights. If the law simply declared that flying over private property was lawful, it would accomplish the same end without inadvertently jeopardizing radio or other conceivable uses of the air. Perhaps, Freund added, state legislatures would find this streamlined version of the law easier to accept.

Bogert and some of his colleagues responded with obvious exasperation. By then several states had already adopted the uniform law. Were the committee now to strip away one of the sections, the states that enacted it in the future would be adopting a statute different from the one that was already law elsewhere. The entire purpose of the National Conference was to create uniform state law, but if the Conference changed the law midstream it would be responsible for a uniform aeronautics law that was not uniform. W. H. Washington, a commissioner from Tennessee, one of the states that had already adopted the act, told the Conference that "he would feel very much crestfallen and very much ashamed" if the Conference were to amend a statute he had just persuaded his home state legislature to enact. In any event, Bogert insisted, an easement for airplanes hardly implied the absence of an easement for radio waves. "The bill has to do with aeronautics only," he concluded. "It is not attempting to settle all questions with respect to the subject of ownership and use of space."[47] The Conference kept the uniform law intact.

New York never did adopt the uniform law, perhaps because of this objection from radio broadcasters and their lawyers. The act ran out of steam, in any event, in the early 1930s. There were still twenty-seven states left that had not enacted it. None of them ever would.

Chester Cuthell, for one, was untroubled that more than half the states had declined to adopt the uniform law. "We believe that the Courts will determine that aviators have a legal right of flight," he told the assembled delegates at the International Civil Aeronautics Conference held in Washington in 1928. Even without statutory authorization, he predicted, courts would side with aviators over landowners. "By the overwhelming opinion of the members of the Bar," Cuthell explained, there is "a legal right of flight over private property."[48] Within a few years, courts throughout the United States would put that claim to the test.

FIVE

Interstate Commerce in the Air

One answer to the problems posed by inconsistent state laws was to turn regulation over to the federal government. "If air navigation becomes as general and extensive as people now expect," the lawyer Burdett Rich predicted in 1910, "the control of the Federal government over it must necessarily be very comprehensive." If Congress were to establish a single uniform law of the air, pilots would be spared the difficulties of trying to comply with multiple sets of rules in the course of an interstate trip. Around 1910 and 1911, as planes reached astonishing speeds and began to cover equally astonishing distances, many calls arose for federal regulation. "When air-craft travel at speeds of 40 to 80 miles an hour, it is possible to traverse more than a single State in a day," one lawyer remarked. "Must the aviator take out licenses for every State in the Union? Would it not be more desirable to receive a Federal license which would enable him to fly where he pleased?"[1] The same simplicity could be achieved with a federal rule governing trespass, altitude, and the like, which would allow aviators to be confident that the law at takeoff would not change before landing.

Every lawyer knew that the federal government's power was

limited to the areas specified in the Constitution, but one of those areas was the regulation of interstate commerce, and the proponents of federal control had no doubt that air travel was a form of interstate commerce. "'Commerce,' as used in the Federal Constitution, is not limited to the mere interchange of commodities," one lawyer insisted. "It includes navigation without regard to whether the purpose of such navigation be business or pleasure." Congress had long passed laws governing interstate travel by water and railroad, so there was precedent supporting similar laws for the air. "The new mode of interstate commerce is at hand," proclaimed the Denver lawyer Wayne Williams. "Congress will be called upon to pass laws regulating aeroplanes as interstate carriers."[2]

The first proposal to receive serious attention came from Simeon Baldwin. Baldwin was between jobs in 1910: he had just reached the mandatory retirement age as chief justice of the Connecticut Supreme Court and was preparing to run for governor, a post he would assume the following year. In the interim he pursued a long-standing interest in aviation. He drafted an "Act to Regulate Commerce by Airships," which he proposed to the American Bar Association, for the ABA to recommend to Congress.[3] The act would have required a federal license, for both the pilot and the plane, before embarking on an interstate flight, and would have set forth many of the requirements for obtaining a license. Baldwin had been one of the founders of the ABA back in the 1870s and was a former president of the organization. He was still an active and respected member in 1911 when the ABA took up his suggestion at its annual meeting—he was simultaneously the chair of its section on legal education and the director of its comparative law bureau. He may well have expected some deference from his colleagues, particularly on a subject like aviation, about which he surely considered himself more knowledgeable than most.

But not everyone was so sure about the desirability of federal regulation. The ABA rejected Baldwin's proposal, in part because Baldwin's colleagues were not convinced that the issue was sufficiently important. The amount of interstate commerce conducted by airplane was still negligible in 1911. "The navigation of the air has not become so general as to permit uniform legislation," the ABA concluded. Most undoubtedly expected that to change, but there would be time enough to revisit the issue when the need for federal control became more pressing.

More ominously, for proponents of federal regulation, some of Baldwin's colleagues in the bar association were uncertain about the scope of federal power over aviation. The ABA put the question off to another day, with a half-joke that only hinted at the issue's complexity: "How far the man who 'goes up in a balloon' engages in interstate commerce, when he happens to be accidentally blown across an imaginary state line, your committee is not prepared at this time to decide."[4] Baldwin's fellow bar members were evidently still thinking of aviation as a sporting pastime rather than a means of commercial transportation. It must have seemed incongruous to them to place airships in the same regulatory category as railroads or steamboats.

Lurking beneath the humor, however, were some difficult questions of constitutional law. Clearly Congress could regulate interstate commerce by airplane, just as it regulated interstate commerce on land and water. But most flights were not interstate: most never crossed a state boundary. When Wilbur Wright, say, flew around above a field for several minutes at a time, was that interstate commerce? There were some flights over which the power of Congress was clear, but there were many more as to which federal authority was far murkier.

It would have been possible, in principle, to create a regulatory scheme in which the federal government would provide one set of rules for interstate flights and the states would be free to provide their own rules for the rest. Baldwin's proposal would have done just that: it exempted flights that never crossed a state line, and allowed states to regulate them as they wished. Baldwin, who had a conservative view of congressional power, most likely thought it impossible to let the federal government do anything more.[5] But such a scheme would have defeated the purpose of federal regulation. If the law governing *inter*state flights differed from the law governing *intra*state flights, aviators within a single state might face inconsistent rules of the road, or contradictory rules pertaining to altitude or trespass over private property, depending on their destinations. Conduct that was lawful at one moment might become retroactively unlawful a moment later, when the aviator crossed a state line. To make matters worse, aviators often could not know whether or when they were crossing state lines, so they would have no way to know which set of rules they were supposed to follow. Government officials on the ground, looking up and seeing a plane in the sky, had no way to know whether the pilot intended to stay within the state's borders, so they too would be unable to determine which set of rules to apply. A system of dual federal and state regulation could easily have been worse than no federal regulation at all.

To be effective, a plan of federal regulation would have to cover *all* flights, whether interstate or not. That was the only way to achieve the uniformity that was the main purpose of federal control in the first place. But did Congress have the power to regulate flights that didn't cross any state line? There could be no federal aviation law until this question was answered.

The federal government was of course much smaller in the nineteenth century than it is today, but it did more than we sometimes remember. It ran a pervasive postal network that reached thousands of tiny communities spread over an enormous area, a system that in 1841 already employed over fourteen thousand people. It built and operated lighthouses, buoys, and other aids to navigation by water. It mounted ad hoc but regularly recurring programs of disaster relief, compensating victims of floods, fires, and the like. It distributed pensions to war veterans, whose numbers ballooned after the Civil War, until by 1900 the Bureau of Pensions was paying benefits to nearly 750,000 former soldiers.[6] It fought and treated with Indians, sold off public land to settlers, collected customs, and governed the parts of the country not yet populous enough to be states. None of these programs aroused sustained constitutional opposition. Though the wisdom of each new step was extensively debated, few doubted that the federal government had the power to pursue it. Each program fell within a constitutional grant of authority that was either explicitly specified in the text (as with the post office) or generally accepted by contemporary lawyers as encompassed within a broadly worded provision (as with the lighthouses and disaster relief).

Controversies over the federal government's power erupted from time to time, when the government contemplated departing from these well-worn grooves and intervening in the economy in other ways. Proposals for federal spending on roads or canals consistently drew opposition on the ground that such spending was unauthorized by the Constitution.[7] Whether the federal government could operate a bank was always a point of dispute. But while high-profile incidents like these were unfolding, the federal government was building up a portfolio of lower-profile and less controversial functions, some of which were no more firmly based in the text of the Constitution than a federal bank or a federal road.

One of the most important of these functions involved the regulation of shipping. The first U.S. Congress passed statutes providing for the registration and inspection of ships, as well as a labor law for merchant seamen that guaranteed rights such as the timely payment of wages and adequate medicine. Congress enacted a similar labor law for fishermen in 1813. In addition to providing lighthouses and other navigational aids, the federal government improved rivers and harbors by removing sandbars and other impediments. In 1838, after a series of gruesome steamboat accidents caused by exploding boilers, Congress required inspections and licenses for steamboats, a scheme that was beefed up in 1852 (after many more explosions) with detailed regulations governing boilers, pumps, tubes, and valves. In the 1840s and 1850s Congress enacted a series of safety statutes for all ships, not just steamboats, with restrictions on matters like the number of passengers and the quality of ventilation.[8] Shipping was a subject generally understood to be within the federal government's power to regulate.

The constitutional source of that power was never quite clear. The most obvious candidate was Congress's authority to regulate interstate commerce, but these statutes did not limit themselves to interstate voyages or to commercial voyages—they applied to all shipping, regardless of its location or its purpose. Members of Congress and other proponents of these shipping statutes may have been implicitly relying on a broad definition of congressional power, of the sort that would become law in the middle of the twentieth century, as encompassing subjects affecting or relating to interstate commerce even if they were not interstate commerce themselves. This broad conception, however, tended not to be applied at the time to roads or canals, which affected interstate commerce at least as much as intrastate shipping did.[9] It seems more likely that contemporaries instinctively placed shipping on natural waterways in a different category from other forms of transport and assumed that the federal government could regulate it, perhaps because rivers and lakes (and especially the ocean) were so obviously part of an interstate, indeed international, network of pathways, and because so much interstate commerce traveled by water.

Judges were, on occasion, troubled by allowing Congress to regulate ships not engaged in interstate commerce. In a few cases, for example, the steamboat licensing statute was held not to apply to local ferries with routes that did not cross state lines.[10] Nevertheless, by the early twentieth century the many federal laws governing shipping were a salient example of federal regulatory power. Travel by water would serve as a common analogy for travel by air. If Congress had the power to regulate one, many lawyers would assert, it must have the power to regulate the other.

Until the middle of the nineteenth century, shipping was the only industry that was, by its very nature, a form of interstate commerce. By the early twentieth century there were a few others. Congress used its authority over interstate commerce to enact statutes governing each. By the time federal regulation of aviation became a serious possibility, the federal government was much more active than it had been a few decades earlier, and lawyers' understanding of the federal government's power over interstate commerce had expanded accordingly.

The telegraph business was a clear example of interstate commerce, and the federal government intermittently promoted the telegraph from the very beginning. A congressional appropriation in 1843 financed the first telegraph line in the United States. In 1866 Congress authorized telegraph companies to build lines along public land, navigable waterways, and post roads. A decade later, when the Supreme Court held that this grant was within

Congress's power to regulate interstate commerce, Chief Justice Morrison Waite explained that Congress's power would grow along with technological change. "The powers thus granted are not confined to the instrumentalities of commerce . . . in use when the Constitution was adopted," Waite observed, in words that would be frequently quoted by proponents of federal aviation regulation, "but they keep pace with the progress of the country, and adapt themselves to the new developments of time and circumstances. They extend from the horse with its rider to the stage-coach, from the sailing-vessel to the steamboat, from the coach and the steamboat to the railroad, and from the railroad to the telegraph, as these new agencies are successively brought into use."[11] New methods of transportation and communication were increasingly tying the states together into a single national market, and as they did, the scope of Congress's regulatory power would increase.

The railroad industry was another clear example of interstate commerce, and one that was on Waite's mind, because whether and how Congress should regulate the railroads were big issues in the 1870s and 1880s. The Interstate Commerce Act of 1887, which placed various restrictions on the rates railroads could charge, would be interpreted very narrowly in its earliest years by the Supreme Court, but it was just the first in a long series of statutes in which the federal government would govern the railroad business. The Safety Appliance Act of 1893 required all trains to have power brakes and automatic couplers. The Elkins Act of 1903 and the Hepburn Act of 1906 further regulated rates. The Employers' Liability Act of 1908 governed injuries suffered by railroad workers, and the Adamson Act of 1916 placed an upper limit on their hours and a lower limit on their wages. These statutes and others were all upheld by the Supreme Court as falling within Congress's power over interstate commerce.[12]

The same pattern occurred with the invention of the telephone and the radio, two more intrinsically interstate technologies. Federal regulation of the telephone industry began in 1910, when Congress added the telephone to the jurisdiction of the Interstate Commerce Commission. In the Radio Act of 1912, Congress required broadcasters to obtain federal licenses and authorized the Commerce Department to regulate the airwaves. With each new form of transportation or communication, federal regulation followed.

Indeed, as technology integrated the states into a single American market, the federal government increasingly began regulating the markets themselves, not just the technology. The best-known early example may be the Sherman Antitrust Act of 1890, but more specialized statutes followed quickly, including regulations of traffic in animals in 1903 and 1905, a Pure Food Act in 1906 and a meat inspection act the following year, plant quarantine laws in 1905 and 1912, statutes prohibiting certain narcotics in 1909 and 1914, laws regarding the quality of agricultural products in 1910, 1912, and 1916, and even a law prohibiting child labor in 1916. By the second decade of the twentieth century, it was apparent that the federal government was more powerful than it had ever been before. "We have been won over more or less unconsciously to the belief that Congress has, or ought to have, authority to pass any salutary law in the interest of the national welfare," remarked the political scientist Robert Cushman. "Instead of surprise that Congress should have the temerity to penetrate into a new field of legislation, there is impatience to find that there is any such field into which Congress may not penetrate."[13]

But if the federal government was regulating more aggressively than before, lawyers were well aware that the Constitution still required the subject of that regulation to be interstate commerce, and that the Supreme Court often defined the phrase quite narrowly. In 1918 the Court struck down the child labor law of two years before as beyond the power of Congress. Four years later the Court found that the Antitrust Act did not apply to a baseball league with teams in different states, on the theory that the league was not engaged in interstate commerce.[14] As Americans generally grew more accustomed to federal regulation, people interested in aviation naturally turned to the federal government. But the federal government was wielding an uncertain power. Lawyers disagreed sharply over its scope. Court decisions defining interstate commerce could change the legal landscape dramatically from one year to the next. Drafting a federal law to govern aviation would turn out to be a trickier business than most nonlawyers realized.

With the end of World War I, calls for federal regulation of the incipient aviation industry grew sharply in volume. "If the old distinction between interstate and intrastate commerce is to be transferred to the air, how is a State to know whether an airplane appearing in the clouds is on an interstate or intrastate journey?" asked the Chicago lawyer Carl Zollman. "The entire control should be in the hands of the Federal authorities." *Scientific American* expected that "the economic future of the world may well depend upon the development of aviation," and insisted that "legislation controlling the nation's air-ways should be undertaken by the Federal government, that we may not have 48 sets of laws regarding air travel." Laurence Driggs, the president of the American Flying Club, agreed that without strong federal control, "a riot of senseless and contradictory statutes among the various state legislatures will so hamper aviation that it will be strangled at this delicate period in its infancy." W. Jefferson Davis, a member of the American Bar Association's Aviation Committee, pointed out that merely to fly from Washington, D.C., to New York required an aviator to pass over six different states within the space of two hours. "Were it necessary for him to familiarize himself with different laws obtaining in each of these states," Davis worried, "not to say anything about the different city ordinances which might be enacted, it would be impossible for him to devote his attention to anything other than a study of the conflicting laws."[15]

Some of the support for federal regulation came from people concerned for their own safety as potential crash victims. "To make air-travel safe," the *Literary Digest* insisted in 1920, the federal government would have to begin inspecting and licensing planes, just like it already did for ships. "At present there is no inspection of planes or examination of airmen," complained the *Buffalo News* a year later. "Must our legislators wait until some overwhelming catastrophe so inflames public opinion that they will be forced to act?" But there was no grassroots movement for federal aviation regulation. The vast majority of Americans still had little or no contact with airplanes.[16]

The loudest voices clamoring for federal regulation came instead from the aviation industry itself. Insiders wanted the federal government to begin inspecting planes and licensing pilots, to make flying safer and, perhaps more important, to make it *look* safer to prospective customers. As a delegation of aircraft manufacturers explained at a 1921 meeting with the U.S. Department of Commerce, federal regulation would reduce the frequency of accidents, and limiting the number of accidents was the only way to "prevent civil aviation from getting into bad repute." For the same reason, the industry urged the creation of a national system of air traffic control. The lack of such a system, they argued, "was one of the main causes of accidents in the air, which give rise to the belief that flying is extremely dangerous—one of the severest handicaps to the development of transportation by air." Through the early 1920s, presidents of aviation firms repeatedly pleaded with Herbert Hoover, the secretary of commerce, for help in getting the attention of Congress. The industry's trade association established an Information Department, which wrote magazine articles and published reports urging the importance of federal regulation.[17]

Additional pressure came from insurance companies, for whom the development of commercial aviation promised to open a lucrative line of business. They banded together as the National Aircraft Underwriters Association to lobby for federal regulation. Federal licensing of pilots and aircraft "will make it possible for airplane owners and operators to procure insurance at lower rates," assured H. P. Stellwagen, the association's secretary, but one may suspect that the association's member firms were less interested in lowering their rates than in creating a large pool of new policyholders. The Chamber of Commerce joined in as well. In the Chamber's view, federal regulation was "undoubtedly one of the conditions of interesting capital in this field."[18]

"I believe this is the first time, certainly to my knowledge, sir, that an industry has come to the Congress of the United States and asked for regulation," testified Frank Russell, vice president of the Curtiss Aeroplane and Motor Corporation, before a Senate subcommittee. Russell may have been exaggerating a bit—it was hardly unknown for business representatives to seek regulation, particularly in the form of laws that would make it more difficult for newcomers to enter an industry—but in an era when business interests and the federal government were often understood as opponents, others were struck by what they saw as the same incongruity. "Congress has been denounced unsparingly for passing legislation regulating and controlling business," declared the House Committee on Commerce. "It is rather startling, to say the least, to have an industry really in its infancy and capable of boundless development asking and urging legislation putting the business completely under Federal control."[19] Startling or not, the main proponents of federal regulation were within aviation itself.

Much of the industry's pressure for legislation was coordinated by the Chicago lawyer William MacCracken. Like so many of the early aviation experts, MacCracken learned about flying during World War I, in the Army Air Service. When he returned to law practice at the war's end, he became chair of the American Bar Association's committee on aviation law, general counsel to the National Aeronautic Association (the industry's trade association), and the lawyer for National Air Transport, the largest of the early airmail carriers. While holding these positions simultaneously, MacCracken had a hand in drafting bills and lobbying for their enactment. In 1926, when Congress created the Bureau of Aeronautics within the Commerce Department, MacCracken was the natural choice to run the bureau as assistant secretary of commerce, a post he would hold until 1929.[20]

The industry had sympathetic ears throughout the government. The National Advisory Committee for Aeronautics, created by Congress in 1915 primarily to conduct aeronautical research, consistently recommended federal legislation from 1918 onward. The Post Office, whose managers correctly expected would be the single largest user of airplanes, wanted federal control, too. "It took a generation to find out that it was absolutely necessary to have interstate regulation of railroads," recalled E. H. Shaughnessy, assistant to the postmaster general. "It never worked satisfactorily when the States themselves tried to regulate interstate railroads, and you might just as well, in my opinion, start off with the benefit of that experience and try to give aviation people the sort of help and control they ask for." The U.S. Navy also pressed for federal legislation. Assistant Secretary of the Navy Theodore

The Chicago lawyer William MacCracken learned to fly in World War I and then became the leading aviation lawyer of the 1920s. In 1926, Herbert Hoover, then secretary of commerce, put MacCracken in charge of the federal government's new Bureau of Aeronautics. LC-USZ62-101771, Prints and Photographs Division, Library of Congress.

Roosevelt, Jr., the former president's son, urged the "formulation of a comprehensive code of air laws," a task he considered "essentially a Federal duty, for aircraft moves so fast that most of its work will be inter-State." The Navy, which already had many planes of its own, was concerned that the United States would fall behind other nations in aeronautic technology unless it developed a robust commercial aviation industry.[21]

Within the government, support for federal control ran straight to the top. Herbert Hoover, who would supervise any federal regulation as secretary of commerce, was strongly in favor. Without a body of federal air law, he argued, "aviation can only develop in a primitive way." The President's Aircraft Board, established to recommend policy on military and commercial aviation, agreed that federal regulation was necessary. So did Presidents Harding and Coolidge. So, most likely, did most members of Congress. "It is utterly ridiculous that the United States Government, while not allowing any person to take passengers across Long Island Sound in a steamboat unless the captain, mates, engineers, boilers, hull, lifeboats, and life preservers have all been passed as satisfactory to Federal inspectors, nevertheless, permits anyone to take passengers across the Sound in any type of aircraft without any examination or certificate whatsoever," huffed the Senate Committee on Commerce. "No wonder our insurance companies decline to believe that the present risks of commercial aviation are such as to warrant as low rates as are granted to ocean navigation."[22] Federal officials were virtually unanimous in believing that aviation should come under federal control.

As a result, there was scarcely a day between 1918 and 1925 in which Congress did not have before it one bill or another that would have established a federal law of the air. But by 1925, despite seven years of study, Congress had enacted none of them. The principle underlying the bills, that it would be desirable to have federal aviation regulation, encountered no real opposition. No one, least of all the industry itself, had any interest in perpetuating the patchwork of state law that federal regulation would replace. Part of the reason for the lack of any legislation was simply the press of other business. "The individual Congressman has not been brought to feel the vital necessity of lending immediate and intelligent encouragement to aviation in America," the lawyer W. Jefferson Davis complained in 1925. Davis was sure that one of the recent bills would have passed nearly unanimously, if only it could have been brought to a vote.[23] But much of the delay was due to a more serious concern: it wasn't clear that the federal government even had the power to regulate the air. As aircraft manufacturers, insurers, and government officials clamored for federal law, lawyers wondered about how much regulation the Constitution could support.

In 1920 the American Bar Association formed a Special Committee on the Law of Aviation, to report on how the law could best be changed to facilitate the growth of commercial flight. Within a year, members of the committee were already exasperated. There were times when it seemed like they were the only ones who remembered that the Constitution divided power between the federal government and the states. "Many persons interested in the practical development of flight through the air have no conception of the existence, at the threshold, of a constitutional problem arising from this division of power," the committee complained in its first report. "They are impatient of our apparent inaction; and practically with one accord they appear to look to the national government for relief; they see other governments active with international conventions and national laws, and cannot and do not care to comprehend why anyone hesitates to believe that the powerful government of the United States has not every power which any other government exercises to promote and to regulate air flight." For lawyers, or at least for thoughtful lawyers, in the 1920s the extent of the federal government's authority over the air posed a knotty question of constitutional law, but the intricacies of constitutional doctrine held "no appeal to those who are impatient to see the actual commercial development of air flight."[24]

But if nonlawyers could not fathom why the bar association was taking so long, lawyers understood perfectly. They all knew the basic axiom of American constitutional law, that the federal government possessed only whatever powers were granted to it in the Constitution. Any legislation enacted by Congress needed a hook somewhere in the Constitution's text. Of course, air travel had not been contemplated in the late eighteenth century when the Constitution was drafted, so its framers had no occasion to specify whether the federal government had the power to regulate aviation. To find a textual home for that power, lawyers would have to manipulate language that had originally been written with other ends in mind. As the ABA's aviation law committee suggested, "it seems advisable for constitutional minds to get busy."[25] They soon did.

Many suggested that federal power over the air could be based on the Constitution's grant of admiralty jurisdiction to the federal courts, a provision that had recently come to be used to support federal regulation of shipping on navigable waterways. The idea of a congressional admiralty power made little sense as a textual matter, because the relevant provision is a grant of power to *courts* rather than to Congress, so until the late nineteenth century it was understood not to confer upon Congress any power to regulate. Toward the end of the century, however, the Supreme Court held that the provision *did* authorize Congress to legislate on maritime matters, even those with no effect on interstate commerce. By the early twentieth century, lawyers understood admiralty as a distinct category of federal power, separate from the power to regulate commerce.[26] Congress's admiralty power clearly did not authorize it to regulate transportation by land. But did the admiralty power extend to the air? Air was like water in some respects—the two were similar enough to give rise to the extended debate in the first two decades of the century over whether there was an international freedom of air navigation comparable to the international freedom of water navigation. Could Congress use its admiralty power to legislate for the skies?

The air was navigable too, insisted Godfrey Cabot, president of the National Aeronautic Association; it was "an ocean that is navigable over the whole earth." If the federal government could control transportation on water, he reasoned, it could a fortiori control transportation in the air. "This is somewhat analogous to admiralty jurisdiction," mused Florida senator Duncan Fletcher, a former lawyer and president of the Gulf Coast Inland Waterways Association, and thus a man with occasions to reflect on the legal nature of water. "This should give the courts jurisdiction over the air." The Columbia law professor Charles Thaddeus Terry, representing the National Aircraft Association, thought the analogy between water and air "is perfect. The Federal Government, through its agencies, lays down rules of the road, so to speak, with reference to the vessels, what signals shall be and how vessels shall pass. Why not aircraft?"[27]

The most enthusiastic exponent of the admiralty theory was the Indianapolis lawyer William Rooker, who used his position as chairman of the Conference of State and Local Bar Associations of America as a platform for publicizing his view. He printed a pamphlet with his arguments, copies of which he mailed to the governor of each state; the mayor of every city in the country with a population exceeding thirty-five thousand; the president and faculty of every college and university in the United States; the president and directors of all the stock exchanges, railroad and steamship companies, banks, insurance companies, and aircraft manufacturers; and all the judges and government officials he thought would benefit from it. Rooker's argument was so idiosyncratic, however, that his efforts could not have convinced many readers. "I say the right of the admiralty jurisdiction can be proven," Rooker declared; "it can be proven with biology; it can be proven with the philosophy of language." How this was so was never entirely clear; apparently it had something to do with Rooker's belief that "neither the ocean nor the atmosphere is exposed to geometrical measurement," which meant that "there can be no such municipal organism in the ocean or the atmosphere as functions under the common law," and with no common law, the law of admiralty was the only available alternative. (Simeon Baldwin, one of the recipients of Rooker's barrage, politely responded: "I should deprecate founding any air craft law on the certainties of mathematics.")[28] Rooker was a crank, but he was a crank attempting to prove a proposition many lawyers found intuitively right, that the federal government's control of the water implied the authority to exert similar control over the air.

For all the similarities between air and water, however, air was obviously not the same thing as water, and many other lawyers found this too high an obstacle to get past. In 1914, while the debate over federal regulatory power was just getting started, a federal court in Washington State had held that it lacked admiralty jurisdiction over an airplane that had crashed into Puget Sound. The sound was navigable water, the court acknowledged, but aircraft, "not being of the sea or restricted in their activities to navigable waters," did not lie within the federal admiralty power. Commentators found the decision clearly correct. Seven years later, when the debate was near its peak, the New York Court of

Appeals reached a similar result, in an opinion by Benjamin Cardozo, then the most respected state court judge in the country. A hydroplane was subject to federal admiralty jurisdiction while in the water, Cardozo reasoned, but not while in the air, "because it is not then in navigable waters, and navigability is the test of admiralty jurisdiction." For many lawyers, these cases were enough. "There isn't the faintest likelihood of any court, supreme or otherwise, departing upon purely scientific analogy from the historic doctrine that admiralty means admiralty," insisted the D.C. lawyer Henry Glassie when the ABA took up the question at its annual meeting. The lawyers who labored in the Legislative Drafting Service of the House of Representatives agreed. The admiralty power was limited to "matters which are maritime in their nature," they concluded, and air travel simply was not maritime.[29] If it were to predicate aviation regulation on the admiralty power, Congress would run a considerable risk that its work would be found unconstitutional.

An alternative and particularly timely source of federal authority was the Constitution's treaty clause. The Constitution makes treaties, along with federal statutes and the Constitution itself, "the supreme Law of the Land," and authorizes Congress to make "laws which shall be necessary and proper" for exercising its powers. There had long been uncertainty as to whether these provisions permitted Congress to implement a treaty by enacting legislation that, in the absence of the treaty, it would have lacked the power to enact. The question reached the Supreme Court in 1920, just as the aviation debate was heating up, in a case challenging the constitutionality of a federal statute protecting migratory birds, a statute enacted to implement a recent treaty between the United States and Great Britain. (The birds migrated to Canada, which was still part of the British empire.) Before the treaty, lower courts had found a similar statute beyond the authority of

Congress. After the treaty, however, the Supreme Court gave its approval. Justice Oliver Wendell Holmes explained that Congress's power to implement treaties was a source of authority independent of its other powers. The implication, never stated in the opinion but widely noted at the time, was that the federal government could expand the power of Congress by entering into treaties.[30]

Lawyers with an interest in aviation recognized that this principle could remove most doubts, or maybe even all doubts, as to Congress's authority over air travel. The Convention Relating to International Air Navigation had recently been negotiated at the Paris Peace Conference. The Convention required signatories to take many of the same steps that were being urged on Congress, such as certifying the competence of pilots and the safety of aircraft. If the United States would simply ratify the Convention, lawyers pointed out, the problem of federal power would be solved.[31] This was yet another argument in favor of ratification, a course already being urged on the Senate by aviation lawyers. The Senate never did ratify the Convention Relating to International Air Navigation, however, because it was too closely connected to the League of Nations and similar postwar institutions. The treaty power thus could not serve as a textual hook for a federal law of the air.

Another possibility was to amend the Constitution, to provide explicit textual authority for federal regulation. This was the recommendation of a committee of the New York State Bar Association, whose members disapproved of the linguistic manipulation that seemed necessary to squeeze aviation into one of the Constitution's existing clauses. "If the power of Congress and the jurisdiction of the National government are to be extended to new subject matter," the committee insisted, "it should be by proper Constitutional amendment in a Constitutional way." The lawyers on the ABA's Aviation Committee unanimously agreed. "The power should be conferred by *constitutional amendment* and should not be seized in the guise of the exercise of existing powers," they urged. "Every exercise of existing powers which goes beyond the obvious or necessarily implicit extent of these powers is fraught not only with the visible danger of attack on the ground of unconstitutionality and of invasion of the essential or reserved powers of the states, but with the more insidious danger of a further weakening of constitutional limitations deliberately incorporated in the bill of rights."[32] Over the preceding decades the reach of government, especially the federal government, had been increasing, particularly with respect to the regulation of business. Those who argued for the constitutionality of these new laws normally did so, not by proposing to add new language to the Constitution, but by urging judges to reinterpret the old language. Lawyers who had participated in these debates on behalf of business clients were aware that aviation was just one battle in a much larger war. Victory in that one battle, if it meant contributing to a more flexible mode of constitutional interpretation, could imply losses in more important battles in the future.

But corporate lawyers were not the only ones who favored a constitutional amendment. The most frequently quoted proponent was Elza Johnson, a lawyer for the Army Air Service, who advised the Air Service that nothing in the Constitution allowed the federal government to regulate the air. "The navigation of air presents problems that have no precedent," he counseled, and it was foolish to pretend otherwise. "The question should be stripped of all camouflage and hope of getting by, and met squarely as it is." He accordingly recommended making the Constitution as clear as possible, by giving Congress the explicit power of "regulating the use for air travel of all air space over the earth and within the borders of the United States."[33] Johnson, whether on his own behalf or on behalf of the Army, had no reason to be apprehensive about federal regulation of business. He simply thought a constitutional amendment was the only intellectually honest route.

Then again, securing a constitutional amendment would be no easy matter, and that was the argument against it. One Illinois lawyer, upon hearing the recommendation of the ABA's Aviation Committee, bemoaned "the loss of time and the overwhelming cost of procuring an amendment to the National Constitution, when it is obvious that such an amendment might ultimately be held to have been absolutely unnecessary." If Congress could just enact a law, the courts could resolve its constitutionality in a test case, and "a test case is much cheaper than a constitutional amendment." The next year, at the joint meeting of the relevant committees of the ABA and the National Conference of Commissioners on Uniform State Laws, there had been considerable turnover of personnel on the ABA committee, and many of the participants thought that amending the Constitution would be an utter waste of time and money. "If we have to get a constitutional amendment it will take many years, and I do not know who will finance it," William MacCracken explained. William Moffat, chief of the Navy's Bureau of Aeronautics, agreed that an amendment would not be worth the wait. "We are the only country in the world that does not regulate aviation, and we are waiting because we think it would be unconstitutional," Moffat complained. "I would rather take a chance on it and pass something and find out perhaps in the next few years whether it is constitutional or not." In the end, both committees voted to stop considering a constitutional amendment, on the theory that further discussion would only delay the enactment of legislation they all agreed was necessary.[34]

With that decision, only one alternative remained. If Congress was to regulate the air, its authority would have to come from the Commerce Clause.

There was no doubt that Congress's power over interstate commerce allowed it to regulate commercial air travel that crossed state lines. "The air lends itself more peculiarly to interstate commerce than do navigable waters," explained the law firm hired by the National Advisory Committee for Aeronautics, "because in the air State lines can be crossed in any direction at any point."[35] That much was easy. Power over noncommercial flights was no trouble either. "Commerce," in the sense of business, had never been a literal prerequisite for federal authority. The many federal statutes regulating travel by ship or by train had never distinguished between trips taken for commercial purposes and trips taken for fun; all trips, regardless of their nature, were subject to the same regulatory schemes. This may be because lawyers were still interpreting "commerce" in its broader (and today nearly extinct) sense of "contact among people," a sense in which contact for the purpose of business would be just one special kind of commerce. Or it may have had a more pragmatic cause; perhaps lawyers tacitly recognized how complicated the law would be if federal power extended to interstate travel for business but not for pleasure. Either way, few lawyers, if any, seriously contended that Congress could not regulate interstate noncommercial air travel.

The question of *intra*state air travel was much harder. "Regardless of how a bill is drawn," declared one lawyer, "it is inevitable, if it is to be sustained under the present conditions, that a considerable field of intra-state flying will be left to the states." Because of such doubts, some of the bills before Congress in the early 1920s explicitly left the regulation of intrastate aviation to the states, in the earnest hope that the states would pass identical statutes of their own.[36]

There was a line of recent Supreme Court cases, however, that gave proponents of federal regulation hope that Congress had the power to govern even intrastate flights as part of a general scheme of aviation law. In 1905 the Court had allowed the federal government to break up the "Beef Trust," a combination of the country's largest meatpackers, despite the fact that the acts alleged by the government all involved trade within a single state. "Commerce among the states is not a technical legal conception, but a practical one, drawn from the course of business," Justice Oliver Wendell Holmes explained in his opinion for a unanimous Court. So long as the acts at issue were part of "a current of commerce among the states," they were subject to federal control. Might aviation likewise be described as a nationwide "current of commerce," embracing all flights, even those that never crossed state lines? In 1914, only a few years before the onset of the debate over federal aviation regulation, the Court had upheld an order of the Interstate Commerce Commission affecting *intra*state railway rates. "Wherever the interstate and intrastate transactions of carriers are so related that the government of one involves the control of the other," Justice Charles Evans Hughes had reasoned, "it is Congress, and not the state, that is entitled to prescribe the final and dominant rule." This opinion seemed even more helpful. It was obvious that intra- and interstate aviation were related. If the courts could be persuaded that one could not be regulated without the other, perhaps the authority of Congress would be complete.[37]

While aviation bills were before Congress, the Supreme Court decided three more cases in 1922 and 1923, all of which reinforced federal power over certain intrastate activities. In another case involving railroad rates, the Court again allowed the Interstate Commerce Commission to regulate intrastate fares. When the federal government "cannot exercise complete effective control over interstate commerce without incidental regulation of intrastate commerce," the Court unanimously held, "such incidental regulation is not an invasion of state authority." A few months later the Court upheld the Packers and Stockyards Act of 1921, which authorized the Department of Agriculture to regulate a variety of aspects of the stockyard business, even those that did not directly involve interstate commerce. Chief Justice William Howard Taft cautioned that courts should not interfere with the reasonable judgment of Congress that the stockyards were part of a broader current of interstate commerce in meat. The following year the Court upheld the Grain Futures Act of 1922, over the objection of the Chicago Board of Trade that all of its trading took place within a single building in Illinois. "Sales on the Chicago Board of Trade," the Court concluded, were "indispensable to the continuity of the flow of wheat from the West to the mills and distributing points of the East," and so could be regulated by Congress as a component of interstate commerce.[38] The timing of these cases was fortuitous in a narrow sense, in that they had nothing to do with the pending aviation bills. In a broader sense, however, their timing was anything but fortuitous. The federal government was expanding its reach in the early 1920s, in response to the technological changes that were giving rise to an increasingly national market. It took in stockyards in 1921 and commodity futures in 1922. Perhaps aviation would be next.

Proponents of federal regulation seized on these Supreme Court cases as evidence that constitutional law was changing in the right direction. The two railroad cases were enough, William MacCracken believed, to prove "that legislation for the regulation of aeronautics by the Federal government would be sustained as constitutional notwithstanding the fact that its scope would be broad enough to regulate both inter and intrastate aerial navigation." Even the members of the National Conference of Commissioners on Uniform State Laws thought so, and, as MacCracken informed a House committee studying the question, "they are last-ditch men on State rights." As a result, by the mid-1920s some of the bills before Congress explicitly provided for federal regulation of *all* aviation, regardless of whether it crossed state lines, in language crafted to mirror the words the Supreme Court had used to justify federal regulation of intrastate railroads and stockyards.[39] With some timely help from the Supreme Court, Congress seemed to be on the way to enacting a truly uniform federal statute.

The point of a uniform federal aviation law was to make flying safer, by eliminating inconsistent state regulation. Part of the discussion of proposed federal bills, perhaps the greater part, focused on the licensing of pilots and the inspection of aircraft, issues that had nothing to do with the ownership of airspace. But much of the discussion was about the dangers of inconsistent state "rules of the road" for airplanes, and one rule of the road involved the question of aerial trespass. What would happen if states had differing minimum altitude requirements? What if one state followed the *cujus est solum* maxim and recognized a landowner's control up to the heavens, while a neighboring state did not? The likelihood that Congress would enact a federal aviation law prompted a vigorous debate about whether federal law should answer the airspace question and, if so, what the answer should be.

In 1925, after Congress had been considering a federal aviation law for several years, the Department of Commerce and the American Engineering Council convened a Joint Committee on

Civil Aviation, chaired by Assistant Secretary of Commerce J. Walter Drake, to make recommendations about what form federal legislation should take. One of the committee's suggestions was that federal law should recognize a "public right of flight in navigable air space," regardless of who happened to own the land beneath. The committee's report received a lot of attention; it was summarized in major newspapers and printed in full by a commercial publisher.[40]

The notion of declaring a public right of flight, however, was already a controversial one. When the American Bar Association's Aviation Committee had made a similar suggestion a few years earlier, many of the ABA's members thought it would be a terrible strategic mistake even to bring the issue up, because they worried that a public right of flight implied that the owner of the ground owned the space above. *Cujus est solum* "is not the law," insisted W. Jefferson Davis, "but is merely a theory which has come down to us from mediaeval days." William Rooker found it "humiliating that the thing should be presented to an intelligent audience—the old doctrine of ownership in the air." Simply mentioning a right of flight in legislation, they believed, would grant more dignity to the *cujus est solum* maxim than it deserved, by implying that it was weighty enough to require legislation to counteract. "That rule has been so long exploded that it is not worth serious attack," MacCracken sniffed. The House of Representatives' lawyers agreed. Courts would allow planes to fly over private property, they predicted, even without any explicit statutory mention of a public right of flight.[41]

But worries about declaring a public right of flight also stemmed from precisely the opposite concern—that it would require compensating all the landowners below, because of the *cujus est solum* maxim. "Even if the 48 States did permit the Federal Congress to legislate on this subject," wondered Laurence Driggs, president of the American Flying Club, "is it not the individual land owner whose consent must be obtained, to permit a trespass on his air?" Elza Johnson, legal advisor to the Army Air Service, came to the same conclusion. "There are no authorized public highways established in the air," he insisted, "nor could there be until such highways were definitely taken and established under eminent domain, and this involves payment to the individual for property taken for such purpose."[42] *Cujus est solum* was still alive, despite the best efforts of many aviation lawyers to declare its death. It still lurked behind any attempt to declare a public right of air navigation.

Despite these doubts, by the mid-1920s some of the bills before Congress included declarations of a public right of flight above privately owned land, although on occasion members of Congress evinced some skepticism about their power to do what was being asked of them. At one 1924 hearing, when MacCracken analogized the proposed public right of air navigation to the familiar terrestrial highways that ran alongside private property, Alabama representative George Huddleston could only think of the landowner beneath. "The highway is made public property, made so through regular processes of law," Huddleston fumed. "The air, at least a part of it, is his, and I am just now about to ask you the authority for the holding that it is not all his." MacCracken was at a loss. He could only cite Lord Ellenborough's dictum from 1815 about the rights of balloonists, one judge's opinion from another country and another century. Huddleston understandably remained unconvinced.[43]

By 1926, when Congress finally passed a statute to govern the air, it had considered bills that would have established a public right of flight and bills that were silent on the matter. It had considered bills that would have explicitly governed intrastate flights, bills that would have explicitly disclaimed any governance over

intrastate flights, and bills that remained ambiguous by not saying anything one way or the other. The future of the airspace
question would depend on which combination of these two features would be in the final legislation.

The Air Commerce Act of 1926 took a middle ground between
the two competing views of federal power over intrastate flight.
It directed the Department of Commerce to set air traffic rules
throughout the country and mandated penalties for anyone who
violated them, regardless of whether the violation took place during an intrastate flight. The Commerce Department was also to
establish a registration and rating system for aircraft and pilots,
but the act imposed penalties for violating these provisions only
where unregistered aircraft or pilots flew in interstate commerce.
The registration system, unlike the air traffic control system, was
thus optional for planes and people who never crossed state lines.
Aviation lawyers nevertheless expected most intrastate flyers to
seek federal registration, because federal licenses would be useful
in demonstrating airworthiness to prospective customers, because
the fraction of purely intrastate aircraft would inevitably decline
as average flights grew longer, and because many states were themselves likely to require a license as a condition of flight. The result
would be a de facto national system of registration that was im-
mune from constitutional challenge.[44]

The Air Commerce Act embodied a similar compromise on
the airspace question. It included an explicit declaration of a
"public right of freedom of interstate and foreign air navigation"
in the nation's "navigable airspace," a term defined as all the airspace above the minimum safe altitudes of flight to be prescribed
by the Department of Commerce. This was a right to fly above
private property, but only for flights crossing state or national

boundaries. For intrastate flights, state property law would continue to govern ownership of the airspace. The report of the House Committee on Interstate and Foreign Commerce explained that this right of navigation through the air "is analogous to the easement of public right of navigation over the navigable waters of the United States." But because "the primary source of power to impose such an easement is the commerce clause," Congress limited the easement to interstate flights.[45]

This was a timid interpretation of the commerce power, even for 1926. A public easement of flight, one that included intrastate flights, could plausibly have been justified as part of a nationwide system of air traffic control that had to be uniform if it was to work at all. A Supreme Court that had recently upheld federal regulation of intrastate commodity futures trading and intrastate railroad rates, on the theory that such regulation was necessary to effectuate a national regulatory scheme, would most likely have placed federal regulation of intrastate aviation in the same category. By 1926, however, the last thing the aviation industry needed was protracted litigation over the constitutionality of federal law, even if the law would eventually be upheld. The industry had been waiting a long time already.

If the Air Commerce Act was weaker than many had hoped for, most observers seem to have been relieved that Congress had at last passed a statute after eight years of dithering. "The long arm of the law has reached up at last into airspace," exulted the *Nation*. The *New York Times* called it "a red-letter day" in the history of aviation, a day that would be remembered as "opening the national airways." Insiders expected that the Air Commerce Act and the ensuing regulations promulgated by the Commerce Department would bring insurance rates down and spur the development of a commercial aviation industry. As things turned out, they were right. Commercial aviation took off, so to speak, after

NORTHWEST AIRWAYS, Inc., in connection with the Transcontinental Air Transport, Inc., announces the establishment of
passenger airplane service between Chicago and St. Paul-Minneapolis, effective September 1, 1928, which will afford connections with trains of the
Pennsylvania Railroad as shown below.

AIRPLANE SCHEDULES

Westbound		Eastbound	
Lv. Chicago (Cicero Field)	3.00 p. m.	Lv. Minneapolis (Wold-	
Ar. St. Paul (Municipal Airport)	7.00 p. m.	Chamberlain Field)	8.30 a. m.
Ar. Minneapolis (Wold-		Lv. St. Paul (Municipal Airport)	8.40 a. m.
Chamberlain Field)	7.10 p. m.	Ar. Chicago (Cicero Field)	12.10 p. m.

WESTBOUND TRAIN

Westbound airplanes connect at Chicago with the following train:

MANHATTAN LIMITED No. 23, DAILY

Lv. New York, N. Y. (E. T.):		Lv. Baltimore, Md.	8.02 p. m.
(Pennsylvania Station)	6.15 p. m.	Lv. Harrisburg, Pa.	10.30 p. m.
(Hudson Terminal)	6.10 p. m.	Ar. Chicago, Ill. (C. T.):	
Lv. North Philadelphia, Pa.	8.05 p. m.	(Englewood)	1.40 p. m.
Lv. Washington, D. C.	7.05 p. m.	(Union Station)	2.05 p. m.

EASTBOUND TRAINS

Eastbound airplanes connect at Chicago with the following trains:

BROADWAY LIMITED No. 28, DAILY		LIBERTY LIMITED No. 58, DAILY	
Lv. Chicago, Ill. (C. T.):		Lv. Chicago, Ill. (C. T.):	
(Union Station)	12.40 p. m.	(Union Station)	1.10 p. m.
(Englewood)	12.57 p. m.	(Englewood)	1.27 p. m.
Ar. Pittsburgh, Pa. (E. T.)	11.56 p. m.	Ar. Pittsburgh, Pa. (E. T.)	12.10 a. m.
Ar. North Philadelphia, Pa.	7.54 a. m.	Ar. Harrisburg, Pa.	5.40 a. m.
Ar. New York, N. Y.:		Ar. Baltimore, Md.	8.03 a. m.
(Hudson Terminal)	9.41 a. m.	Ar. Washington, D. C.	9.00 a. m.
(Pennsylvania Station)	9.40 a. m.		

While the Manhattan Limited No. 23 westbound, and the Broadway Limited No. 28
and Liberty Limited No. 58 eastbound, make direct connections at Chicago with the
airplanes, passengers desiring to stop over in Chicago, and passengers from other points,
may use any other Pennsylvania Railroad trains to and from Chicago.

All times shown are Standard Time

Connections are made at St. Paul and Minneapolis both eastbound and westbound
with the trains of all lines

The Air Commerce Act of 1926 spurred the development of commercial air travel, including this route, established in 1928, between
Chicago and Minneapolis–St. Paul. Passengers leaving Minneapolis in
the morning would arrive shortly after noon in Chicago, where they
could connect with a train and be in New York City or Washington,
D.C., by the following morning. Portfolio 18, folder 60, Printed
Ephemera Collection, Library of Congress.

1926. That year, the thirteen air carriers in the United States flew a total of 4.3 million revenue-earning domestic miles. Five years later, the number of carriers had tripled, and their mileage had increased by a factor of ten.[46]

But the aerial trespass question lingered, and indeed grew more complicated. Because of continuing uncertainty as to the extent of Congress's powers under the Constitution, the easement of flight established by the Air Commerce Act of 1926 applied only to interstate flights. Yet Congress had authorized the Commerce Department to promulgate air traffic control rules for all flights, including intrastate flights, and minimum altitude requirements would be an important component of those rules. Sure enough, the ensuing Air Commerce Regulations set a one-thousand-foot floor for all flights over populated areas, and a five-hundred-foot floor elsewhere, except of course during takeoffs and landings. Intrastate flights were left in an odd legal position. Under federal law, planes had to be at least five hundred or one thousand feet above the ground, but under state law there was no guarantee that they could be above the ground at all. Everything depended on the law of the particular state. And to make matters even stranger, in the first reported case testing the constitutionality of the Air Commerce Act, a federal judge suggested that the minimum altitude requirements might not be lawfully applied to intrastate flights in the first place. It would not be necessary to apply the federal rule to intrastate flights, he reasoned, because if interstate aircraft flew above five hundred feet, and if intrastate aircraft flew below, they would never crash.[47]

In the wake of the Air Commerce Act, lawyers thus recognized that the issue of who owned the airspace was still open, and still important, with respect to intrastate flights. Indeed, they realized, it had not yet been definitively settled for interstate flights either, because of the possibility that landowners might claim that the act unconstitutionally took away their right, under the *cujus est solum* maxim, to exclude planes from their airspace.[48] As the growing commercial aviation industry filled the skies with planes, meanwhile, conflicts between landowners and pilots would only grow in volume. More than two decades after the Wright brothers' first flight, the problem of airspace was as pressing as ever.

SIX

Landowners against the Aviation Industry

As air travel grew more frequent in the late 1920s and early 1930s, so did disputes between aviators and landowners. "I am a poultry raiser keeping about 2,500 Longhorn hens," wrote the proprietor of the Cackle Corner Poultry Farm in Garrettsville, Ohio. "About once in two or three weeks an airplane, sometimes it is a U.S. mail plane, flies over my place so low that the hens become so frightened that they pile up, thus injuring each other and my egg yield drops one or two hundred eggs per day, and by the time I get them back to normal along comes another low flying machine and sends the egg yield down again." Garrettsville, southeast of Cleveland, was located beneath the airmail route between Chicago and New York. The poultry farmer was complaining to the postmaster general, the only person he could find with authority over any of the planes that crossed through his airspace. "The loss to me is so great that I fear it may put me out of business," the farmer concluded. "I wondered if the planes could not be requested to fly higher." The postmaster general accordingly asked National Air Transport, the Post Office's airmail contractor, to fly a bit higher over Garrettsville.[1]

But most of these disputes were not so easily resolved. At a resort in Rhode Island, vacationers complained of low flights over their cottages. On Long Island, where Roosevelt Field airport bordered the Old Westbury Golf Club, golfers were repeatedly disturbed by planes taking off and landing. The club built a 125-foot-high fence on the boundary between the two properties, a fence high enough to force aviators to take off and land from the other direction. In White Plains, New York, a grand jury indicted the Westchester Airport Company for maintaining a public nuisance, after neighbors complained that the dust raised by ascending planes flying over their houses so clogged the air that they were forced to keep their windows shut. A fox breeder in Nebraska sued Boeing Air Transport on the ground that Boeing's planes flying overhead so frightened his foxes that they suffered miscarriages. Katherine Meloy filed a similar suit against the city of Santa Monica, California, after the city opened its Clover Field airport across the street from Meloy's farm. Planes "continually fly over plaintiff's residence at an elevation of less than one hundred feet," Meloy complained, creating "terrific and unusual noises in the vicinity of plaintiff's dwelling which are startling in the extreme and wearing upon her nerves." The airplane, once a novelty, was becoming an annoyance, especially to those who lived near an airport. "The very people who thrilled at the sight of the first plane in their vicinity are tiring of airport dust and low-flying planes," the law professor Fred Fagg realized. Uncertainty about the relative rights of fliers and landowners only made matters worse. "The higher one proceeds above the surface of the earth," mused the Indiana judge Byron Elliott, "the thinner becomes the legal atmosphere." By 1930, Syracuse insurance lawyer Joseph Murphy could already remark that aviation "has become a prolific source of litigation."[2]

Much of that litigation involved claims of trespass. Landowners would battle it out against aviators all through the 1930s. By the end of the decade, there would be a substantial body of law on the question of whether landowners could exclude airplanes as trespassers.

The first of the trespass cases was *Smith v. New England Aircraft Company*, decided by the Massachusetts Supreme Court in 1930. The plaintiff was the well-known sportsman Harry Worcester Smith. Smith was most famous in British and American foxhunting circles as a master of hounds, but he was also a champion steeplechaser, the author of several books on hunting, and an inventor with forty patents to his credit, most relating to improvements in textile machinery. When he died in 1945, the *New York Times* said that "Mr. Smith's name was a household word among horsemen and sportsmen."[3]

It was also a household word among aviation lawyers. One of Smith's homes was a 270-acre country estate called "Lordvale" in Grafton, Massachusetts, just outside of Worcester. Lordvale was surrounded by farms until 1927, when a group of Worcester businessmen and flying enthusiasts, worried that the post–Air Commerce Act boom in aviation was passing Worcester by, determined they needed an airport. They purchased a farm and built an airport on it, which they named Whittall Field after the man who did most of the organizational work.[4] The farm they chose happened to adjoin Smith's estate. They leased the airport to the New England Aircraft Company, a firm in the business of operating airfields and flying schools. New England Aircraft would not survive Smith's lawsuit: while the suit was pending, the firm was acquired by Curtiss Flying Service, another airport operator, one of the many companies that would be merged together in 1929 to form the Curtiss-Wright Corporation, which remains an important aerospace company today.

Now that it was next to an airport, Harry Worcester Smith's peaceful country home was no longer so peaceful. Because of the prevailing winds, most takeoffs and landings—several every day, except in bad weather—were over Smith's land, at altitudes as low as one hundred feet. Smith's house was surrounded by his own trees and brush, which created a buffer of over a half a mile between the house and the airstrip. Planes were thus usually at an altitude of five hundred feet or more by the time they flew over the house. Under Massachusetts equity procedure, Smith's suit was referred for fact-finding to a master, who determined that the noise created by the planes did not materially interfere with the physical comfort of Smith or his wife. "There was no evidence in this case that either the plaintiffs, their guests or any member of their household had suffered from fear or fright by reason of airplane flights over their land," the master found. "There was no evidence of damage occasioned to their property, nor interference with the present use made of their land." Smith and his wife, the master observed, were being a bit too sensitive. "I find the plaintiffs are persons accustomed to a rather luxurious habit of living," he concluded, "and while the noise from the airplanes in flight over their premises has caused them irritation and annoyance, yet gauged by the standards of ordinary people this noise is not of sufficient frequency, duration or intensity to constitute a nuisance." Smith was represented by the prominent Boston attorney Charles Francis Choate. Choate's failure to file any exceptions to the master's report suggests he realized that the report was accurate.

The Smiths alleged that the overflights were both a trespass and a nuisance, but the master's factual findings effectively knocked out the nuisance claim. A nuisance is simply an unreasonable interference with the use of property, and the airport was not interfering with the Smiths' use of Lordvale at all. The Smiths could win, therefore, only if the Massachusetts Supreme Court found that the airplanes using Whittall Field were trespassing when they flew through the Smiths' airspace.

The court began by noting that both the federal air commerce regulations and a state statute required planes to fly at least five hundred feet above the ground, except during takeoffs and landings. These laws, the court held, implicitly authorized overflights of private property, because they presumed the existence of people and buildings below. (Overflights were *explicitly* authorized by the Air Commerce Act, but only for interstate flights, and there was no evidence about where pilots headed when they left Whittall Field. Perhaps this is why the court did not rely on the Air Commerce Act.) On the other hand, the court acknowledged all the pre-aviation cases finding aerial trespasses committed by overhanging parts of buildings, wires, animals, and so on. From those cases, the court derived the principle that "private ownership of airspace extends to all reasonable heights above the underlying land." The court then struggled, over several meandering pages, to reconcile the right to fly with the private ownership of airspace. In the end, the court concluded that flights above five hundred feet, the statutory minimum altitude, were not trespasses, but that flights at one hundred feet, including takeoffs and landings, *were* trespasses. "Air navigation, important as it is, cannot rightly levy toll upon the legal right of others for its successful prosecution," declared Chief Justice Arthur Prentice Rugg in his opinion for a unanimous court. "No reason has been suggested why airports of sufficient area may not be provided so that take-offs and landings of aircraft may be made without trespass upon the land of others."

But having handed the Smiths a seeming victory, the court whisked it away at the last moment. Because the Smiths had not suffered any actual damage, the court held, they were not entitled to an injunction ordering the cessation of overflights. All they could get from the defendants was money, and only a nominal sum in light of the lack of damage. Curtiss-Wright, the successors to the New England Aircraft Company, could continue to operate Whittall Field and fly over Harry Worcester Smith's property, even though the planes were committing trespass with each flight. Whittall Field remained in operation until it was replaced by a larger and better-situated airport in 1945. Lordvale was destroyed by fire in 1940, in an accident unrelated to the airport. In the first big battle between aviators and landowners, the aviators had won.

As many commentators noted, however, it was not entirely clear *why* the aviators had won, and the murkiness of the court's opinion limited the utility of *Smith v. New England Aircraft* as a precedent for future cases. If federal regulations and state statutes could authorize overflights at five hundred feet, free from liability for trespass, why couldn't they also authorize takeoffs and landings at one hundred feet, or indeed any other altitude? How could the common-law property rights of a landowner depend on the particular altitude that happened to be mentioned in a statute? In the absence of a statute, what would the landowner's rights be? How could aviators ascend to and descend from the permissible height of five hundred feet without trespassing in their neighbors' airspace, unless airports were made impossibly large? What about flights at altitudes between one hundred and five hundred feet— were these trespasses or not? Why did the court require a finding of actual damage as a prerequisite to an injunction, when the normal rule, for trespasses in the air or on the ground, was to award an injunction regardless of the presence of actual damage? The Massachusetts Supreme Court had decided the case before it, but in such an incoherent way as to provide little guidance for later cases presenting different facts.[5]

Lawyers would be disappointed again the following year by a lawsuit in New York.[6] After an airplane plunged into the plaintiff's house, he sued the plane's owner and then, perhaps seeking deeper pockets, sued Nassau County and the town of Hempstead, on the theory that they had "invited" airplanes to trespass in his airspace by operating an airport in Hempstead. In granting the town's and county's motions to be dropped from the case, the trial judge wrote a brief opinion in which he said that the *cujus est solum* maxim was "not now to be taken too literally." But that was all he had to say about aerial trespass. He held that he would dismiss the complaint against the town and county because it failed to allege any wrongdoing on the part of any public officials, a conclusion that might or might not have rested on a determination that airplanes were not trespassing. Once again, a case involving a claim of aerial trespass had been resolved in a way that would not be helpful in the future.

The most important aerial trespass case of the 1930s arose from a dispute outside Cleveland, Ohio, a dispute that closely resembled the conflict between Harry Worcester Smith and the New England Aircraft Company. The plaintiffs were the brothers Frederick and Raymond Swetland, whose 135-acre country estate in Richmond Heights had been surrounded by farms for decades. Like Harry Smith, however, the Swetlands were victims of the boom in aviation that followed the Air Commerce Act. In 1929 a neighboring parcel of land was acquired by the Curtiss Airports Corporation, another Curtiss-Wright subsidiary, which built runways, hangars, facilities for a flying school, and a large parking lot. The airport was scarcely open before the Swetlands filed suit.

Swetland v. Curtiss Airports Corporation came before a new federal judge, George Hahn, who had been appointed by the lame duck Calvin Coolidge only a few months earlier. Nothing in Hahn's background suggested he would bring any particular wisdom or experience to the question of who owned the air. He was a Republican lawyer from Toledo who became a judge largely because his law partner was Walter F. Brown, Herbert Hoover's assistant secretary of commerce (and later postmaster general when Hoover became president). Hahn would not live long enough to compile a distinguished record as a judge; he died of influenza in 1937, after a career remembered only, if at all, for his supervision of the reorganization of the Willys Overland Company, one of the important early automobile manufacturers.

Hahn nevertheless produced a learned and thorough opinion incorporating much of what had been written about aerial trespass over the preceding three decades.[7] The airport itself, he decided, was not a nuisance. "It is obvious that although aviation is still to some extent in the experimental stage," Hahn explained, "it is of great utility in times of peace, and will be a great protection to the nation in times of war. In fact, it is indispensable to the safety of the nation that airports and flying schools such as contemplated by the defendants be encouraged in every reasonable respect. An airport, landing field, or flying school can be regarded as a nuisance only if located in an unsuitable location." An agricultural setting, a few miles away from a major city, was not an unreasonable spot for an airport, even if it inconvenienced its neighbors. "No one will contend that the plaintiffs will have the same enjoyment of peace and quiet which they have had in this locality for nearly a quarter of a century," Hahn conceded. But years of quiet did not give one a right to continued quiet. The Swetlands "at no time had a right to prevent the adjoining owner from using this property for any reasonable purpose. They have been fortunate in that they have been able to enjoy their country estate as they have for so long a time. They must now yield to change and progress of the times."

The Swetlands also alleged that airplanes were trespassing by flying over their land, and it was to this point that Hahn devoted the greater part of his attention. He reviewed the English and American cases on aerial trespass, from the early disputes about overhanging parts of buildings to the recent cases involving bullets and telephone wires. "It is safe to say," he concluded, "that there are no cases which involve an adjudication of property rights as appurtenant to land in the air space which would normally be used by an aviator." The offending items were all too low. The *cujus est solum* maxim was routinely quoted in these cases, Hahn acknowledged, "but it is the points actually decided in the cases, not the maxim, which establish the law." And those cases demonstrated only that landowners owned their airspace up to a point, not that they owned up to the heavens. In reaching this conclusion, Hahn drew heavily on the legal scholarship of the previous two decades.

It would be no easy matter to decide precisely at what altitude the landowner's right to exclude aircraft ended, but Hahn realized he had no need to answer that question. Both the United States and Ohio had set five hundred feet as the minimum altitude for flight, and, Hahn found, five hundred feet was no less reasonable a height than any other, because flying at that altitude would not interfere with the Swetlands' enjoyment of their land. Takeoffs and landings, on the other hand, took place well below five hundred feet above the Swetlands' estate. After visits to the airport to experience them firsthand, Judge Hahn determined that takeoffs and landings below five hundred feet were nuisances—not necessarily at all airports and over all property, but just over the Swetlands' property, because of the effect of the noise and the dust on the Swetlands' use of their land. He accordingly enjoined the airport from allowing flights in the Swetlands' airspace at altitudes below five hundred feet.

The decision was national news. Should Hahn's view of the law be applied everywhere, fretted *Time* magazine, "the effect would be equivalent to creating a fence 500 ft. high around every airport. And as approved aircraft have a minimum gliding ratio of 7-to-1, airmen have computed that 3,500 ft. would have to be added to each dimension of the present average airport for planes to clear the edges at the prescribed altitude." The *Los Angeles Times* reported that Curtiss-Wright was planning to shut down the airport, because there was not enough room to get planes to five hundred feet before they left the property. Judge Hahn's ruling was a "menace to aviation," complained Curtiss-Wright's Cleveland manager.[8] These were overreactions. Hahn had explicitly *not* found that flights below five hundred feet were trespasses or *per se* nuisances. He had carefully explained that at other airports in other locations, very low takeoffs and landings might not be nuisances, because they might not be bothering any neighbors.

The reaction among lawyers was much more positive, because the lawyers were more attentive to detail. "This certainly is not a holding that mere flight above the surface of the ground, even at a height of less than 500 feet is a trespass," declared law professor Thompson George Marsh. Most who wrote about the case were pleased that Hahn had affirmed the near-consensus of the previous decade in the law reviews and legal treatises, that the *cujus est solum* maxim was not to be taken literally, and that ordinary overflights were not trespasses. The new *Journal of Air Law* called Hahn's decision "an admirable compromise of the conflicting interests involved—those of the land owner to be undisturbed in the use and enjoyment of his land, and those of the public in the newest medium of travel." The *Journal* was particularly happy that the decision was "based entirely on the finding that a nuisance was maintained, and not the ground that trespass was committed." A ruling based on nuisance was confined to the unique facts of the case, but if flights below five hundred feet were trespasses over one piece of land, they would have been trespasses everywhere.[9]

Both sides appealed Judge Hahn's decision. Curtiss Airports wanted to keep taking off and landing above the Swetlands' land, and the Swetlands wanted to bar *all* overflights, regardless of their height. The Court of Appeals slightly modified Judge Hahn's injunction, but again gave a victory to the Swetlands.[10] Not all overflights were trespasses, the court ruled. A landowner did not have exclusive rights to the "upper stratum" of the air, which he could not reasonably expect to use himself. Aircraft could fly in this upper stratum without committing trespass. The landowner's remedy for bothersome flights in the upper stratum was limited to nuisance. In the "lower stratum" of the air, by contrast, the landowner had a "dominant right of occupancy for purposes incident to his use and enjoyment of the surface," a right that would support an action for trespass. The tricky question, as always, was where to draw the line between the two strata, and, like Judge Hahn, the Court of Appeals determined that it had no need to establish any rule. "We cannot fix a definite and unvarying height below which the surface owner may reasonably expect to occupy the air space for himself," the court acknowledged. "That height is to be determined upon the particular facts of each case. It is sufficient for this case that the flying of the defendants over the plaintiff's property was not within the zone of such expected use." Planes were accordingly not trespassing when they crossed over the Swetlands' estate.

The Court of Appeals was less charitable, however, about the airport itself. "We cannot doubt from the evidence," the court

declared, "that the brightly illuminated field with the noises incident to its operation, however careful defendants may be, will un-
avoidably interfere with, if not destroy, the plaintiffs' enjoyment
of their property." Judge Hahn had found that takeoffs and landings were nuisances, but the Court of Appeals found the airport
itself to be a nuisance as well. The court enjoined Curtiss Airports
from continuing to operate an airfield on its property.

The appellate decision was the occasion for another round of
commentary from lawyers, who were again happy to see an official repudiation of the *cujus est solum* maxim. "The higher space
will be left free to air travel, much the same as navigable waters
over private property are free to public navigation," exulted one
California lawyer.[11] Some airports would have to be relocated farther from settled areas if the view of nuisance law taken by the
Court of Appeals were to be followed by other courts, but the
right of flight itself was growing more secure. And the Court of
Appeals decision was written more clearly and logically than the
earlier effort of the Massachusetts Supreme Court, which made it
more useful as a precedent. The boundary between trespasses and
permissible overflights was located at the limit of the airspace the
landowner could reasonably expect to occupy.

In the war between airplanes and landowners, the outcome of
the first two battles, *Smith* and *Swetland,* had been mixed. Airplanes were not trespassers in the upper air; they *were* trespassers
in the lower air; and whether any particular overflight was a nuisance depended heavily on the subjective view of the judge. But
there would be more battles to come, and some of the most important would not be fought in a courtroom.

Construction on the Empire State Building began in early 1930,
while *Smith* and *Swetland* were working their ways through the

courts. Completed the following year, at 1,048 feet it was the tallest building in the world, and it would remain the tallest until 1972, when it was passed by the World Trade Center. But there was more to the Empire State Building than just the building. Sitting on top was a pole, two hundred feet high. The pole was intended to be a mooring mast for dirigibles. The idea was that dirigibles could be anchored to the mast, to allow passengers to embark and disembark, and to take on provisions, by a gangplank that would connect the ship to an elevator in the tower. The plan no doubt had its dangers for passengers, but it must have seemed promising from the pilot's perspective, because in crowded Manhattan there was no place more accessible to dirigibles.[12]

But could the mooring mast even be used without breaking the law? To reach it, dirigibles would have to fly over adjacent properties. While anchored, they would likely extend into the airspace above neighboring buildings. In either case, would they be trespassing? The owner of the Empire State Building was a corporation headed by Al Smith, the former governor of New York, and formed by some prominent businessmen, including John Jakob Raskob and members of the du Pont family. These were men accustomed to top-quality legal advice, so they naturally turned for answers to the New York law firm of Chadbourne, Stanchfield & Levy. The firm had a diverse practice—it had recently represented James Joyce in litigation over an expurgated American edition of *Ulysses*—but most of its clients were railroads and other large corporations. They included some of the leading aviation firms of the era, including the Wright Aeronautical Company. Thomas Chadbourne was a Wright director. He was also a close friend of Al Smith.[13]

Chadbourne, Stanchfield & Levy replied with a lengthy memorandum, in which it concluded that use of the mooring mast would probably be legal, but that the law was so uncertain that

The Empire State Building, shown here soon after its completion in 1931, boasted a mooring mast for dirigibles at the top. The lawyers for the building's owners advised that dirigibles would probably not be committing trespass by passing over adjoining buildings, but the lawyers admitted that the law was uncertain. LC-USZ62-70108, Prints and Photographs Division, Library of Congress.

one could not be sure.[14] The mast was high enough that dirigibles would not violate the federal air regulations or any state statutes while tied up or flying there or back. The harder questions were whether they would be committing trespass or nuisance. The Empire State Building was several hundred feet higher than all the surrounding office buildings, so flights would not come close to any already-existing uses of land. In light of *Smith* and *Swetland*, the firm counseled, this was probably enough of a gap to immunize dirigibles from liability for trespass, particularly because the people working in the surrounding buildings had no interest in privacy or quiet comparable to that of the owner of a secluded country estate, the sort of land at issue in the two cases. If the neighboring buildings grew much higher, dirigibles would no longer be able to reach the mooring mast, so the legal problem would disappear. As for nuisance, dirigibles passing overhead would be loud, but New York was already so noisy that the sound would scarcely be noticed. They would attract crowds, but New York was already very crowded. They might cause people below to fear dangerous accidents, but the city was already full of comparable dangers. When all these risks were balanced against the undoubted benefit of having an airport in the heart of the city, the firm concluded, the mooring mast was unlikely to be enjoined as a nuisance. The same considerations applied to dirigibles anchored to the mast, when the wind caused them to stray over adjoining properties.

But all these predictions, the firm advised, had to be taken with a grain of salt. The memorandum ended with some words of caution: "The answer is too speculative to be given with any assurance, and one enlightened guess is as good as another." The question was still too new, and the court decisions too few, to say anything with certainty about trespass or nuisance in the air.

That was enough encouragement for the owners of the Empire

State Building, who opened the mooring mast for business. "In a comparatively short time the Zeppelin airships will establish transatlantic, transcontinental and transpacific lines," Al Smith declared. He expected them to land atop his skyscraper, from which their passengers would emerge at the bottom, seven minutes later, directly onto the corner of Fifth Avenue and Thirty-fourth Street. The first dirigible to anchor was a small private ship, which tied up for three minutes on a windy weekday morning in September 1931, while pedestrians watched from below in amazement and traffic ground to a halt. The pilot did not attempt to disembark. Two weeks later a blimp owned by the Goodyear Tire & Rubber Company moored briefly to the mast in order to deliver a stack of newspapers, in a publicity stunt meant to demonstrate the feasibility of roof-to-roof mail delivery. Despite these efforts, however, the Empire State Building never became a terminal for dirigibles.[15] The winds at twelve hundred feet were so strong, and the surrounding area so crowded, that the risk of a terrible accident was always unacceptably high. Within a couple of years the mooring mast was converted to a television transmission tower. It was not much longer, in any event, before the prospect of commercial zeppelin travel was only a memory.

But the Empire State Building mooring mast was done in by engineering problems, not legal ones. The legal climate, although uncertain, was welcoming enough to cause some experienced entrepreneurs to go forward with the plan, and their expectations about the law turned out to be correct. During the mooring mast's brief life, just as Chadbourne, Stanchfield & Levy predicted, the owners of the Empire State Building were not sued for trespass or nuisance by any of their neighbors. To the extent that the common law bubbled up from below, as a product of repeated practice and the expectations that practice engendered, the experience

of the Empire State Building was one more step in the consolida-
tion of a public right to use the upper airspace.

In the conflict between airplanes and landowners, the airplanes
had a big advantage. The aviation industry was well organized,
with trade associations and lobbyists seeking to influence the law.
Landowners were not organized at all. There were too many of
them and their interests were too varied. The aerial trespass question, meanwhile, was a life-or-death issue to the aviation industry.
Without the ability to fly over privately owned land, there could
be no industry at all. Aerial trespass was much less important to
landowners. Most lived nowhere near an airport, so most had no
reason to worry about low-flying planes overhead. Landowners
were also beneficiaries of aviation, some as passengers and many
more as senders and receivers of mail. Whatever interest they had
in preserving their airspace was thus counterbalanced by their recognition that planes had to fly somewhere overhead. Many of the
people employed by the aviation industry were also landowners,
of course, so they too had to see both sides of the issue, but they
had much more to gain from a thriving industry than they had to
lose from planes flying over their land. In the political economy
of aerial trespass, landowners had the odds against them.

The industry's clout had been demonstrated in the lobbying
for the Air Commerce Act of 1926. In the 1930s, aviation representatives turned their attention to the law of trespass, which for
non-interstate flights was still a question of state law. The Uniform State Law for Aeronautics, promulgated in 1922 and adopted in twenty-two states and territories, had accommodated the
cujus est solum maxim by declaring that all the space above land
was owned by the surface owners, subject to a public "right of

flight" at altitudes high enough to avoid interfering with the then-existing use of the land. In 1930, however, both the Massachusetts Supreme Court (in *Smith*) and a federal district court (in *Swetland*) published opinions suggesting that in fact landowners did not own all the airspace, but only the airspace closest to the ground. Aviation lawyers saw an opening. "There are those who would wish the maxim to be destroyed in its entirety rather than have it adapted to present needs," remarked the law professor Carl Zollman, and it was clear enough who they were.[16]

One vehicle for legal change was the *Swetland* case itself. When the case reached the Court of Appeals, it attracted two amicus curiae briefs (that is, briefs filed on behalf of parties who are not involved in the case but who care about its outcome). One was filed by the Aviation Corporation, a holding company with interests in many small airlines. It argued that there could be no such thing as aerial trespass because landowners owned *none* of their airspace. The other was filed by the Aeronautical Chamber of Commerce, whose 772 members accounted for 98 percent of miles flown by scheduled airlines and 96 percent of all aircraft and motors produced in the previous year. The Chamber of Commerce argued that air, no matter how low, was a public thoroughfare much like navigable water.[17]

These briefs had no discernable effect on the Court of Appeals, but litigation was not the only route to victory. The American Bar Association had a standing committee on aeronautical law, chaired by the St. Louis lawyer George Logan. Logan was an aviation man: he was also the chair of the legislative committee of the St. Louis Air Board and a member of the advisory committee of the Air Law Institute recently established at Northwestern University. Before long he would become legal counsel to the National Association of State Aviation Officials. Logan may have been best known to aviators as the author of the 1928 book

Aircraft Law—Made Plain, a guide for pilots and owners of airplanes. In the very first section of the book, Logan denounced the *cujus est solum* maxim as a legal fiction with no place in the modern world. The other three members of the bar association committee were also aviation lawyers. Howard Wikoff, of Chicago, was general counsel to the American Air Transport Association, the organization representing the largest air carriers. The Jacksonville lawyer John Cobb Cooper was soon to become vice president of Pan American Airways. Mabel Walker Willebrandt, one of the pioneer woman lawyers of the era, had recently left her position as assistant attorney general of the United States (which made her the highest ranking woman in the federal government throughout the 1920s) to become counsel to the Aviation Corporation. She was the author of the Aviation Corporation's amicus curiae brief in the *Swetland* case.[18]

This was a committee more interested in the welfare of aviation firms than of landowners. Shortly after the publication of *Smith* and *Swetland,* the committee drafted a new "Uniform Aeronautics Code," which it hoped would replace the old Uniform State Law for Aeronautics. The new code omitted the old law's declaration that airspace was owned by the surface owner. In its place was a new provision, one that pointedly refused to acknowledge the *cujus est solum* maxim. It read simply that "flight in aircraft over the lands and waters of this state . . . is lawful unless at such a low altitude as to interfere with the then existing use" of the land or water. In its report, the committee explained its belief that the old law's treatment of the airspace "proclaims a legal untruth. No decided case has ever held that 'airspace' was 'owned' by the landowner to unlimited heights," the committee insisted. "It is manifest that prior to the use of aircraft and prior to the use of upper airspaces, there could have been no authoritative pronouncement on the subject." And now, after *Smith* and *Swetland,*

After serving as assistant attorney general from 1921 to 1929, Mabel Walker Willebrandt became counsel to the Aviation Corporation and one of the leaders of the industry's effort to have airspace declared unownable. LC-USZ62-88097, Prints and Photographs Division, Library of Congress.

"enough has been said in these two cases apparently in opposition to the old pronouncement, to indicate that the broad statement as contained in the old Uniform Aeronautics Act, was, as it stood, incorrect."[19]

Members of the ABA who weren't paying close attention might have thought this a metaphysical dispute. The old uniform act had said that surface owners owned all their airspace, but that planes could fly through it anyway, so long as they didn't interfere with the landowners below. The committee's new proposal also said that planes could fly through the airspace, so long as they didn't interfere with the landowners below. Either way, flight would be lawful above a given height, and the height would be the same in both cases. The aviation lawyers who were members of George Logan's aeronautics committee, however, considered the difference between the two formulations very important. Retaining the old language, they concluded, "would simply lend color to the assertion of non-existent and unnecessary rights by litigiously inclined persons, to the great nuisance and possible destruction of aviation." Logan explained why, while discussing the proposal at the bar association's annual meeting. The committee meant to espouse the same theory Mabel Walker Willebrandt had argued as amicus curiae in *Swetland*—that there could be no such thing as ownership of airspace. A plane that flew too low, so low that it interfered with the landowner's use of his land, might be liable for nuisance, but it could not be committing trespass.[20]

This was indeed a bigger change than it seemed. Under the old uniform act, a pilot who flew too low was trespassing in someone else's airspace. He was committing a tort—a civil wrong—regardless of whether he caused any actual damage to the landowner below, because trespass was wrong independent of its effect on the owner of land. The landowner could accordingly go to court and obtain an injunction ordering the pilot to stop. It was not hard to envision the people who lived near airports doing exactly that, and indeed some were already trying. Under the new proposed code, by contrast, a pilot who flew too low was not doing anything wrong unless, considering all the circumstances, he unreasonably inflicted harm on the landowner below. While the outcomes of such cases were obviously impossible to predict without knowing all their facts, one could assume that under such a rule the landowners near airports would obtain injunctions in a much smaller class of cases, particularly if courts, in deciding what sorts of activities were reasonable, took into account the public need for air travel. *Smith* and *Swetland* had created an opportunity for a small group of aviation lawyers to press for a seemingly technical change in language that could be of great benefit to their clients.

The implications of the change did not go unnoticed. "One may be pardoned for registering alarm," remarked James Hayden, the director of research in aviation law at Catholic University, "when it is suddenly proposed to discard the legal learning and beliefs of centuries." Hayden pointed out that the ownership of airspace had hardly prevented the aviation industry from growing over the past three decades. "Why should this industry deliberately cultivate the ill will and antagonism of every landowner in the nation," he wondered, "by a legalistic denial of a principle of law which has been considered sound . . . for more than five hundred years?" Worse, landowners in built-up downtowns were accustomed to conveyances of "air rights"—the right to build above land or even buildings owned by others. If unenclosed airspace was not capable of being owned, what exactly were these landowners conveying? Did the committee's view of the law mean that all these transactions had been void from the beginning?[21]

Although landowners were not organized like the aviation industry was, they had something close to a spokesman in Nathan

MacChesney, the general counsel to the National Association of Real Estate Boards, the predecessor to today's National Association of Realtors. MacChesney was very active in lawyers' civic organizations. He had been president of the National Conference of Commissioners on Uniform State Laws in the early 1920s, when NCCUSL had promulgated the uniform aeronautics law. He had been president of the Illinois State Bar. He was a member of several ABA committees and a regular attendee at ABA meetings. As Charles Hine, the Cleveland lawyer who represented the Swetlands, put it to him: "You are the logical man to lead the fight against special and unwise legislation on behalf of the aviation interests." MacChesney did just that, although without much support from his client. "It seems unbelievable to me," he complained, "that the landowners of this country, through their various organizations, should not be willing to put up a fight to protect themselves in a matter such as this." He repeatedly encouraged the National Association of Real Estate Boards to intervene on behalf of landowners in cases like *Swetland,* but the association never thought getting involved was worth the investment. "Those of us who have the interest of the landowner at heart should be put in a position to make some sort of a fight on the subject," he lamented to Hine. "It sometimes seems to me as if those who represent the landed interests had no idea of what is necessary to protect them. They are immersed in the immediate business, apparently, without a care as to general movements which are undermining their fundamental rights." MacChesney could fight the aviation interests only on the cheap, in nonjudicial forums like bar association meetings.[22]

Putting up a fight was worthwhile only for landowners who lived near airports. Perhaps the most pugnacious was Frederick Swetland himself, who seems to have been fired up by the experience of litigating against Curtiss-Wright. "All existing laws having to do with the operation of aircraft have been written solely in the interests of the owners and operators of such aircraft, and with almost total disregard to the rights or interests of the owners of land over which the aircraft operates," he despaired, a few months after his victory in the Court of Appeals. He bemoaned the fact that aviation law "is almost daily being written in our statute books by persons interested in aviation," because the general land-owning "public has not been aroused to the danger." Swetland barraged MacChesney with letters urging him to fight one injustice or another committed by the operators of airports, which he believed "can be located and should be located in the commercial districts of our country or in remote districts where such use would not infringe on the enjoyment and use of surrounding property by individual owners." Instead, he lamented, "the people interested in the promotion of aviation wish to subject the owner of land to any sort of use of the air," worst of all "landing and taking off from airports at low elevations."[23]

When the ABA's aeronautics committee proposed to do away with the ownership of airspace, MacChesney was ready to defend the landowners. "The real estate interests of this country," he declared to the assembled delegates, were "rather alarmed at the growth of the contention that the rights of land-owners are practically to be wiped out." The entire reason people moved to the country, he argued, was to escape the noises of the city. A quiet environment was "what gives value to large areas of land in the country adjacent to our great cities." He urged that flight over land owned by another ought to be unlawful, not just when it interfered with the landowner's *use* of his land, but also when it affected the *value* of his land, a much larger class of instances. Without such a rule, he concluded, the law of aviation would effectively allow "the confiscation of the rights of the land-owner without compensation."[24]

When the meeting was over, MacChesney continued the fight with a vigorous letter-writing campaign targeted at sympathetic lawyers and law professors. "It seems to me that interests other than those especially interested in aviation should be represented in the American Bar Association Committee," he complained to Francis Bohlen, a law professor at the University of Pennsylvania. "Land owners have a very substantial stake in this matter," he declared to a group of like-minded lawyers, "which is gradually being chiseled away without full consideration of their rights."[25]

The American Bar Association never did approve the new Uniform Aeronautics Code proposed by George Logan and his committee. Thanks largely to Nathan MacChesney, the landowners won this round. Neither side could rest, though, because the next round had begun, and this one did not take place in a courtroom either.

The American Law Institute was a self-consciously elite organization, formed in 1923 to draft "restatements," or summaries of areas of the common law. Unlike the American Bar Association or the National Conference of Commissioners on Uniform State Laws, the ALI was deliberately *not* representative of the profession as a whole. Its leaders were law professors and judges. Lawyers were members too, but the first set were a handpicked group, and membership thereafter required the approval of existing members. The idea was to create an organization of experts insulated as far as possible from political pressure, and then to bring their expertise to bear on the task of organizing complex and unsystematic bodies of law.[26]

This goal necessarily limited the legal fields the ALI would enter. As the organization's founders explained, "the fact that a man is a lawyer does not make him an expert on the tariff, or on the proper organization of city government, or enable him to speak with authority on hundreds of other questions of existing or proposed law debated on public platforms and in legislative assemblies." The ALI would focus instead on subjects that were not politically controversial, areas of law in which neutral, apolitical expertise might be useful—"such matters as the form in which public law should be expressed, the details of private law, procedure or the administration of law, and judicial organization." The Institute would "not promote or obstruct political, social or economic changes," but would strive instead to clean up doctrinally messy fields for the benefit of the profession as a whole.[27] Members thought of themselves as technicians, not lawmakers.

The ALI's first finished project was the *Restatement of Contracts,* completed in 1932 under the leadership of Harvard law professor Samuel Williston. Soon after came restatements in other common-law fields—agency (1933), torts (1939), security (1941), judgments (1942), and property (1944). These works served their intended purpose; they streamlined thousands of court decisions into a form easily used by lawyers and judges. By 1998 the ALI's restatements had been cited as authority in more than 140,000 court opinions. The *Restatement of Torts* was the most useful of all, if utility can be measured by citations. It had been cited as authority nearly sixty thousand times.[28]

Volume 1 of the *Restatement of Torts,* published in 1934, covered "Intentional Harms to Persons, Land, and Chattels." One of the intentional harms to land was trespass. In its discussion of trespass, the authors of the restatement necessarily had to discuss the possibility of trespass above and below the surface of the earth, and in the course of that discussion they had to say something about airplanes. The issue of aerial trespass was thus on the ALI's agenda, but not because members had any particular interest in the aviation industry or in the peace and quiet of landowners.

Aerial trespass was simply one variant of trespass, and trespass was only one kind of intentional tort. Charged with organizing and summarizing the law of torts as a whole, members of the ALI had a perspective very different from that of the aviation lawyers who made up the aeronautics committee of the American Bar Association.

They were also people with different interests. The "Reporter," or initial draftsman, of the restatement's provisions on aerial trespass was Edward Thurston, another Harvard law professor, the author of casebooks (compilations of cases for students) on topics like quasi-contracts and (later) torts. His work was reviewed by a committee of advisors consisting of four law professors, four judges, and only two practicing lawyers, one of whom, Owen Roberts, left the committee in 1930 when he was appointed to the U.S. Supreme Court.[29] None of these men represented aviation companies and none represented landowners. They were exactly the sort of people the ALI's founders had hoped would "restate" the law of aerial trespass—people whose allegiance was not to one side or the other in a political debate but to the intellectual coherence of the law.

By 1931 Thurston had drafted a rule confirming that at least some airspace was owned by the person who owned the land below. "A trespass on land may be committed by entering or remaining," his draft read, "(a) on the surface of the earth, or (b) beneath the surface thereof, or (c) above the surface thereof." He explained that there had been so many cases supporting proposition (c), from the early cases involving overhanging parts of buildings right up through *Smith* and *Swetland,* that it could hardly be in doubt. Nevertheless, he observed, "if possible some method should be found by which the great and growing industry of commercial aviation can be recognized as lawful. The only question on which there can be a doubt is as to which of several alternative methods best attains this end." He accordingly suggested that aircraft ought to have a privilege to fly through airspace owned by another, so long as they did not unreasonably interfere with the landowner's enjoyment of his land or airspace. This was, he acknowledged, the same strategy adopted in the Uniform State Law of Aeronautics and in the federal Air Commerce Act of 1926.[30]

This suggestion did not please aviation lawyers, who at that very moment were using the American Bar Association's aeronautics committee to press for a rule stating that airspace could not be owned. John Cobb Cooper, one of the members of the ABA committee, led a delegation to the 1931 meeting of the ALI to protest. The ALI accordingly referred the issue back to Thurston and his advisors. Thurston stood his ground. He responded two years later with a revised draft that included a much more detailed statement of the privilege of flying through airspace owned by another. The new provision read: "An entry above the surface of the earth, on the air space in the possession of another, by a person who is traveling in an aircraft, is privileged if the flight is conducted (a) for a legitimate purpose, and (b) in a reasonable manner, and (c) at such a height as not to interfere unreasonably with the possessor's enjoyment of the surface of the earth and the air space above it." Thurston provided some hypothetical fact situations to demonstrate how clause (c) of the proposed privilege would work. If A were producing "talking moving pictures," and B, knowing that, flew over A's land at a height that interfered with A's filming, B would be a trespasser. If A maintained a fox farm, and B flew over A's land low enough to frighten the foxes into miscarrying, B would be a trespasser. By twice including the concept of reasonableness in his rule, once in clause (b) and again in clause (c), Thurston was going a long way toward merging the concepts of trespass and nuisance. Aviators would be trespassing only if they flew at unreasonably low altitudes, which would be virtually the same circumstances under which they would also be liable for committing a nuisance.[31]

The aviation lawyers protested yet again. At the 1933 ALI meeting it was Mabel Walker Willebrandt who spoke on their behalf. She objected even to these weak limitations on the ability of flyers to traverse airspace. The New York County Lawyers Association also had a committee on aeronautical law, which was also controlled by aviation lawyers, and it too protested that air travel should be a matter of "right and not of privilege." The mere existence of controversy on this point, some suggested, meant that the ALI ought not to attempt to prescribe any rule at all, because any rule would require making the very sort of contested policy decision the restatements were supposed to avoid.[32]

The ALI nevertheless adopted Thurston's proposed rule by an overwhelming vote.[33] Aviation lawyers continued to grumble,[34] but the mandarins of the bar had spoken. The *Restatement of Torts* was not the law itself, but it was as close to the law as any such text could be, because it would become the standard reference for judges throughout the country. According to the *Restatement of Torts,* landowners owned their airspace, subject only to a privilege of reasonable flights at reasonable heights.

Meanwhile the courts were deciding more aerial trespass cases. Sky Haven Airport opened in rural Chester County, Pennsylvania, in 1930 and was promptly sued by three of its neighbors, two farmers and a tuberculosis hospital.[35] They complained of noise, dust, and one occasion on which a stunt plane flying at three thousand feet had dropped a cushion on one of the farms. In *Gay v. Taylor,* published in the fall of 1932 while lawyers were arguing at meetings of the ABA and the ALI, the court found that the airport was a nuisance. The noise and dust, it concluded, were "most objectionable, especially to persons who have sought the peace and quiet of the farming and agricultural community under consideration to establish their homes and bring up their children." Having already ruled against the airport, the judge acknowledged that he had no need to decide whether airplanes were also committing trespass, but he nevertheless offered his opinion that they were. "Invasions of the air space over one's real property are trespasses only when they interfere with a proper enjoyment of a reasonable use of the surface of the land," he reasoned, in language closely tracking the view emerging in drafts of the *Restatement of Torts.* The law of trespass, he concluded, was thus coterminous with the law of nuisance. Any overflight that was a nuisance would also be a trespass, because the same standard of reasonableness applied to both legal theories.

Atlanta's first airport gave rise to a similar dispute. Candler Field was constructed in 1927 on land near the property of Clovis Thrasher, who sued the city four years later for trespass and nuisance.[36] The trespass claim caught Justice Reason Chesnutt Bell of the Georgia Supreme Court in a philosophical mood. "What is the sky?" he wondered. "Who can tell where it begins or define its meaning in terms of the law? When can it be said that a plane is above the sky or below it?" The unanswerability of such questions moved Bell to conclude, in *Thrasher v. City of Atlanta,* that unused space could never be owned, because it could not be possessed. "The space is up there," he reasoned, "and the owner of the land has the first claim upon it," but so long as he had not built anything, the space was available for others to pass through. This was the view that aviation lawyers had unsuccessfully tried to persuade the American Bar Association to adopt, a view inconsistent with the earlier cases.

A federal appellate court in California reached the same conclusion soon after, in *Hinman v. Pacific Air Transport*.[37] Burbank's airport was located next to land owned by Mr. and Mrs. F. R. Hinman, who sued two air carriers for repeatedly flying over their land at altitudes below one hundred feet. The court rejected their claim for trespass. "The air, like the sea, is by its nature incapable of private ownership, except in so far as one may actually use it," reasoned Judge Bert Haney. "The owner of land owns as much of the space above him as he uses, but only so long as he uses it. All that lies beyond belongs to the world."

Between 1930 and 1936 there had been five reported cases addressing the question of aerial trespass, and their outcomes had been mixed. An aviation lawyer could take solace in the fact that all five cases had concluded that flights at high altitudes were not trespasses.[38] Such was also the view of the federal Air Commerce Act, the Uniform State Law of Aeronautics, and the *Restatement of Torts*. This unanimity meant there was no longer any serious argument that landowners owned up to the heavens. Overflights were lawful, so long as they were not too low.

In the Civil Aeronautics Act of 1938, Congress would ratify this consensus. The Air Commerce Act of 1926 had recognized a public right of *interstate* travel through the nation's "navigable airspace," the airspace above the minimum altitude prescribed by the Department of Commerce. By 1938, however, the federal government's power to regulate interstate commerce was growing substantially, amidst a series of U.S. Supreme Court cases that left lawyers with little doubt that even flights within a single state fell within federal authority. The Civil Aeronautics Act accordingly declared, for *all* flights, interstate or not, "a public right of freedom of transit in air commerce through the navigable air space."[39] The upper air was free.

For lower flights, by contrast, the law was in disarray. Three of the cases (*Smith, Swetland,* and *Gay*) had found that flights below a certain altitude were trespasses, while the other two (*Thrasher* and *Hinman*) had held that flights in unused airspace could never be trespasses, no matter how low. To make matters worse, the three cases in the first group had provided three different ways of defining the upper boundary of the landowner's property: It was located either somewhere between one hundred and five hundred feet *(Smith),* or at the border between the "upper" and "lower" strata of the airspace *(Swetland),* or at the point where a flight became low enough to interfere unreasonably with the landowner *(Gay).* The leading lawyers' organizations had tried to resolve the confusion on their own, but all they had done was replicate it, as the American Bar Association's aeronautics committee favored one rule and the American Law Institute another. All this uncertainty affected only the landowners who suffered the lowest overflights, the people with the misfortune to live next to airports, but they were the only ones likely to file suit in the first place.

More airport cases were decided in the early 1940s, but they did not clear things up. The Massachusetts Supreme Court surveyed the jumbled field in 1942 and reaffirmed its decision from twelve years before in *Smith.* The Georgia Supreme Court revisited the question eight years after *Thrasher* and reached a different outcome, because in the interim the Georgia legislature had enacted the Uniform State Law for Aeronautics. The court held that flights fifty feet above the ground *were* trespasses. The Delaware Court of Chancery and the Michigan Supreme Court, facing the question for the first time in 1942 and 1944, respectively, simply followed the restatement rule and disregarded all contrary views.[40]

The problem was one of balancing irreconcilable interests. "We all recognize that flight over private property must in some way be legalized," remarked the Seattle lawyer William Allen. Allen represented a new aircraft manufacturer called Boeing, so he was hardly unbiased, but it was true that one could scarcely find a person who did not want to encourage the growth of aviation. "It seems to be inevitable," another lawyer noticed, "that almost every writer who deals with aviation from any and every angle, legal, commercial or mechanical, always thinks and writes of the good of the trade, the growth of an infant industry and the effective evolution of the discovery." On the other hand, it was no easier to find a person who thought that landowners should be unduly bothered by low-flying aircraft. "The industry must realize," one law professor lectured, "that the right of the landowner in the airspace above his land is a property right which cannot be blown down by huffing and puffing." The pace of technological change was increasing so quickly, meanwhile, that no one could predict what adjustments in property rights might be desirable a decade or two in the future. "It is for this very reason," warned a New York lawyer, "that fundamental property rights should not be too readily cast aside. That which may be denied to subjacent owners today may be an urgent necessity to them and the world in general tomorrow."[41]

The disagreement was not over the value of protecting aviation or of protecting landowners, both of which commanded virtually unanimous support, but rather over how to balance the two. Some suggested that the precise verbal formulation did not matter much, because the outcomes of cases would be identical under any of them,[42] but this was surely an overly optimistic view. The Hinmans had been forced to submit to flights less than one hundred feet above their Burbank home, flights that would have been deemed trespasses under Massachusetts law. The aviation industry had been lobbying for its view of the law with a vigor that would have been nonsensical unless industry lawyers believed their clients stood to gain. Different verbal statements of the law had real consequences for airports and the adjoining landowners.

Forty years after the dawn of flight, the law of aerial trespass was still partially uncertain. Planes could fly at high altitudes, but whether they were trespassing at low altitudes was still up in the air.

SEVEN

The Rise and Fall of Air Law

Before the 1920s, the participants in the aerial trespass debate were dabblers. Some were lawyers and some were not, but even the lawyers were not specialists in aviation law, because there was no such thing. That changed quickly. From the 1920s on, the debate was dominated by aviation lawyers. By the 1930s, many even began to speak of "air law" as a distinct field of law, with its own legal doctrines. They taught air law courses, wrote air law treatises, and established air law institutes. A subject that did not exist ten years earlier had become its own discipline.

Ten years after that, however, the field had nearly disappeared. The rise and fall of air law raises some questions that are not often addressed about the organization of legal knowledge. Why do some changes in the world, but not others, cause us to reorganize our categories of thinking? Why would lawyers start to think of air law as a category separate from others? And why would they stop? What exactly do we mean when we say that air law, or any other type of law, is or is not a distinct field?

Lawyers had long been predicting that aviation would one day be a legal specialty. Less than a year after the Wright brothers' first flight, the Pennsylvania lawyer Archibald McClean foresaw a world in which aircraft would be commonplace. "In those flying days," he mused, "it is even conceivable that there shall be lawyers, who, having made a specialty of the laws of moving things that be above the firmament, as well as that through which they move, will have well established reputations as legal sky pilots." By 1910 the *New York Times* already knew that "airship law is surely destined to take its place with railroad law, telephone law, and all the other novelties of the last century at which Coke and Blackstone would have rubbed their eyes in astonishment."[1] Railroads had their lawyers—some as corporate employees, others as proprietors of their own law firms—who spent their days tending to the myriad legal matters that arose in the ordinary course of the railroad business. If the airplane became as popular as the train, aviation companies would need their lawyers, too.

After World War I, as aviation changed from a hobby into a significant commercial enterprise, there emerged a cohort of lawyers specializing in aviation.[2] Some had learned about airplanes as pilots in the war. William MacCracken, counsel to National Air Transport in the early 1920s and later assistant secretary of commerce, had been a flight instructor in the Army Air Service. Fred Fagg, the founder of Northwestern's Air Law Institute, had flown night patrols over the English Channel. Others had no flight experience but acquired aviation clients by happenstance and gradually built an air practice. Chester Cuthell, who served for many years as chair of the ABA's committee on aeronautics law, was the lawyer for the early aviator and inventor Glenn Curtiss, and thus had a hand in the formation and representation of all the enterprises in which Curtiss was involved, even after Curtiss's death. Once an industry gets to be a certain size, there will be lawyers who specialize in catering to the legal needs of that industry, and aviation was no exception. Contracts had to be drafted, regulations had to be complied with, lawsuits had to be litigated, and in all these activities it was useful to have a lawyer familiar with the world of commercial aviation.

A specialized professional literature helped create a group of people who identified themselves as aviation lawyers. Journal articles on aviation law began to appear before the Wright brothers first flew. The first English-language book on the topic was *Air Sovereignty* (1910), by the Dutch scholar Johanna Lycklama à Nijeholt. That was followed closely by English law professor Harold Hazeltine's *The Law of the Air* (1911), a book that received lavish praise in American legal periodicals. In the United States, Henry Woodhouse's *Textbook of Aerial Laws* appeared in 1920. By the late 1920s, after the Air Commerce Act, Americans had their choice of many more books, most of which were treatises focusing on U.S. domestic law and targeted at lawyers rather than general readers. "New legal problems present themselves," explained federal judge Benjamin Bledsoe in his introduction to W. Jefferson Davis's *Aeronautical Law*. "Into and through this field, soon to become very important in the onward march of our civilization, the lawyer must accompany the business man." As time went on, the lawyers who read books like these came to think of themselves as aviation lawyers. "I have no doubt," Chester Cuthell predicted, that "there will be an Aviation Bar just as there is an Admiralty Bar." He was right.[3]

This sort of professional self-identification has persisted right up to today. The industry is of course much bigger than it was in the 1920s, so there are many more people today who identify themselves as aviation lawyers, and many firms with distinct aviation practices. To draft an aircraft lease, one has to know something about the law governing leases, but much more about the world of aircraft, so a lawyer expert in, say, real estate leases would be little help in negotiating an aircraft lease. There are aviation lawyers and there are real estate lawyers, but there are no lease lawyers: in this instance it is industry, rather than legal form, that divides up practice areas.

Much of the legal profession is similarly divided up accord-ing to the nature of the client rather than the nature of the law. Banks, movie stars, and telephone companies all need lawyers to take care of their contracts, but there are no contract lawyers; rather, there are lawyers who represent banks, lawyers who repre-sent movie stars, and lawyers who represent telephone companies. On the other hand, much of the profession is organized by legal function rather than by client. There are lawyers who try cases for every kind of litigant, lawyers who obtain patents for clients in any sort of industry, and lawyers who navigate the environmental permitting process for anyone who needs a navigator. There are lawyers who specialize in writing wills, in getting divorces, and in calculating taxes. Some of the bar specializes in a particular type of client, while some of the bar specializes in a particular type of law, and it is hard to say which is more common.

In describing what they do, lawyers often call their practice a kind of law, whether they specialize in representing a particular sort of client or in performing a particular legal function. A law-yer who represents movie stars will say he practices "entertain-ment law," while a lawyer who calculates taxes will say she prac-tices "tax law," but they are really saying two different things. The field of entertainment law is defined by the needs of clients in the entertainment industry. The field of tax law is defined by the tax code and the court cases interpreting it. There is no entertain-ment code or body of entertainment cases; entertainment law is whatever law happens to come up in the course of the enter-tainment business. Contract law, labor law, intellectual property law—so long as it is applies to the client as an entertainer, it is part of entertainment law. While entertainment lawyers represent clients in the entertainment industry, tax lawyers do not represent clients in the tax industry—there is no such industry. Tax lawyers represent clients in any industry, who happen to have tax problems. "Tax law" describes a category of *law* that cuts across several client industries, while "entertainment law" describes a field of *practice* that cuts across several categories of law.

There are also some cases in the middle, involving specialized statutes or other bodies of law that apply only to a single industry. There are complicated statutes that apply only to banks, for example, so to say that one practices "banking law" means both that one represents banks and that one is expert in the statutes governing them. Much the same could be said of "oil and gas law" or "insurance law"—they are defined simultaneously by the nature of the client and the substance of the law.

By the 1920s there was clearly a field of "aviation law" in the practice sense. There were aviation lawyers, who represented clients in the aviation field. Around 1930 many of these lawyers began to claim something more. They began to argue for the existence of "aviation law" or "air law" as a category of law as well as a field of practice. They did not just handle matters of contract law, or tort law, or property law that happened to arise in the aviation business. Rather, the issues they dealt with constituted an entirely new legal category. This was not a claim to one of the intermediate cases, like banking law today, because there were not yet enough statutes or doctrines unique to aviation. It was a claim to one of the pure cases, like tax law. "The new field of law of the air," exclaimed one of its early proponents, was marked by "the absence of ancient and inflexible methods and rules and impenetrable precedents." Musty old doctrines might appeal to lawyers in older fields, "lawyers who harked back to 1850," but when it came to air law, those old fogies "were left behind so fast they never really knew what had gone past them." Another lawyer declared that "the function of law schools in the past has been largely to teach the law established by precedents," but the proper teaching of air law required "enlightening students with regard to the law of the future." Aviation lawyers began to speak of "the young science of air-law," or "the beginnings of a law for the air."[4] They believed they were witnessing the birth of air law—not just a specialized kind of practice, but a new field of law.

The law school curriculum is mostly organized around fields of law rather than types of client. This was even more true in the 1930s than it is today. The Association of American Law Schools publishes a directory of law professors every year. In 1931, the first year in which the directory listed professors by courses taught as well as by surname, virtually all the courses were fields of law. From agency and bankruptcy through water rights and wills, students learned areas of legal doctrine rather than the needs of particular industries. There were occasional courses that did not cover fields of doctrine, but these were mostly interdisciplinary classes like jurisprudence and legal history. The only courses organized by industry were insurance, mining, and oil and gas, which were already businesses regulated by statutes of their own, and only a handful of schools offered courses in mining, or oil and gas.

If air law was a field of its own, like bankruptcy or wills, it deserved to be taught in law school. In 1929 Northwestern became the first law school in the country to take this step, by establishing an Air Law Institute. "In the course of legal history," explained John Henry Wigmore, the law school's long-serving dean, "new economic and social activities have from time to time found the Law not prepared." He provided a series of examples. The "copious literary activity" of the early eighteenth century had given rise to the law of copyright. The growth in the number of businesses bearing trade names had produced the law of trademarks. The geography of the American West had required a new law of water rights. And in the aerial age, Wigmore declared, "we are confronted with a new, and this time a vaster, field for the definition of legal rights—Rights in the Air." The time had come for an Air Law Institute, "to furnish a clearing-house for experiences" of scholars and students alike.[5] The Institute would be modeled on the University of Königsberg's Institut für Luftrecht (Institute for Air Law), established four years earlier.

To run the Institute, Northwestern hired one of its own former students, Fred Dow Fagg. After serving as a pilot in World War I, Fagg had taught economics at Northwestern and then enrolled in Northwestern's law school from which he graduated in 1927. He joined the faculty at the University of Southern California but was in Los Angeles for only one year. He spent the 1928–29 school year in Königsberg, at the Institut für Luftrecht, and then returned to Chicago to become managing director of Northwestern's new institute. Fagg founded and edited a new scholarly periodical, the *Journal of Air Law,* an American version of already-existing air law journals in France, Italy, and Germany. The *Journal of Air Law* published its first issue in 1930. The Air Law Institute sponsored lectures, maintained a reference library, provided fellowships, taught summer classes, and hosted conferences. Befitting an organization intended to bridge the worlds of theory and practice, the Institute's board of directors included, along with Northwestern professors and some local lawyers, the presidents of the Chicago Tribune Company, the General American Tank Car Company, and the Peoples Trust and Savings Bank.

Fagg also occasionally taught a course in air law. It began with a survey of the history of the subject, dating back to the work of the prewar European theorists of air sovereignty. The course then

covered the international conventions pertaining to air navigation, the Air Commerce Act of 1926 and the regulations promulgated by the Commerce Department, the state regulation of aeronautics, the vexed question of aerial trespass, and issues of liability
and insurance for accidents, before concluding with a variety of
minor topics such as the taxation of aircraft fuel and the regulation of airmail.[6]

Soon after, other law schools followed suit. In 1929 New York
University established a research program in air law, funded in
part by the Aeronautical Chamber of Commerce. "The need for
such research in a school of law is obvious," noted Frank Sommer,
the dean of the law school. "A few years ago no aviation law existed. With the development of the industry, however, court decisions and legislative activity have contributed to indicate a solution of many problems." A year later NYU began publishing a
journal of its own, the *Air Law Review,* edited by NYU law professor Alison Reppy. In the spring of 1930 the school sponsored a
series of lectures by prominent aviation lawyers, including Chester Cuthell, William MacCracken, and Mabel Walker Willebrandt.[7]

NYU's interest in air law was sparked by a major gift from the
Guggenheim family. Harry F. Guggenheim had been a naval aviator during World War I. After the war, he and his father, Daniel
Guggenheim, wishing to use some of their wealth to aid the strug-
gling aviation industry, established the Daniel Guggenheim Fund
for the Promotion of Aeronautics. Although the fund was in existence only from 1926 to 1929, it established schools or research
centers at universities all over the country, including aeronautical
engineering schools at the Massachusetts Institute of Technology
and the California Institute of Technology. One of the lucky institutions was New York University, which opened the Guggenheim
School of Aeronautics.

At the NYU law school, the air law program continued to expand as the university sought ways to use its Guggenheim money. In 1931 the school formed the American Academy of Air Law, to serve as an umbrella organization along the lines of Northwestern's Air Law Institute. Like Northwestern's institute, the Academy amassed a reference library, funded research fellowships, and sponsored lectures and conferences. Like Northwestern, NYU offered occasional courses in air law. George Sprague, who had been at the law school since 1911, taught the subject in 1933, but then went back to his usual subject, the law of admiralty. The following year the law school hired a local attorney named Arnold Knauth to teach air law, but he too stopped after one year, and the school never seems to have resumed teaching it.

Many other schools, meanwhile, began offering air law courses. In 1931 there were only three professors of air law in the United States: Fred Fagg at Northwestern, James Hayden at Catholic University in Washington, D.C., and Robert Kingsley at the University of Southern California. The next year there were fourteen, more than taught patents and nearly as many as taught water rights. Air law was part of the curriculum at De Paul and Loyola in Chicago; at Ohio State, Marquette, and Denver; and at Mercer, Kentucky, Florida, and Vanderbilt. Catholic and Denver each had two faculty members teaching the subject. These were individual courses, not elaborate programs like at Northwestern or NYU, but they represented the schools' recognition that air law was a field worth studying in its own right. USC even lured Otto Schreiber and Rudolf Hirschberg from the University of Königsberg to deliver a series of lectures, which the law school's dean proudly declared to be "the first course in air law to be given by any class 'A' law school in the United States."[8] Air law seemed poised to take its place in the law school canon. Lawyers' mental organization of the law was mostly learned in school, so as of

1932 one might reasonably have expected that one day air law would be like bankruptcy or wills—one of the ordinary subdivisions of the law.

Instrumental and intellectual motives alike lay behind the promotion of air law as a distinct field. Aviation lawyers, whether in practice or in law schools, no doubt hoped to be acknowledged as experts in a domain of their own rather than viewed as dabblers across many fields already dominated by others. To be an esteemed authority on air law was better than to know a small fraction of the law of torts, the law of contracts, and the like. In any human endeavor, legal or otherwise, there are advantages to defining a field around the expertise one already possesses. None of the professors of air law in the 1930s had much prestige in the legal academy, and few of the aviation lawyers were leaders of the bar. They were small fish trying to look bigger by shrinking the pond.

But there was much more to the concept of air law than the vanity of aviation lawyers. Traditional legal categories like torts or contracts were not found in nature; they were nothing more than ways of organizing legal knowledge that lawyers had found useful in the nineteenth century, when the categories had come into being. Life had obviously changed quite a bit by the 1930s. There was no reason to assume that the old categories were still the best, particularly in the fields that had been most affected by technological change. This was one of the main principles of the loose agglomeration of thought known as legal realism—the idea that the old abstract categories had lost their value, and that a fresh look at the actual operation of the law would reveal the need for new ones that more closely tracked the experience of lawyers and clients. Columbia law professor Herman Oliphant, president of the Association of American Law Schools, urged "a radical reclassification of most of the law in terms of the human relations affected by it," a reorganization necessary because of the way real life was "hopelessly mixed and confused in such broad and outworn categories as property, trusts, torts, and contracts." Many of the realists shared the belief, as Karl Llewellyn explained, "in the worthwhileness of grouping cases and legal situations into narrower categories than has been the practice in the past." Different sorts of contracts, for example, might in practice be treated differently by judges, despite a single set of doctrines ostensibly governing all contracts, so a realistic assessment of the law might require reclassifying the law of contracts in a different way.[9] The notion of chopping the law into different, and smaller, categories was very much in the air in the 1930s, particularly in elite academic circles.

Air law was a realist-sounding legal category. Instead of being an abstract concept like torts or contracts, it was a functional category delineated by a feature of the real, physical world. A course in air law shared a worldview with Leon Green's 1931 torts casebook, which was divided into chapters with concrete titles like "Keeping of Animals" and "Traffic and Transportation" rather than the traditional abstract headings like "Negligence" and "Proximate Cause." It shared the perspective of Harold Havighurst's 1934 contracts casebook, which was organized by topics like "real estate brokers" and "physicians" rather than the traditional abstract concepts like "consideration" and "breach." None of the leading realists ever took up air law as a specialty (although two of them, Myres McDougal and Harold Lasswell, would later coauthor a 1,100-page treatise on space law).[10] But they would have been sympathetic observers.

The time was thus right for air law. It was a category with a growing constituency behind it, and it promised to be more useful than the older, broader categories in predicting how judges would rule. If all the hubbub over aerial trespass had demonstrated anything, it was that the stodgy old terrestrial law of property was not especially useful in deciding aviation cases. If the same were true about other legal fields, like torts and contracts, perhaps it would make sense to take aerial matters out of the old abstract categories and put them into the single narrow field of air law.

But not everyone thought air law a useful category. "In reality the subject is merely an application of familiar principles to a new set of facts," insisted one skeptical reviewer of Henry Woodhouse's early treatise on the topic. Aviation lawyers were so enamored of their supposed field that "your swivel-chair becomes a Pegasus in clouds of theory, Spad-mounted speed cops lurk behind their fleecy ambushes, and colored kite balloons direct your flight of imagination." So-called air law was nothing more than "hypothetical cases that involve familiar enough legal principles," he concluded. There was no need to create a new field of law.[11] The common law had accommodated technological change in the past, another lawyer pointed out, and it was in the midst of doing the same for aviation. "No greater tribute to the genius of the common law can be found," he declared, "than the manner in which the law of this recently developed science has fitted itself into the existing body of principles without any perceptible change or enlargement."[12]

When law schools began to add air law to the curriculum, that too drew some skeptics. "The students," admitted Sayre MacNeil of Harvard, "seem hungry for all that there is of it." But did student demand mean that air law deserved to be taught in law school as a separate course? Or "should 'air law' be treated like 'horse law' of yore or 'automobile law' of today, split up and assigned to different existing courses?" MacNeil taught some of the traditional subjects in which issues related to aviation might arise, like property and municipal corporations (a course about the powers of cities, some of which were beginning to operate airports). He estimated that the substance of a course in air law could be covered in less than two lectures of property (for rights in airspace), an hour in torts (for crashes), less than half a lecture in criminal law (for whatever criminal issues might occur in aeronautics), some time in municipal corporations (to discuss the ability of cities to acquire land, issue bonds, and so on), and maybe some fractions of an hour in agency, insurance, public util ities, administrative law, and equity. By studying all the aviation issues in a single course, students would miss the extent to which court decisions depended on legal doctrines applicable to all sorts of other fields besides aviation. "The thesis is at least arguable," he declared, "that for some years to come the best groundwork for students is to partition 'air law' in divers old fashioned compartments of legal doctrine."[13]

Even some of the aviation lawyers had their doubts as to the existence of the field. Philadelphia lawyer Hazleton Mirkil was a member of the Air Law Institute at Northwestern and the author of several articles on the subject. Yet he conceded that there really was no such thing as air law, at least not yet. "Certainly there exists today no such distinct branch of law, as peculiar to the subject of the air, to air navigation and to airmen, as is Admiralty Law to the sea, to the ships upon it, and to their crews and cargoes," Mirkil admitted. "It is impossible that there should be, because public opinion is slow in forming." Byron McCormick was a law professor at the University of Arizona who attended Otto Schreiber's lectures on air law at USC. Yet even McCormick agreed that "it would probably be extravagant to speak of Air Law as a separate branch of judicial science; it is hardly that as yet. Problems arising may be determined by the application of established rules of International Law, Constitutional Law, Criminal Law, Torts or some other recognized branch of the law." Like Mirkil, he held out the hope that air law might one day be its own field. "In another ten or twenty years," he speculated, "Air Law may be treated as a branch as distinct at least as Water Law and Mining Law of our Western states." But not yet.[14]

As time went on, the skeptics gained the upper hand. There were fourteen professors of air law in 1932, but there would never be that many again. The directory of law professors listed eleven in 1933, five in 1934, and only four in 1935. In 1936 there was not even a listing for air law; the four law professors listed for 1935 still taught it, but the Association of American Law Schools no longer considered the subject important enough to get its own entry. Air law would not return to the directory until 1942, when there were only three professors on the list. None of them had taught the subject in the 1930s.

The institutions that had been built in the 1930s to promote air law did not last long. As early as 1930 New York University was already proposing to Northwestern that the schools' institutes and journals of air law be merged into one, to save the expense of maintaining duplicate programs. Fred Fagg was amenable to the merger but the governing board of Northwestern's Air Law Institute was not. At the time Northwestern was the more highly regarded school, and the prevailing view there was that Northwestern had nothing to gain from an association with NYU. By the mid-1930s little was left of NYU's air law program but the *Air Law Review,* and even that ceased publication in 1941. Alison Reppy, the editor, claimed that a journal devoted to air law was no longer necessary because the law had become so stable, but journals specializing in equally stable areas of law kept on publishing, so the decline of institutional support seems the more likely culprit.[15]

Things were no better at Northwestern. Fred Fagg was away

in Washington in a series of government positions beginning in 1934, and then he left the Air Law Institute completely in 1937 to become the dean of Northwestern's School of Commerce. By 1939 he was vice president of the entire university, and in 1947 he left Northwestern to become president of USC. Meanwhile the Air Law Institute was chronically short of money. Its initial budget came mostly from a group of grants, including one from the Daniel Guggenheim Fund, but when these expired in 1932 the Institute's funding plummeted. Without Fagg and without much of a budget, the Air Law Institute crumbled. One day in 1938 Wigmore opened the door of the Institute's office and found unopened packages all over the floor. By then, Dean Leon Green admitted, the Institute was "only a paper organization," which did nothing but publish the *Journal of Air Law.* It no longer sponsored fellowships or offered courses, it had no staff, and its collection of books and journals had been transferred to the Northwestern law library.[16]

The *Journal of Air Law* lived on, but in a modified form; in 1939 it began to be funded half by the law school and half by the school of commerce, it changed its name to the *Journal of Air Law and Commerce,* and it began to publish articles about the aviation business in addition to articles about law. Northwestern tried to give the changes a positive spin, by claiming that law and economics were inseparably related and that a journal could not sensibly incorporate one without the other. It is likely, though, that the journal's new focus had more to do with Fagg's move from the law school to the school of commerce and with the decay of the Air Law Institute. Northwestern would eventually give up on the journal completely in 1960. After a one-year hiatus, Southern Methodist University began to publish it.[17]

If air law was scarcely taught in school—indeed, if air law might not even exist—there was no point in funding institutes and journals devoted to it. By 1946 even John Cobb Cooper was

Fred Dow Fagg examines a map of the major air routes in the United States. Fagg was the founding director of Northwestern's short-lived Air Law Institute, which began to fade away soon after he left in 1934. Photograph by Theodor Horydczak, LC-H814-2363-002, Prints and Photographs Division, Library of Congress.

having second thoughts. Cooper had been one of the early aviation lawyers. He chaired the ABA's committee on aeronautical law in the early 1930s and was vice president of Pan American Airways from 1934 to 1945. Leaving Pan Am for a position at the Institute of Advanced Study allowed Cooper some time to think about the nature of air law. "Over the past two decades," he recalled, "many ambitious young men have asked, 'What should I study to become an aviation lawyer?' Even ten years ago I tried valiantly to answer and felt I had done so fairly well. Now I am not so sure." Cooper had lost his faith in air law. "Whether such a subject for separate study as 'aviation law' exists seems now a very debatable question," he reflected. "Aviation is nothing more than another form of transportation—aircraft the mobile instruments employed, airports the passenger and freight stations or docks used. The legal principles applicable to aviation generally, and air transport, particularly, range through the old student categories of contracts, torts, personal property, real property, etc."[18] As aviation became a normal part of life, the legal issues thrown up by aviation were becoming normal legal issues, to be decided with reference to the normal categories. The airplane, Sayre MacNeil would have said, was becoming like the horse or the automobile.

Air law had come and gone. When John Cobb Cooper went to McGill University in 1951 to be the inaugural director of its Institute of International Air Law, there were no longer any comparable institutions in the United States. Many years would pass before there would be another.[19]

As a field of practice, aviation law never went away; indeed, it grew right along with the aviation industry. By 1947 the New York lawyer John Eubank, a self-professed "authority on aeronautical jurisprudence," could identify himself as the chair of the Committee on Aeronautical Law of the Federal Bar Association of New York, New Jersey, and Connecticut, and a member of the

Aeronautical Chamber of Commerce, the Institute of Aeronautical Sciences, the National Aeronautic Association, the Soaring Society of America, the Aircraft Industries Association of America, the Aero Club of New York, and the Committee on Aeronautical Law of the New York State Bar Association and the New York County Lawyers Association. There was no shortage of professional organizations for a busy lawyer to join, and there never would be. In 2007 the American Bar Association's Forum on Air and Space Law had more than 1,500 members, lawyers who represented airlines, airports, and government agencies.[20]

The law school curriculum meanwhile became much more diverse in the second half of the twentieth century, and the number of law professors and law students skyrocketed, which meant that the number of people teaching *any* course was likely to grow substantially. Air law (and later, aerospace law) gradually returned to legal education, not as a field of law in its own right but as a course introducing students to the issues they would confront as aviation lawyers, issues that properly belonged to a variety of legal fields. By 2002 the directory of law professors listed all sorts of similar courses, covering topics like agricultural law, entertainment law, and sports law—topics defined by the client's business rather than by the way lawyers classified the law. The number of air law or aerospace law professors never grew very large. It reached thirty-four in 1972, when the space program was in the public eye. That would have been a large number in the 1930s, when the world of legal education was much smaller, but in the 1970s it made air law a tiny niche in the curriculum, on the same scale as courses in "legal problems of education" or "law and science." By 2002, when outer space no longer loomed as large, the directory listed only eighteen professors of aviation and space law.

The law itself, meanwhile, had hardly stood still. New fields came into existence in the second half of the twentieth century, fields that succeeded where air law had failed. The 1962 directory did not include a listing for environmental law, but by 1972 there were more than one hundred professors of the subject, and by 1982 there were approximately three hundred. Lawyers thought of environmental law as a category of law, not just a type of practice.[21] The 1962 directory did not include a listing for civil rights. In 1972 the directory noted that professors of civil rights were included in the category of constitutional law. By 1982, civil rights was its own category, with over three hundred professors. Civil rights was not just a kind of law practice, it was also understood to be a distinct area of law.

Environmental law and civil rights clearly had something that air law lacked, but what was it? They both had a growing cadre of lawyers practicing in the field, but air law had that, too. They both had, at their foundation, a few complex federal statutes. When they began, much of environmental law was based on the National Environmental Policy Act of 1969, the Clean Air Act of 1970, and a series of similar laws enacted in the 1970s, while much of the law of civil rights was embodied in the big civil rights acts of the 1960s. But air law was just the same. It too was governed largely by a series of increasingly detailed federal statutes, from the Air Commerce Act of 1926 to the Civil Aeronautics Act of 1938 to the Federal Aviation Act of 1958. A specialized bar and some specialized statutes weren't enough to make air law a useful category of law.

A clue to the demise of air law may be found by looking at technological changes analogous to the invention of flight. The railroad and the automobile were at least as transformative of ordinary life. They likewise spawned specialized regulatory schemes and specialized bars, the railroad perhaps to a greater extent than the automotive industry. We could say the same about the telegraph, the telephone, the radio, and the television, all of which brought dramatic changes to everyday life, and all of which were eventually regulated by specialized statutes and counseled by lawyers whose practice was defined by the needs of the industry. Yet none of these technological changes gave rise to new areas of law, in the sense of categories of legal doctrine rather than types of practice. There were never many law school courses in automobile law or television law, never any institutes of railroad law or telegraph law. A lawyer for General Motors might confront issues of contract law and tort law, administrative law and labor law, but he would not think of them as constituting a field called automobile law. We might infer that technological change, in itself, does not cause lawyers to create new categories of law. New inventions are assimilated into the old categories. The new fact patterns thrown up by technological change might require some rethinking of particular legal doctrines, but they don't cause the reconfiguration of entire legal fields.

Environmental law and civil rights, by contrast, were not created by technological change. They were created by cultural changes—the growth of popular interest in protecting the environment and in requiring racial equality. These were changes in normative beliefs, not in physical things. These changes did not merely produce new sets of facts that had to be slotted into the old rules; rather, they produced a strong desire for new rules, which were then applied to the same old facts. The new rules did not fit into any of the old subdivisions of legal doctrine, so they required the elaboration of entirely new legal fields.

We have the makings here of a tidy theory—the proposition that cultural change, but not technological change, will give rise to new areas of law. We might hesitate, however, before making this assertion with any confidence, because of the possible existence of one very large counterexample: the Internet.

Like any major technological innovation, the Internet spawned a host of novel legal questions. Is it lawful to download copyrighted music? to send unwanted email? to conduct automated searches of another person's website? How should domain names be allocated? And whose law applies to issues like these? The jurisdiction in which the computer user sits? The jurisdiction that houses the server that hosts the web page? It was not long before there was a group of lawyers and law professors who specialized in such questions. Many of them began to insist that the legal issues surrounding the Internet were best understood not as divided among a variety of legal fields but as constituting a new field in its own right. They were practitioners and analysts, they declared, of something called cyberlaw.

Cyberlaw grew even more quickly than air law had. In 1992 there were 42 law professors who listed themselves as teachers of a course the directory called "computers and the law," a topic that in 1992 must have embraced much more than the Internet. By 2002 there were approximately 170, and in 2006 there were roughly 250, to which should be added many of the nearly 150 teaching communications law, a topic that often included regulation of the Internet. The Social Science Research Network, the major online forum for professors to circulate their papers, had a category devoted to cyberspace law. Several law schools, including Harvard and Stanford, established institutes devoted to the subject. In law school, at least, cyberlaw seemed pervasive. "The course names," declared some of the new field's academic enthusiasts, "bespeak the scope of change underway. Cyberlaw is emerging as a doctrinal area of its own, on par with contracts and torts." Cyberlaw was a useful category, one of its leading theorists explained, because "we see something when we think about the regulation of cyberspace that other areas would not show us."[22] The same claims had once been made about air law.

And as with air law, these claims had their critics. Cyberlaw's most prominent skeptic was the federal judge Frank Easterbrook, who drew the same analogy Sayre MacNeil had drawn about air law sixty-five years earlier. Cyberlaw, Easterbrook scoffed, was no more worthy of study than "the law of the horse." Horses were involved in all sorts of legal issues: there were contracts for the sale of horses, people were injured by horses, and special regulations governed the licensing of horses. Yet no one thought the law of the horse a useful category of law. (Well, hardly anyone. Easterbrook's critique produced at least one spirited defense of equine law as a useful category.) Instead, disputes regarding horse sales were referred to the law of contracts, cases of injury were resolved according to the law of torts, and so on. "Only by putting the law of the horse in the context of broader rules about commercial endeavors," Easterbrook concluded, "could one really understand the *law* about horses." The Internet, in his view, was just the same.[23]

Who is right? If the rise and fall of air law is any guide, Easterbrook's view will eventually come out the winner. Air law ceased to be a useful category when the airplane was no longer a novelty. One day the Internet will be thought of as just another method of communication, like the telephone or the mail, and when that day comes (if it has not come already), a legal category called cyberlaw may have as much usefulness as a field called postal law. The Internet, like the airplane, created new sets of facts, not new normative beliefs. In this sense, cyberlaw seems more like air law than like environmental law or civil rights.

Then again, if cyberlaw seems a useless category, an arbitrary collection of cases and doctrines that happen to arise in Internet-related disputes, it bears remembering that the old abstract categories may be no less arbitrary. Perhaps it does make sense to apply the same general rules to all contracts, regardless of what the contracts are for, and to lump those rules together under a heading called "contracts," but if so, it is not because of anything inherent in the nature of contracts. There is no law of nature that tells us to classify all different sorts of injuries under a heading called "torts." We do so simply because we find those methods of organization more convenient than any other. But what is a convenience in one era often becomes a hindrance in another. Lawyers from two centuries ago would not recognize our current scheme for organizing the law, and we would likely be baffled if we could see the way the law will be organized two centuries from now. For all we know, one day cyberlaw may be a fundamental category. If so, who could blame lawyers for looking back on the air law pioneers of the 1930s as visionaries unacknowledged in their own time?

EIGHT

William Douglas Has the Last Word

After nearly half a century of debate over whether airplanes were trespassers, the U.S. Supreme Court finally resolved the issue in a 1946 case called *United States v. Causby,* a case students still read in law school because of its importance in establishing the basic structure of rights in airspace. *Causby* was yet another dispute between an airport and its neighbors, but if the facts of the case sounded familiar to aviation lawyers, the law did not. The defendant happened to be the government of the United States, so *Causby* was decided as a matter of federal constitutional law rather than state property law. And while the decision was formally reached by the Supreme Court as a whole, in fact it was the work of a single idiosyncratic justice, William Douglas, who made a law that none of his colleagues wished to have made.

At first the Causbys didn't mind living next to an airport. The Greensboro–High Point Airfield, a few miles west of Greensboro, North Carolina, was one of the many airports built in the late 1920s, soon after the enactment of the Air Commerce Act of 1926. Greensboro was not a big city—it had a population around fifty thousand when the airport was built—so it never had much air traffic, just some mail planes, some private aircraft, and the occasional commercial flight. These were all small planes that didn't make much noise and didn't need a long runway. In 1934, when the Causbys bought the neighboring parcel of land, the airport was "just a little old landing field," as Thomas Causby put it, nothing more than a short airstrip, a wooden hangar, and a small administration building.[1]

"It was just a good place to live," Causby recalled several years later. The Causbys were chicken farmers, with nearly three acres on the eastern edge of the airport. "Yes sir," Causby declared, "I was making a comfortable living, had a good business." Between 1934 and 1937 the Causbys built a small five-room frame house with hot and cold running water and a few smaller houses for the chickens. They had approximately four hundred breeding hens, whose eggs Causby sold to commercial hatcheries. They also raised young chickens, which they sold as fryers. The farm produced enough income to support Thomas and his wife, Tinie, as well as their youngest son, who was born in 1935. When World War II began and their older son, Lewis, joined the army, the chicken farm also had to support Lewis's wife and their baby daughter, who moved in with Thomas and Tinie.

It was the war that ruined the Causbys' chicken business. When the United States entered the war, one of the many urgent tasks facing the military was a sudden need for airports. In November 1941 the Army Air Forces had 114 airfields in the continental United States, but by the end of 1942 the Army would have 614, and by the end of 1943 it would have 783.[2] Most of these, including the one in Greensboro, were not built from scratch but were converted from civilian use. In 1942 the U.S. government leased the Greensboro airfield, for a term renewable every year at the government's option for the ensuing twenty-five years or "six

months after the end of the present National Emergency, whichever shall occur first." The government extended the runway to
accommodate the heavy military planes that would be using the
airport, and built a control tower to handle the increased traffic.

Life on the farm would never be the same. Army and Navy
planes took off and landed constantly, at all hours of the day and
night. It was "one plane right after another," Tinie Causby testified, "and they would swoop so close to the house it seemed they
were taking the roof off." The end of the lengthened runway was
only about 2,200 feet from the Causbys' house. At the prescribed
30-to-1 glide angle necessary for the heavy planes (that is, one
foot of elevation or descent for every thirty feet of horizontal distance), planes often came within 67 feet of the Causbys' roof, 63
feet of the roof of one of the chicken houses, and 18 feet of the
top of their highest tree. "The noise waked me up three to five
times every night," Thomas Causby complained, "and when they
swooped down in there right over us it was bad. Lighted up the
whole earth." At night, each plane would "light the whole house,"
Tinie added. Their granddaughter "can't hardly sleep day time or
night time, it disturbs the baby so," she explained. "I have walked
the floor for as much as 30 minutes to an hour at night when they
would come one right after another. I would be so nervous I
couldn't stay in bed."

The noise and the lights at night were hard enough to deal
with, but what bothered the Causbys even more was their worry
that one of the planes would crash into their house. They had
seen military planes plunge to the ground on a few different occasions, some of them fatal to local residents. "I don't know how to
explain it," Thomas said of his apprehension. "I have stood there
and watched and scringed for fear they were going into the house."
After watching the earlier accidents he was "completely a nervous
wreck, that is all the way I can put it." His wife felt the same way.

"It made me kinder nervous," she said after one military plane crashed into the short space between her house and the runway. "I began to shake, thinking that if it had been a little bit further it would have been right in the house." After a different accident on a neighboring parcel killed a mother and three children, Tinie began taking sleeping pills.

The chickens were in even worse shape. "They would jump off the roost, get excited and jump against the side of the chicken house and the walls and burst themselves open and die," Thomas testified. "I have taken out as high as six or 10 in one day." When somewhere near 150 chickens had been killed, the Causbys had to give up chicken farming. They sold their remaining chickens at a loss.

In late 1943, after selling their chickens, the Causbys took their problem to William Comer, a local lawyer. Comer must have realized that their story presented a classic case of both trespass and nuisance. Planes flying so low—only sixty-seven feet above the Causbys' roof—were clearly trespassing under one view of the law expressed in some of the key cases of the 1930s. Noise and bright lights at night were paradigmatic nuisances. The problem, however, was that the airport and the planes were controlled by the government of the United States. Under the ancient legal doctrine of sovereign immunity, the government could be sued only where Congress, by statute, had waived that immunity and allowed the government to be sued. Comer knew, perhaps after a little research, that Congress had never enacted a statute waiving the government's immunity for committing a trespass or a nuisance. Nearly all the airport litigation of the 1930s had involved private parties as defendants; none had involved the federal government. For the Causbys to sue the government, Comer would have to find a different legal theory.

With a little more research, he found one. The Takings Clause of the Fifth Amendment to the Constitution bars the government from taking "private property . . . for public use without just compensation." By repeatedly flying at such low altitudes over the Causbys' land, Comer must have reasoned, the government was taking their property and putting it to public use. The claim of a constitutional violation was functionally almost the same as a claim for trespass. Either way, Comer would have to prove that the government was infringing on the Causbys' property, either on the ground or in their airspace. But the value of casting the claim as a constitutional violation was that Congress *had* waived the government's sovereign immunity for lawsuits based on the Constitution. In the Tucker Act of 1887, Congress had authorized the Court of Claims, a specialized court in Washington, D.C., to hear a variety of claims against the government, including those "founded upon the Constitution of the United States." That was the only way the Causbys could sue the government.

When Comer filed the Causbys' lawsuit in early 1944, therefore, he filed it in the Court of Claims rather than in a local court, and he alleged neither a trespass nor a nuisance, as in the earlier airport cases, but rather a violation of the Takings Clause. "While the War Department has not actually condemned the property of the claimants," Comer's petition asserted, "the use made of their property is tantamount to a taking of the same in that it has become uninhabitable." The petition alleged that the value of the Causbys' land and buildings had been reduced from $6,035 to zero, and that the loss of the chicken farming business had cost them another $1,000. Comer accordingly requested $7,035 in damages. Because most of the witnesses were in or near Greensboro, the Court of Claims ordered that testimony be taken before a commissioner in Greensboro, who then forwarded a transcript of the proceedings to court. The suit would probably have stalled without the local commissioner, because the Causbys would likely have been unable to afford a trip to Washington to testify.

The Takings Clause is a restriction on the government's inherent power of eminent domain, the power to take property from its owner and put it to public use. While early American practice seems to have been inconsistent—colonial governments usually compensated the owner when taking property, but not always— the Fifth Amendment made compensation a requirement when the federal government exercised its power of eminent domain, and by the middle of the nineteenth century most state constitutions required state governments to compensate property owners as well. Long before the invention of the airplane it was clear that compensation was required for the functional equivalent of government takings, even where the government never formally acquired title to the property. In the famous case of *Pumpelly v. Green Bay Company*, for example, the Supreme Court required compensation where a government-built dam had flooded the plaintiff's land. Although the government had never actually taken the land, Justice Samuel Miller explained, "it would be a very curious and unsatisfactory result" to allow the government to escape liability for utterly destroying property, simply "because, in the narrowest sense of that word, it is not *taken*." By the time the Causbys lost their chicken farm, landowners' suits against the federal government seeking compensation for intentional flooding were a routine part of the docket of the Court of Claims.[3]

The government had to compensate a landowner for flooding his land with water, but what if the government flooded the air with planes? The closest precedent was the Supreme Court's 1922 *Portsmouth Harbor* case, which arose from the protracted litigation in the early part of the century between the United

States government and the owners of the Pocahontas Hotel, a fashionable turn-of-the-century summer resort on Gerrish Island, the southernmost point in Maine. The resort, virtually a self-sufficient community, included the hotel building, several cottages, a water tower and a water supply system, a windmill, an icehouse, a stable and carriage house, bath houses, and a steamboat pier. In the days before air conditioning, affluent urbanites often spent much of the summer at such resorts, and the Pocahontas was easy for them to reach; there were bridges connecting Gerrish Island with the New Hampshire coast near Portsmouth, close to the train station and the trolley line. The Pocahontas had a sandy beach, a golf course, sailboats, and horses. Every room had an unobstructed view of the ocean. Nearly two hundred acres of land had been developed in a spot perfect for a resort but suitable for little else.

The Pocahontas Hotel was not, however, the only thing on Gerrish Island. It shared the island with Fort Foster, a military base that defended the entrance to Portsmouth harbor. The government had bought the land for the fort in the 1870s, before the Pocahontas Hotel opened, but for lack of money the fort was not completed until 1901, by which time the hotel was a successful business. The fort included a battery of guns, placed to fire missiles toward incoming ships out at sea. But because the resort had the better location, the missiles could not reach the ocean without crossing through the airspace above the resort. The first time the army tested the guns, in the summer of 1902, vacationers were no doubt ill at ease, and when the second test at the end of the summer damaged one of the resort buildings, bookings for the following summer plummeted. The guns would not be fired for the next several years, but the resort never recovered. The Pocahontas lost money in the 1903 summer season and closed for good in 1904.[4]

The owners of the resort sued the government in the Court of Claims under the Tucker Act, seeking compensation for a taking of their property. The case reached the Supreme Court three times. The resort lost the first two cases, in 1913 and 1919, because by then the guns had not been fired in many years and there appeared to be no prospect they would be fired again. When World War I was over, however, the army replaced the old guns, which had been sent to France, with new ones, and it began testing the new ones by once again firing them across the defunct resort's land. Grasping at his last chance for compensation, the owner of the land filed suit yet again. The Court of Claims dismissed the suit on a demurrer—that is, it held that even if the facts alleged by the landowner were true, the suit would still lack merit. This time the Supreme Court reversed. If the guns were fired frequently and continuously enough, Justice Oliver Wendell Holmes reasoned, the government might be deemed to have taken property from the landowner. Justice Louis Brandeis dissented, but he did not quarrel with the proposition that the firing of shots over land, in peacetime, could justify a court in finding a taking. He argued instead that when the guns were tested the United States was still formally at war, that renewal of the conflict was still a possibility, and that the government should have the right during wartime to send weapons across private land without compensating the owner.[5]

The opinions were no more detailed than that, so there remained some ambiguity as to whether the property the government might be taking was in the air or on the ground. On one hand, the briefs in the case focused entirely on property rights in the land. "The United States has ruined a tract of land on the coast of Maine," the hotel's brief insisted. Firing guns across the land, the brief argued, was tantamount to "depriving claimants of the use and profit thereof."[6] The briefs never once considered the possibility that the government might be taking property in airspace. With the litigation framed as presenting a question that pertained only to land, it is likely that the members of the Court thought of the case that way as well. On the other hand, the case was litigated in the early 1920s while aviation regulation was a prominent issue, in Congress, in state legislatures, and in lawyers' organizations such as the American Bar Association and the National Conference of Commissioners on Uniform State Law. Members of the bar who were not themselves involved in the case read the opinion but not the briefs, so they might reasonably have suspected that the justices had an eye toward property rights in the air. If the opinion was read in that frame of mind, Holmes's implication seemed to be that the airspace, or at least the airspace near the ground, was property and that it belonged to the owner of the land.

Despite Justice Holmes's stature within the legal profession, his opinion in *Portsmouth Harbor* did not play a large role in the debates over aerial trespass throughout the 1920s and 1930s. It was scarcely cited in any of the airport cases of the 1930s. This was in part because of its brevity and its failure to say explicitly that the invasion of another's airspace constitutes trespass. The opinion's lack of influence was no doubt also due to the fact that it formally addressed a question of constitutional law rather than trespass. Substantively the issues were almost identical, but as a doctrinal matter lawyers placed them in different categories. *Portsmouth Harbor* was a takings case, not a trespass case.

Had Thomas and Tinie Causby sued an ordinary airport for trespass in state court, their lawyer would likewise have had little use for *Portsmouth Harbor*. But because their opponent was the federal government, and because they were claiming that the government had taken their property without just compensation,

Justice Holmes's opinion in *Portsmouth Harbor* became William Comer's most important weapon.

The hearing before the Court of Claims commissioner in Greensboro did not take very long, because there was no real dispute about the facts. The government conceded that military planes were flying at low altitudes across the Causbys' land day and night. The only disagreement between the Causbys and the government was over the legal significance of those facts—whether they amounted to a taking of the Causbys' property. Comer scored some rhetorical points by having Tinie Causby testify that back when the military was lengthening the runway, government engineers came to the house and declared that they would have to condemn the Causbys' farm. They "came with blueprints and showed me right in the back yard," she recalled. One of the engineers "said, 'According to my blueprint every building you have got is directly in the runway and will have to be moved,' and he was not the only one." In the end, of course, the government decided to leave the buildings in place and simply fly over them. Strictly speaking, these aborted plans were not relevant to the legal question whether overflights were a taking. The engineers might have misunderstood the law, or they might have been planning to have the government assume an obligation it had no constitutional duty to assume. Mary Fagan, the Justice Department lawyer sent down to Greensboro to represent the government, objected to Tinie Causby's testimony for this reason, but the commissioner overruled the objection and allowed the testimony in. While not relevant in a strict sense, it gave a bad odor to the way the Causbys had been treated by the government.

The hearing took place in the spring of 1944; the transcript must have arrived at the Court of Claims soon after that. The court normally decided cases in panels of five judges, but one of the judges, former Texas congressman John Marvin Jones, was on leave to run the War Food Administration, so only four judges were available for the Causbys' case. From their backgrounds, one might have expected them to have some sympathy for the military. All four had spent much of their careers in the federal government. Samuel Whitaker had worked in the Justice Department all through the 1930s. Joseph Madden had chaired the National Labor Relations Board under Roosevelt. Benjamin Littleton had been a lawyer for the Internal Revenue Service and a member of the Board of Tax Appeals, while Richard Whaley was a former congressman from South Carolina. Whitaker was the only one with military experience in World War I—Whaley was too old, while Madden and Littleton simply had not served—but Madden would soon take a leave of absence from the court, at the end of World War II, to be legal advisor to the U.S. military government in Germany. This was a group of men who might have been expected to defer to the needs of the military during wartime.

But the Causbys won.[7] The Court of Claims opinion relied heavily on *Portsmouth Harbor* and on the airport cases of the 1930s to hold that the government had taken the Causbys' lower airspace. "Since the days of airplanes," Whitaker's opinion conceded, the old *cujus est solum* doctrine "has received substantial modification." No one believed any longer that a landowner owned up to the heavens. "But even so," he continued, "there can be no doubt that today a landowner owns the air space above his land as completely as he does the land itself or the minerals beneath it, at least insofar as it is necessary for his full and complete enjoyment of the land itself." The Court of Claims was siding with the *Restatement of Torts* and with the state courts that had found low overflights to be trespasses. It was disagreeing, Whitaker acknowledged, with the U.S. Court of Appeals for the Ninth Circuit, which in *Hinman v. Pacific Air Transport* had held that airspace was incapable of being owned. "Under the facts of this case," he declared, "there can be no doubt that defendant has committed numerous trespasses upon the plaintiffs' property. It has traversed many times the air space above their property at such an altitude and with planes of such a character as to seriously interfere with plaintiffs' use and enjoyment of their property, even to such an extent as to make it necessary for them to abandon it as a chicken farm."

In an ordinary trespass case, that would have been enough. But because the Causbys were alleging not just a trespass but a taking, the court had to take another step. "A trespass upon the property of another," Whitaker explained, "does not ordinarily constitute a taking, but if it is sufficiently frequent or if there is otherwise shown an intention to continue it at will, such continued trespasses or intention may amount to a taking, if they destroy the owner's use and enjoyment of his property." Whitaker's authority for this proposition was Justice Holmes's opinion in *Portsmouth Harbor.* Just as Holmes had envisioned in *Portsmouth Harbor,* Whitaker reasoned, "a servitude has been imposed on the property which constitutes an appropriation of it." The court did not award the Causbys all the money they had requested, because it found that their parcel was not rendered valueless. It awarded them two thousand dollars, the amount by which it found that the overflights had reduced the property's value.

Judge Madden dissented, for a reason that would have been familiar to the participants in the aerial trespass debate of the previous four decades. "When railroads were new," he recalled, "cattle in fields in sight and hearing of the trains were alarmed, thinking that the great moving objects would turn aside and harm them. Horses ran away at the sight and sound of a train or a threshing machine engine. The farmer's chickens have to get over being alarmed at the incredible racket of the tractor starting up suddenly in the shed adjoining the chicken house." Times changed, new technology brought new expectations, and the courts should not stifle progress by stubbornly adhering to legal doctrines devised in a different era. "These sights and noises are a part of our world," Madden argued, "and airplanes are now and will be to a greater degree, likewise a part of it. These disturbances should not be treated as torts, in the case of the airplane, any more than they are so treated in the case of the railroad or public highway." If chickens or humans were frightened by planes overhead, it was the chickens and humans, not the planes, that needed to adapt.

But Madden was outvoted three to one. William Comer and the Causbys, a small-town lawyer and two chicken farmers, had won the first round against the government of the United States.

From the government's perspective, the damage award of two thousand dollars was not a serious matter. The government had likely spent much more than that on the litigation already. The real problem was the opinion of the Court of Claims, which invited lawsuits from the neighbors of the hundreds of military air bases scattered throughout the United States. "The issues raised by the instant case are of great general importance," Solicitor General J. Howard McGrath informed the Supreme Court in the government's petition for a writ of certiorari, the document asking the Court to hear the case. "The War Department alone administers some 847 airports which are either owned in fee or operated under leases." The government had purchased many of the surrounding properties and had acquired easements over many of the others, McGrath explained, but "if the judgment of the court below is correct, rights of flight would have to be obtained" over hundreds and perhaps thousands of additional parcels. And that was just for airfields currently in use. The Court of Claims decision would also make it harder for the military to construct airports in the future. When the Causbys had filed their suit, it looked like just another of the countless small cases in which the government was involved, but once the Causbys won, the case became very important to the government.[8]

The Supreme Court had no obligation to hear the case. It could decide for itself whether the case was sufficiently important. In making that decision, one key factor was whether the opinion of the court below created or contributed to a conflict among the lower courts, so the solicitor general emphasized the inconsistency of the lower court's decision with *Hinman v. Pacific Air Transport.* In *Hinman,* McGrath pointed out, the Court of Appeals for the Ninth Circuit "held that flying through air space within 100 feet or even 5 feet of the surface was not a technical trespass upon the property of the landowner." By the mid-1940s *Hinman* was the outlier; the other courts that had addressed the trespass question had all held, like the Court of Claims, that extremely low overflights could constitute trespasses (although they disagreed on exactly how low). But there was indeed a conflict among the lower courts, one that could not be resolved without the Supreme Court's intervention.

The solicitor general's petition and William Comer's short and ineffectual response arrived at the Supreme Court in early 1946. When the justices met to discuss whether to hear the case, Justice William Douglas agreed that there was "a clear conflict" between *Hinman* and the decision of the Court of Claims. He urged his colleagues to hear the case. Justice Wiley Rutledge was less certain of the conflict—he thought that in the opinion of the Court of Claims "the legal theory is perhaps a little different" than in *Hin-*

man—but he nevertheless wanted to hear the case, too. "I think the question is an important one or is likely to be," Rutledge explained. He was "not sure this Court is particularly well adapted to working out a solution to these air problems," but he overcame his doubts.[9] The Court agreed to hear the case and set oral argument for May.

United States v. Causby landed in a depleted Supreme Court. Chief Justice Harlan Fiske Stone died suddenly of a stroke in late April, shortly before oral argument in *Causby.* The Senate would not confirm his replacement, Fred Vinson, until after *Causby* had been decided. Justice Robert Jackson was away in Nuremberg, serving as lead American prosecutor in the trials of Nazi war criminals, for the Court's entire 1945–46 term. His absence was a lucky break for the Causbys, because Jackson was the only member of the Court who had already expressed a view on the issue the Court would be deciding, and he was quite skeptical about the notion that a landowner owned any part of the airspace. "Aviation has added a new dimension to travel and to our ideas," Jackson had written in a concurring opinion in 1944. "The ancient idea that landlordism and sovereignty extend from the center of the earth to the periphery of the universe has been modified. Today the landowner no more possesses a vertical control of all the air above him than a shore owner possesses horizontal control of all the sea before him. The air is too precious as an open highway to permit it to be 'owned' to the exclusion or embarrassment of air navigation by surface landlords who could put it to little real use."[10] This assessment of the issue had no real bearing on the case the Court had been deciding, which had to do with whether a state could impose property taxes on a fleet of airplanes that spent most of their time in other states. Had Jackson been in Washington rather than Germany, he might have reconciled his 1944 statement with a victory for the Causbys by distinguishing be-

The Supreme Court was down to seven members when it decided
United States v. Causby, because Fred Vinson (bottom, center) had not
yet replaced Harlan Fiske Stone as chief justice, and Robert Jackson
(top, second from right) was in Nuremberg. The majority opinion was
written by William Douglas (bottom, right), the dissent by Hugo Black
(bottom, second from left). Photograph by Harris and Ewing, Collection of the Supreme Court of the United States.

tween ordinary overflights and exceptionally low ones. Nevertheless, the government's lawyers wished Jackson was participating.
In their brief they twice quoted his opinion in support of the argument that airspace could not be owned.

   The case was thus decided by a Court with only seven justices.
Aerial trespass was not a topic on which they could have been expected to divide along political or jurisprudential lines. The issue
did not belong to any cluster of frequently litigated constitutional
questions, such as the power of the government in regulating the

economy or in curtailing civil liberties, so no member of the Court had a track record that would be useful in predicting his vote. The only bit of biographical detail the lawyers might have taken into account as they prepared for the case was that five of the seven had served in the military during World War I. Hugo Black, Harold Burton, Frank Murphy, and Stanley Reed had all been in the army, while Felix Frankfurter had been a special assistant to the secretary of war. Only Wiley Rutledge, who was suffering from tuberculosis at the time, and William Douglas, who was too young, had missed the war. (Douglas joined a student training corps and then claimed for the rest of his life to have served in the army.)[11] All were men who might have been expected to be solicitous of the needs of the military during wartime. The Causbys may well have been fortunate that the war was over by the time the case reached the Supreme Court.[12]

The government's lead argument was that landowners did not own the airspace above their land, so that by definition they had no property the government could have taken.[13] The government's brief quoted extensively from the two lower-court cases that had so held, *Hinman* in the U.S. Court of Appeals for the Ninth Circuit and *Thrasher v. City of Atlanta* in the Georgia Supreme Court. The brief acknowledged that other lower courts had held to the contrary, but argued that these decisions were simply incorrect. They were based, the government asserted, "on the erroneous notion that airspace conforming to the safe glide angle is not navigable airspace." *Portsmouth Harbor,* the government contended, was not a case about property in airspace at all, but rather an application of the familiar principle that the destruction of all uses of *land* is tantamount to a taking.

But why did it matter whether the airspace at issue was called "navigable airspace"? On what basis was the government denying that navigable airspace belonged to the owner of the land beneath? At bottom, the government's argument in *Causby* required it to take one side of a fundamental and very old jurisprudential debate.

Where does property come from? The law is full of doctrines that protect the rights of property, all of which presuppose a determination that there is actually some "property" that needs protecting. But how is that latter determination made? What is the source of property? Many people have tried to answer this question over the years. Their answers can be divided into two broad categories.

Some argue that property is a product of law. "Property is entirely the creature of law," declared Jeremy Bentham, in perhaps the best-known statement of this side of the argument.

> To have the object in one's hand—to keep it, to manufacture it, to sell it, to change its nature, to employ it—all these physical circumstances do not give the idea of property. A piece of cloth which is actually in the Indies may belong to me, whilst the dress which I have on may not be mine. The food which is incorporated with my own substance may belong to another, to whom I must account for its use.
>
> The idea of property consists in an established expectation—in the persuasion of power to derive certain advantages from the object, according to the nature of the case.
>
> But this expectation, this persuasion, can only be the work of the law. I can reckon upon the enjoyment of that which I regard as my own, only according to the promise of the law, which guarantees it to me. It is the law alone which allows me to forget my

natural weakness: it is from the law alone that I can enclose a field and give myself to its cultivation, in the distant hope of the harvest.

. . . .

Property and law are born and must die together. Before the laws, there was no property: take away the laws, all property ceases.[14]

On this view, what a person can claim as property is no more than what the law defines to be his property at any given time. As the law changes, so too will the scope of a person's property rights. This is a way of thinking about property that has likely become more widespread in the years since Bentham wrote, but it has never swept the field.

The opposite view is that property is defined not by law but by some source outside the law. "Property does not exist because there are laws, but laws exist because there is property," insisted the nineteenth-century French economist and legislator Frédéric Bastiat. "*Property* is a providential fact, like the human *person.* The law does not bring the one into existence any more than it does the other. Property is a necessary consequence of the nature of man. In a full sense of the word, man *is born a proprietor,* because he is born with wants whose satisfaction is necessary to life, and with organs and faculties whose exercise is indispensable to the satisfaction of those wants."[15] On this view, property is anterior to law, and has an existence independent of the state of the law at any given time. Even a society with no law at all would have some property. In Bastiat's era, God and the human nature he created were often cited as the sources of property; more recently, as religion has played less of an overt role in the legal system, the source of property has often been located in customary social practices. Either way, while the contours of property are no doubt shaped by law, and may even be constituted by law much of the time, the important thing in this way of understanding property is that property is not constituted by law *all* of the time. There remains some aspect of property that law has not created.

Which side one takes in this debate often has strong implications for one's opinion of legislation that redistributes property from one person to another. Under Bentham's view, it makes little sense to call such legislation an infringement of the rights of property, because the legislation is itself one of the defining elements of the law of property. If an earlier version of the law said that a certain item of property was owned by A, and a later version reallocates that same property to B, A would have no more ground for complaint than B would have had before the law changed. After all, the property belonged to A in the first place only because the law said it did, and now the law says it belongs to B. Under Bastiat's view, by contrast, A would have a basis for arguing that the new law violates her property rights, because those rights would have a source independent of what the law happens to be at any given time.

These two ways of understanding property are replicated, in different language, within American constitutional law. The Constitution bars the government from taking property for public use without just compensation, and from depriving people of property without due process, but it does not define the term *property* or say where a definition should be found. When called upon to decide whether something is or is not property, the Supreme Court has vacillated between two methods, each of which corresponds to a side of the argument between Bentham and Bastiat. At times the Court has taken the Benthamite position that property is defined by nonconstitutional law. In a takings case just three years before *Causby*, for example, the Court explained that "though the meaning of 'property' as used in . . . the Fifth Amendment is a federal question, it will normally obtain its content by reference to local law." If nonconstitutional law defines a particular interest as property, on this view, it will be protected from infringement by the Constitution, but not otherwise. At other times, however, the Court has said precisely the opposite. Perhaps the most famous example is a 1980 case called *Webb's Fabulous Pharmacies,* in which a Florida statute defined the interest on certain court-managed bank accounts as public money rather than the property of the owner of the principal. Under a Benthamite view, the state statute ought to have been enough to put an end to the owner's claim of a taking; after all, by state law the money was not his property, so he had no claim that the state had taken it. But the Court sounded quite Bastiat-like. "Neither the Florida Legislature by statute, nor the Florida courts by judicial decree, may accomplish the result the county seeks simply by recharacterizing the principal as 'public money' because it is held temporarily by the court," the Supreme Court declared. "To put it another way: a State, by *ipse dixit,* may not transform private property into public property without compensation." On this view, a particular asset can be protected by the Constitution even if state law denies it the status of property, so long as there is some other reason to call the asset property, a reason that typically has its grounding in social convention.[16] The interest earned on bank accounts is customarily thought of as property, and in *Webb's Fabulous Pharmacies* that was enough to trump contrary state law.

The Court has vacillated like this because each strategy leads to a problem. If we define property purely with reference to nonconstitutional law, the protections of the Constitution might become very flimsy, because governments would be able to deprive anyone of anything simply by changing the law to redefine this or that asset as something other than property. A broader definition of property allows courts to escape from this bind. On the other hand, if we define property as whatever strikes judges as resembling property, regardless of the content of nonconstitutional law, we run the risk of granting judges discretionary power over much of the economy. A narrower definition of property allows us to cabin this discretion. Neither solution is perfect, so the Court has not settled on either one. The justices have instead chosen their preferred strategy on an ad hoc case-by-case basis, perhaps subconsciously, in a way that will allow them to rule in favor of whichever side of the case intuitively seems stronger.

In *Causby*, it was in the government's interest to be Benthamite, so Benthamite it was. The government's brief pointed out that under the Air Commerce Act of 1926 there was a public right of transit in the "navigable air space of the United States." The navigable airspace, in turn, was defined in the regulations of the Civil Aeronautics Authority, which prescribed the minimum 30-to-1 glide angle for takeoffs and landings. Military airplanes crossing over the Causbys' land had always stayed at or above the minimum glide angle. By law, therefore, the overflights of which the Causbys complained were within the navigable airspace, where planes had every right to be. How, then, could the planes possibly be trespassing?

At their conference a few days after oral argument, the justices spoke in the customary order of seniority.[17] It was a Court entirely remade by Franklin Roosevelt and Harry Truman. The longest-serving justice, Hugo Black, had been appointed in 1937, only nine years before, while the newest, Harold Burton, was just coming to the end of his first term. Felix Frankfurter was the oldest of the justices at sixty-three, while the youngest, William Douglas, was only forty-seven, which meant that when the Wright brothers took their first flight, Frankfurter would have been twenty-one years old and Douglas only five. The younger justices had little memory of a time before the airplane, while the older ones likely remembered the dawn of flight very clearly. All seven had spent their entire adult lives in elite political and legal circles, however, so they all had ample opportunity to travel by airplane.

Black began by expressing strong disagreement with the idea that the Causbys could own their airspace. The "air is supposed to belong to everyone," he insisted. He declared that he "would not extend property rights in the air." Black had no doubt that the Causbys had been injured by the noise and the lights from the military planes flying over their house, but that injury, in his view, was not the result of having had property taken from them. It was the sort of injury ordinarily redressed by the law of nuisance, not the law of trespass. Black was concerned that the Court should "tread with care," because by imposing liability on the government for a taking, the Court would be creating constitutional law beyond the power of Congress to change. He would "send the parties to Congress"—that is, he would hold that Causbys' only remedy was a petition to Congress, either for compensation directly or for a waiver of the government's sovereign immunity from nuisance suits.

Stanley Reed spoke next. He wanted to reach the same conclusion as Black, he told his colleagues, but he felt constrained by *Portsmouth Harbor* to rule the other way. The airplanes that flew over the Causbys' land, he reasoned, were just like the guns pointed across the hotel's land, so if the latter amounted to a taking, so did the former. But the property the government had taken, Reed thought, was property in the land, not in the airspace. "Air is public property," he argued. Planes could fly through it, "but not in such a way as to take away rights of those on the land." The government had in effect taken the Causbys' land by rendering it nearly uninhabitable. Reed accordingly wanted to affirm the decision of the Court of Claims, but to write the opinion very narrowly, to avoid creating a property right in airspace.

Felix Frankfurter agreed with Reed. He too felt that *Portsmouth Harbor* dictated the outcome, but like Reed he wanted the opinion to be written as narrowly as possible. It was "not a question of an abstract right to the sky," Frankfurter explained, "but if they do take your inhabitance, have they not taken property in the constitutional sense?" William Douglas, Frank Murphy, and Wiley Rutledge all agreed as well. This is a "novel field," Murphy warned. "We should be careful about air," But Murphy was bothered by the fact that if the Causbys were denied a remedy in the Court of Claims, they would have no remedy at all. "*Portsmouth* would have to be overruled if we do not affirm," Rutledge added. "When the U.S. destroys your property, it takes it." With the votes of Murphy and Rutledge, there was a majority of five justices who wished to rule in favor of the Causbys, but none of the five had expressed any support for recognizing property rights in airspace. The property they believed was taken was the Causbys' right to use their *land*, not any right to exclude others from their air.

By the time Harold Burton got to talk, his vote made no difference, but he took the opportunity to caution his colleagues about the course they were about to adopt. There is "great danger for us to enter this field," he advised. The Court was "apt to be led astray by feelings of injury and equity" for the plight of the Causbys. Burton did not invoke the old saying that "hard cases make bad law," but that was his point—that the justices' understandable sympathy for the Causbys was leading them to craft a rule that would have unhappy consequences in other fact situations. An "airport would require the power of eminent domain" to acquire neighboring parcels, Burton worried. He agreed with Black that this was really a case of nuisance, not a trespass or a taking. A "private plane has the right to go through the air," he reasoned, "and if it does wrong it has to pay, but we should say it is a tort" rather than a trespass.

The Supreme Court was not in a Benthamite mood. The government's argument, that the airspace above the minimum 30-to-1 glide angle was by law not the Causbys' at all, had made no impression on any of the justices, not even the two dissenters. Black and Burton sided with the government, but their conception of property was no less intuitive than that of the five justices who sided with the Causbys. All seven were relying, at bottom, on social convention with respect to the use of air—the five in the majority thought that landowners had a right to be left in peace on the ground below, while the two dissenters thought that the air was free for flying so long as the government was flying the planes. None of them cared that federal law had defined as navigable airspace the area in which the planes flew over the Causbys' land.

As the justices left their conference, however, none could have expected that the Court's opinion in *United States v. Causby* would resolve the question that had divided the lower courts, whether landowners owned their lower airspace. They seemed poised to publish an opinion finding a taking, but a taking of land rather than a taking of airspace.

William Douglas was an extraordinarily prolific writer who was better known for speed than for meticulousness. As one generally admiring biographer concludes, Douglas was "interested more in communicating his broad philosophy to the readers of his judicial opinions than in satisfying a scholar's appetite for carefully documented legal arguments. He was not a lawyer's judge or a judge's judge or a scholar's judge. He was a people's judge." This was a working style that enabled Douglas to publish a steady stream of books while on the Court, books on subjects ranging from foreign policy to the environment to his own life. But it was also a style that produced opinions his colleagues often found sloppy and superficial. "Nobody doubted that Douglas could have done a more thorough, scholarly job if he had chosen to," the same biographer acknowledges. "But he did not choose to and that indifference to detail was more infuriating than a showing of incompetence would have been."[18]

When Douglas was assigned to write the majority opinion in *United States v. Causby*, he had two reasons to work even more quickly than usual. The Court was two justices short in May 1946, because of the death of Stone and the absence of Jackson, so everyone had more work to do. And Douglas would likely have felt more time pressure than any of his colleagues, because *Causby* was argued right near the end of the term. Douglas normally spent the summers in his home state of Washington; some years he was so eager to get there that he left the Court even before the term was over. He wrote the opinion in *Causby* very quickly, perhaps too quickly to write as carefully and narrowly as the other members of the five-justice majority wished him to.

Douglas did begin narrowly. "It is ancient doctrine," he explained, "that at common law ownership of the land extended to the periphery of the universe—*Cujus est solum ejus usque ad coelum*. But that doctrine has no place in the modern world. The air is a public highway."[19] The old common-law rule had been superseded by technological change. "Were that not true," Douglas continued, "every transcontinental flight would subject the operator to countless trespass suits. Common sense revolts at the idea. To recognize such private claims to the airspace would clog these highways, seriously interfere with their control and development in the public interest, and transfer into private ownership that to which only the public has a just claim." All of this was common ground by the 1940s. Many years had passed since anyone had seriously contended that landowners owned up to the heavens. The controversy was just about the lower airspace. Thus far, Douglas's opinion had said nothing to resolve the question one way or the other.[20]

In any event, Douglas went on, the demise of the *cujus est solum* maxim had little to do with the Causbys' lawsuit, because the Causbys had lost their *land,* not their airspace. "If, by reason of the frequency and altitude of the flights, respondents could not use this land for any purpose, their loss would be complete," Douglas reasoned. "It would be as complete as if the United States had entered upon the surface of the land and taken exclusive possession of it." The question was what the property owner had lost, not what the government had gained, so if the property owner lost the use of his or her land because of something the government had done, that was a taking. "The fact that the planes never touched the surface" was irrelevant. "The owner's right to possess and exploit the land—that is to say, his beneficial ownership of it—would be destroyed." And the same principle applied when the ability to possess and enjoy land was only partially, rather than completely, destroyed. "The path of glide for airplanes might reduce a valuable factory site to grazing land, an orchard to a vegetable patch, a residential section to a wheat field," Douglas concluded. "Some value would remain. But the use of the airspace immediately above the land would limit the utility of the land and cause a diminution in its value." The government had thus taken the landowner's property to the extent of that diminution. Such was "the philosophy," Douglas asserted, of Justice Holmes's opinion in *Portsmouth Harbor.*

To this point, Douglas had done exactly what his colleagues wanted him to do. He had written narrowly, allowing the Causbys to win without saying a word about whether landowners owned the lower airspace. Had he stopped there, the decision would have had no effect on the aerial trespass debate, and probably little or no effect on commercial aviation at all. The Court's decision in *Causby* would scarcely be remembered today.

But Douglas was on a roll. In his enthusiasm to share his views with the world, he embarked on a discussion of the precise issue the other members of the majority hoped he would avoid—the nature of property rights in airspace. "We have said that the airspace is a public highway," Douglas began. "Yet it is obvious that if the landowner is to have full enjoyment of the land, he must have exclusive control of the immediate reaches of the enveloping atmosphere. Otherwise buildings could not be erected, trees could not be planted, and even fences could not be run." Douglas was characteristically dealing in first principles, as if no one had thought about these matters before. "The landowner," he concluded, "owns at least as much of the space above the ground as he can occupy or use in connection with the land." One can almost see the dismay on the faces of Reed and Frankfurter as Douglas repeated his argument, in increasingly declamatory language. "The superadjacent airspace at this low altitude is so close to the land," he added, "that continuous invasions of it affect the use of the surface of the land itself. We think that the landowner, as an incident to his ownership, has a claim to it and that invasions of it are in the same category as invasions of the surface." With these words, Douglas resolved the aerial trespass question. The lower airspace *was* capable of being owned, and it was owned by the landowner beneath.

It was only after reaching this conclusion that Douglas noted the Court's sporadic practice of determining the meaning of "property" by reference to nonconstitutional law. "If we look to North Carolina law," he ventured, "we reach the same result."

North Carolina had been one of the states that adopted the uniform aeronautics law, according to which landowners owned the airspace above their land, subject to an easement of flight at altitudes high enough to avoid interfering with the landowner's then-existing use of the land. The Court's holding was "thus not inconsistent with the local law." But the nod to North Carolina law was clearly an afterthought. Douglas did not define the Causbys' property by looking to local law; rather, he defined the Causbys' property by invoking his own intuitions about what property must be like, and then only afterward confirmed that his intuitions were not contradicted by the law of North Carolina. His intuitions, in any event, *were* inconsistent with local law. North Carolina law limited the airspace from which a landowner could exclude aircraft to the area that would interfere with the landowner's "then existing use" of the land. By searching his own conscience rather than the law of North Carolina, Douglas had allowed the landowner to exclude planes not just from the airspace he was using at the time but any airspace he might use in the future.

As for the federal law relied upon by the government, Douglas simply denied that it was relevant. He determined that the "navigable airspace" described by federal law included the space above the five-hundred-foot minimum altitude requirement prescribed by the Civil Aeronautics Authority, but not the space within the glide paths established by the CAA. This was not the most convincing argument, and, as later events would show, it was probably not a sincere argument either, because when Congress later redefined the navigable airspace to include glide paths, Douglas held that the redefinition made no difference.[21]

Douglas used a few different verbal formulations to define the boundary between private and public airspace. He twice described the privately owned airspace as lying within "the immediate reaches" of the ground. Once he defined the landowner's property rights as encompassing "at least as much of the space above the ground as he can occupy or use." And once he described the private airspace as the zone in which intrusions would "subtract from the owner's full enjoyment of the property." These formulations were not necessarily equivalent. One could imagine, for example, a layer of airspace that a landowner could not himself use or occupy but that nevertheless had to be kept free from intruders if the owner was to fully enjoy his property. That layer might or might not be within the immediate reaches of the ground—it all depended on what "immediate reaches" was taken to mean. Douglas wrote the opinion so quickly that he was not careful about his language. This was just the sort of thing that drove his colleagues to distraction.

Wherever the boundary was located, it had to be somewhere in the same general area as the boundary established in the earlier lower-court aerial trespass cases, which had been just as vague. In *Smith v. New England Aircraft Company,* the Massachusetts Supreme Court had set the boundary somewhere between one hundred and five hundred feet of altitude. In *Swetland v. Curtiss Airports Corporation,* the U.S. Court of Appeals for the Sixth Circuit had located it somewhere between "upper" and "lower" strata of the air but had declined to be any more specific. In *Gay v. Taylor,* a Pennsylvania court had placed the line at the point where invasions of the airspace interfered with the landowner's enjoyment of the surface.[22]

These earlier cases, however, had rested on the law of the state in which the dispute was located. Each state could have its own law, which could be different from the law of other states, and each state's legislature and courts had the power to change that state's law. Douglas's opinion in *Causby,* by contrast, was not based on the law of any particular state. It was based on Douglas's own interpretation of the word *property* in the Takings Clause of the Constitution, an interpretation informed by his intuitions about the best way to resolve conflicts between landowners and airplanes. The Court was imposing a uniform nationwide rule, a rule that no state legislature and no state court had the power to change. Aviation lawyers had been trying for years to obtain a standardized national law of aerial trespass. They had directed their efforts at state legislatures (through NCCUSL and the ABA) and at Congress, but without complete success. In *Causby,* a case in which no aviation lawyers were involved, William Douglas unexpectedly handed them the uniform law they had long sought. Because the rule derived from the Constitution, no one had the power to change it in the future except the Supreme Court.

Reed, Frankfurter, Murphy, and Rutledge all joined Douglas's opinion, apparently without complaining, even though they had not wanted Douglas to resolve the aerial trespass issue. Such acquiescence would be startling today, but separate concurring opinions were rare for most of the Court's history. *Causby* was decided right near the start of the Court's transition to the current practice, in which concurring opinions are commonplace.[23] Even if the four justices who joined the opinion had been inclined to urge modifications on Douglas or to write separately, they may well have thought twice. Douglas was not a man whose mind was easy to change, so a complaint or a separate opinion was unlikely to cause him to budge. A separate opinion would only split the five-justice majority into two groups, and it was possible that neither group would be large enough to produce an opinion that commanded the assent of four of the seven sitting justices, so writing a separate opinion threatened to prevent the Court from issuing any majority opinion at all. Meanwhile the end of the term was drawing near, which meant a rush to finish up the whole

year's writing assignments, a rush that was worse than normal because the Court was shorthanded. Considering all these circumstances, Douglas's colleagues in the majority kept their disagreements to themselves.

Justices Black and Burton dissented, in an opinion written by
Black. "It is inconceivable to me," Black declared, "that the Constitution guarantees that the airspace of this Nation needed for air
navigation is owned by the particular persons who happen to own
the land beneath." In other areas of constitutional law, Black took
the position that the words of the Constitution should be interpreted as literally as possible, and one needed to read a great deal
into the Takings Clause to reach the majority's conclusion. "No
rigid constitutional rule, in my judgment, commands that the air
must be considered as marked off into separate compartments by
imaginary metes and bounds in order to synchronize air ownership with land ownership," Black insisted. "No greater confusion
could be brought about in the coming age of air transportation
than that which would result were courts by constitutional interpretation to hamper Congress in its efforts to keep the air free.
Old concepts of private ownership of land should not be introduced into the field of air regulation." Black preferred to leave the
regulation of the airspace to Congress and to the Civil Aeronautics Authority, who had the technical knowledge and the flexibil-
ity to adjust the law in response to changing technology. Courts,
by contrast, "do not possess the techniques or the personnel to
consider and act upon the complex combinations of factors entering into the problems." At worst, "they can stand as obstacles to
better adapted techniques that might be offered by experienced
experts and accepted by Congress."

But William Douglas was willing to use the Constitution to
resolve the aerial trespass debate, and four of his colleagues did

not care enough about the issue to try to talk him out of it. The lower airspace belonged to the owner of the land beneath.

"Chickens Upheld in Plane Decision" read the newspaper headline. The Court of Claims, instructed by Justice Douglas to recalculate its damage award in light of the Supreme Court's opinion, reduced the Causbys' recovery. The property actually taken, the Court of Claims found, was an easement of flight through the Causbys' airspace stretching from 83 feet to 365 feet in altitude, the lowest and highest points at which military planes crossed above their land. The easement was taken from June 1942 to November 1946. During that period, the court determined, the rental value of the Causbys' land suffered a decrease of $1,060, and they lost $375 worth of chickens, for a total of $1,435.[24] The award had to be divided with their lawyer, William Comer, who had worked on the case for more than four years, so no one ended up with much money.

Lawyers hailed *Causby* as an important case, although they acknowledged that lower courts would have to decide many more cases before the ambiguities in Douglas's opinion could be resolved. Among aviation lawyers, the case was understood as a victory for landowners. Airports would have to surround themselves with a large enough buffer to allow planes to climb above the upper edge of the neighbors' airspace, counseled the Denver aviation insurance lawyer Lowell White, but "this may be easier said than done." In Denver, for example, "nearly the entire city and county is built up," so any new airport facilities would have to be built far away in adjoining counties. "It must be even more difficult," White lamented, "in populous communities which extend over wide areas, such as Los Angeles where there could not possibly be space for a modern airport within many miles." In White's view,

Causby doomed travelers to airports located inconveniently far from anywhere they might want to go.[25]

One clear effect of *Causby* was to transform the nature of airspace litigation. Landowners had once sued pilots and airplane owners for trespass and nuisance; now, more often than not, they sued government-owned airports for violations of the Takings Clause or its state constitutional analogues. In the 1950s, as they acquired jet engines, planes grew larger and louder, and they needed longer and shallower glide paths on takeoff and landing. Meanwhile the volume of air traffic continued to increase, so there was never any shortage of aggrieved landowners near airports, a problem that was exacerbated by suburban growth, which brought residential developments near airports originally built in rural areas. In 1958, after a spate of suits against airports, Congress redefined the "navigable airspace" to include not just the airspace above the minimum altitude prescribed by regulation but also "airspace needed to insure safety in take-off and landing of aircraft." On a strict Benthamite view of the law, this change would have stripped landowners of some of their airspace; planes would no longer be taking off and landing in *their* airspace, but in airspace that was now dedicated to the public for air travel. The Supreme Court, however, stuck to its own intuitive definition of property. In *Griggs v. County of Allegheny* (1962), another opinion written by William Douglas, the Court declared once again that "the use of land presupposes the use of some of the airspace above it. Otherwise no home could be built, no tree planted, no fence constructed, no chimney erected." Flights that remained within the federally defined navigable airspace were still takings if they crossed low enough over a landowner's property—in *Griggs,* a mere thirty feet above the plaintiff's roof.[26]

Many of the uncertainties surrounding aerial trespass in the years after *Causby* were eventually ironed out, after enough cases presenting slightly different fact situations had made their way through the lower courts. As the law coalesced, landowners in practice had to prove they had suffered some harm on the ground in order to prevail. They also had to prove that the overflights had been at a very low altitude, typically less than around five hundred feet above the ground.[27] The resulting legal standard thus ended up being very close to the formulation of the *Restatement of Torts* from the early 1930s, in that by requiring harm and low overflights as prerequisites it effectively merged the law of nuisance, which required harm but not physical presence on the property, with the law of trespass to land, which required physical presence but not harm. As the law grew clearer, reported cases raising the issue became less common, as airports acquired enough neighboring parcels to forestall litigation, and as the cases that *were* filed became easier to settle because their outcomes were more predictable. After half a century of argument, the aerial trespass debate largely fizzled out.

The issue had not been put to rest by Congress, or by the Civil Aeronautics Authority, or by state legislatures. After decades of debate, in which many of the participants had spent years thinking about the question, it had been resolved by one powerful man, William Douglas, who was likely considering it for the very first time.

NINE

Sovereignty in Space

John Cobb Cooper was the dean of American air lawyers. While an executive at Pan Am, Cooper had represented the United States at the major international aviation conferences, including the 1944 Chicago Convention, where he was one of the drafters of the treaty that still governs international civil aviation today. Toward the end of his career he left the business world for academia, first in Princeton as a member of the Institute for Advanced Study, and then in Montreal as the founding director of McGill University's Institute of International Air Law, the first such organization in North America since the demise of the institutes established in the late 1920s and early 1930s.[1]

In 1951, Cooper was among the first to notice an approaching problem. The Chicago Convention, like the earlier treaties it superseded, was based on the principle that each nation exercised complete sovereignty over the airspace above it. A nation had the right to regulate its own airspace as it saw fit, including the right to exclude foreign aircraft altogether if it wished. In the Chicago Convention, like the earlier treaties, nations mutually consented to foreign overflights of their territory under specified circumstances. As the ever-increasing range of airplanes allowed for more international air travel, this system had facilitated the development of a growing network of international air routes. All seemed to be well. For decades there had been no occasion to think about the scope of national sovereignty over airspace.

In 1949, however, the press had carried accounts of American rocket flights to an altitude of 250 miles above the earth. Did such flights, Cooper wondered, stay within the sovereign "airspace"? Or did they reach an area so high that they flew *above* the airspace, into a zone within no country's jurisdiction? How high up did a nation's sovereignty extend? Was sovereignty unbounded, or did it have an upper limit? And if sovereignty had a limit, where was it located?

It would not be long, Cooper realized, before further technological progress would make these questions even more important. If a rocket could get high enough and then turned parallel to the surface of the earth, it would be in orbit. It would become an artificial satellite, flying high over many different countries several times a day. As it orbited the earth, would such a satellite be infringing the sovereignty of the nations below its path? Before launching a satellite, would one need the consent of each country beneath? Or would the satellite be orbiting above the upper boundary of each nation's sovereignty? "It is obvious," Cooper concluded, "that it is the duty of the trained jurist to suggest an answer to these problems."[2]

The rockets belonged to the U.S. Air Force, which was beginning to grapple with the same questions. The Air Force was already contemplating the eventual use of satellites for military reconnaissance. As an October 1950 report of the RAND Corporation pointed out, however, the legal implications of such satellites were not at all clear. The Soviet Union was likely to argue that its sovereignty had been violated if American spacecraft flew over its territory. Would the Soviet complaint be justified? Or could the satellites avoid Soviet airspace if they flew high enough? No one could be sure.[3]

The scope of national sovereignty over airspace had not been an open question since the period before World War I. Few, if any, had given the issue much thought over the past forty years. But the dawn of the space age brought it back to public attention. Within a few years, as space captured the public imagination, the topic seemed to be everywhere. "Who owns the universe?" Oscar Schachter, deputy legal director at the United Nations, wondered in the pages of *Collier's* magazine. "Will there be national rivalry to plant the Stars and Stripes, the Union Jack and the Hammer and Sickle far off in space, so that governments can then assert exclusive control and keep others away?" "Is discovering space like discovering land?" mused Senator Charles Potter of Michigan. "Can we lay claim to interplanetary space?" Similar questions blanketed the popular press. "Who owns what above the atmosphere?" asked *Newsweek.* "Who owns the unknown?" questioned the *Economist.* "What flags for space?" wondered the *Manchester Guardian.* The science fiction magazine *Galaxy* inquired "Who'll own the planets?" while the *Saturday Review* asked, "Who owns the moon?" "In these momentous days," the president of the United Nations General Assembly informed readers of the *New York Times,* "old conceptions of sovereignty . . . are no longer suitable for the control of the outer universe." Air law had once been settled, advised one general-audience book about space. But now the prospect of space flight has "jolted these concepts of sacred national air-space sovereignty."[4]

The issue was of course most pressing for lawyers. Some, especially lawyers in government or with government contractors like RAND, were providing legal advice to those formulating space policy. Others had the needs of private clients in mind. "My law firm represents some clients who are in the rocket propulsion, electronics, instrumentation and space flight fields," explained the Los Angeles attorney Frank Simpson. "Conceivably, the future might find my client, the rocket engine manufacturer, as the defendant in a tort action, all the pertinent facts of which occurred three hundred miles above the surface of the earth." It was unclear which nation's laws would apply, or even if the rocket was in a nation at all. "Immediately, a number of questions are raised: what forum should be used; what law applies; who has jurisdiction; was the act committed within a sovereign nation or a subdivision thereof, or was it in free space; if it occurred in free space, what are the rules of liability." But whatever their immediate interest, all agreed that, as British lawyer Michael Aaronson put it, "an entirely new situation has arisen. . . . How far up do these political air space frontiers go?"[5]

Some argued that national sovereignty had no upper limit. Throughout the history of air law, reasoned the Taiwanese law professor Ming-Min Peng, lawyers had used the term *airspace* without ever imagining that airspace was bounded at the top. In the Chicago Convention the word was likewise intended to include "all upper space *ad infinitum,*" agreed the Indian law professor R. C. Hingorani. Arnold Knauth, one of the leading American air lawyers, explained that "sovereignty extends as far as the protection of our lives and fortunes requires." In his own lifetime, he recalled, danger had come from as far away as Germany and Japan, and Americans had learned to station troops all over the world—in effect, to exercise sovereignty sideways—to ward off attacks before they could reach the United States. "If that is true *sideways,*" Knauth asked, "is it not just as true *upwards?*" C. L. Sulzberger, foreign correspondent for the *New York Times,* accordingly concluded that all satellites would violate the sovereignty of every nation below their path.[6]

But proponents of unlimited national sovereignty were quickly outnumbered by advocates for an upper bound, who proceeded from the premise that the drafters of the Chicago Convention had never attempted to define the term *airspace* and had given no thought to the future invention of satellites. As in the first decade of the twentieth century, when aerial sovereignty was first debated, some analogized the air to the ocean and contended that just as all were free to navigate the high seas, far from the shores of any country, the upper reaches of space should be open to spaceships of all nations. Another argument from the early days of flight—the idea that sovereignty extended only as far as effective state control—was also revived to support the claim that space had to be an international zone free from national assertions of sovereignty, because no nation could hope to control space.[7] Some of the people who held such views seem to have been unaware that they were repeating the losing arguments from fifty years before, when their predecessors had debated the status of the lower airspace.

In the early part of the century, theoretical contentions about the nature of airspace or of sovereignty had been swept aside by practical concerns of national defense, so other advocates for a ceiling on sovereignty tried to address these concerns. They argued that there was less reason to worry about threats to public safety in space than there was in the air closer to the ground. There was no danger of falling objects, or falling spaceships, once one moved beyond the earth's gravitational field. Allowing free travel in space would not facilitate the violation of customs or immigration laws, as would free travel through the lower air. Some of the fears that had given rise to aerial sovereignty evaporated in outer space.[8] But not all of them. The chilling prospect of space-based nuclear weapons was enough to make anyone think twice before dismissing the danger posed by enemy satellites orbiting overhead.

Perhaps the most common reason to favor an upper bound to sovereignty, and the only one to which there could be no rebuttal, was the simple fact that the earth was always in motion with respect to the rest of the universe. Without some upper limit, each country would be sovereign over a constantly changing sliver of space. "Even the moon, the sun, the planets and other heavenly bodies would be subjected to the successive claims of sovereigns as the universe wheels along," pointed out Chester Ward, the U.S. Navy's judge advocate general. "It is absurd to think that we might be bound to a system as rigid and illogical as this. It is obvious that there must be some upward limit to sovereignty."[9] Close to the ground the airspace rotated along with the earth, so the scope of aerial sovereignty never changed from the perspective of a person on the earth's surface. Matters would be far trickier if sovereignty extended indefinitely into space.

By the late 1950s, therefore, commentators overwhelmingly believed that national sovereignty had to have a ceiling. Somewhere there had to be a dividing line between a lower region partitioned by national boundaries and an upper region open to all. But where?

The UN lawyer Oscar Schachter may have been the first to attempt to draw a line. "The most reasonable rule," he noted in 1952, "would seem to be one that defines the air space in terms of the atmospheric elements necessary to 'lift' aircraft; a limit expressed in these terms would be in keeping with the purpose and intent of the treaties relating to aviation." The established rule of sovereignty over airspace had been devised with airplanes in mind, so sovereignty would end where the air became too thin to support a plane.[10] This was only the first of a long series of similar line-drawing efforts, many of which, like Schachter's, were based on physical features of space.

Some suggested that the ceiling of sovereignty should be located at the end of the atmosphere, where there was no more air. Such a view would be in keeping with the Chicago Convention, argued one English lawyer, because the Convention recognized national sovereignty over "airspace," and airspace implied the presence of air. Albert Moon, a lawyer whose surname no doubt raised eyebrows when he went to work for the Los Angeles–based Aerospace Corporation, thought the dividing line should be somewhere around five miles above the earth, just above the then-current upper bound for commercial flights. Others suggested a height of around fifty miles, just below the orbit of the earliest satellites. The Washington lawyer Andrew Haley, general counsel to the American Rocket Society and a prolific writer on space, urged a more precise version of Oscar Schachter's original proposal. He wanted to place the boundary at the so-called von Kármán line (named for the Caltech physicist Theodore von Kármán), approximately fifty-two miles high, the theoretical limit of air-supported flight. Others drew the line at what they supposed to be the outer limit of the gravitational force of the earth, or about sixty miles.[11]

By the early 1960s, surveys of the subject routinely provided long catalogs of all the various dividing lines that had been proposed by lawyers, ranging from a few miles above the earth to several thousand miles, all backed by ostensibly scientific justifications. "I hope that scientists can solve the problem of re-entry from Outer Space quickly," joked the law professor (and future attorney general) Nicholas Katzenbach. "I am afraid a number of my brethren at the bar are already in orbit. They are traveling very fast and very high in a circular path, and I want them brought back to earth as soon as possible." For all their theorizing about where to locate the upper bound of national sovereignty, none of their proposals was entirely satisfactory. Neither the air nor the earth's gravity came to an abrupt end. Both dwindled away gradually, so it was arbitrary to designate a threshold at which there was too little of one or the other. Airplanes, meanwhile, were repeatedly reaching altitude records as new designs allowed them to fly higher, so any line based on current practice was likely to be out of date in the near future. There was no guarantee that the lowest satellites would remain above the highest planes, so any upper bound to sovereignty drawn between their present-day altitudes might prove permeable.[12] No matter how one tried to draw it, there was no clear line between the lower air and outer space.

An even more fundamental criticism of all these line-drawing efforts became common by the early 1960s. Whether a foreign object far above the earth posed a threat to the people below depended less on its altitude than on its purpose. Foreign scientific research was less dangerous than foreign weaponry, for example, no matter how far away from the earth either was located. As time went on, more and more commentators began to suggest that "the applicable legal regime should be based on the activity undertaken," as two prominent American international lawyers put it, "rather than on the area in which the act occurred." This view quickly came to be called the "functional approach," because it contemplated sorting the lawfulness of spacecraft according to their function instead of their location. "The fundamental regulatory regime for space activities must be along functional lines," insisted Robert Crane, director of Duke University's Space Institute. "This would mean, for example, that if any problems arise concerning the legality of certain communications satellites, we can negotiate with the Soviets without committing ourselves automatically on the legality of specific weather satellites. The principal criterion would be not territorial location but the function and purpose of the particular activity under consideration."[13]

The idea of tailoring a legal rule directly to the function an activity was intended to serve, rather than using location or some other principle as a proxy for that function, was reminiscent of the legal realism of the 1930s. In a well-known 1935 article, for instance, Felix Cohen had contrasted the "transcendental nonsense" of traditional legal reasoning with the "functional approach" characteristic of realism. It was thus not surprising that when the Yale law professor Myres McDougal, one of the realists of the 1930s and 1940s, turned his attention to space law in the 1950s and 1960s, he became one of the leading proponents of the functional approach to sovereignty in space. "There have been hundreds, perhaps thousands of boundaries suggested, but none of them make any sense," McDougal declared. "The most promising mode for accommodating all conflicts," he concluded, would be to assess "the reasonableness of particular types of activities in context. Consideration could be given to such factors as the inclusive or exclusive character of the activities in space (whether benefiting all mankind or only a single state), the importance to the surface state of the interests threatened, the degree and modality of the threat, the availability of alternative remedies to both the surface state and the state engaging in space activity, and so on." This was a long list of factors, and different people might balance them in different ways, but at least they were factors relevant to the real worry about space—that something dangerous might be lurking above. The notion that one could draw a line in the air to mark the boundary between permissible and impermissible space activities was precisely the sort of transcendental nonsense at which the realists would have scoffed. Many accordingly joined McDougal in urging a functional approach to space.[14]

But then the functional approach had its critics, too. Obviously some activities in space, like firing missiles into other countries, would be ruled impermissible, but what about less aggressive uses of space? A reconnaissance satellite, for example, might be used for peaceful meteorological observation, but it might also be used to spy on other nations' armies. Would the satellite be lawful or unlawful? And how would national governments even be able to know the purposes of the satellites orbiting overhead? The functional approach might prove to be even more ill-suited to the problem than the effort to delineate an upper bound to national sovereignty. John Johnson, the general counsel to the National Aeronautics and Space Administration, concluded that "the confusion resulting from the misplaced emphasis on physical characteristics and technological criteria in seeking a solution of the boundary problem quite naturally led to a reaction by others that went to the opposite extreme of denying the problem altogether."[15] Maybe the only solution was to draw a boundary, no matter how unsatisfying any given boundary seemed to be.

Early in the century, the original aerial sovereignty debate also began with a decade of theorizing, mostly by lawyers outside of government who were not in a position to implement any of their proposed solutions. In the end, though, the issue had been resolved not through intellectual effort but by Great Power politics, when the strongest nations of Europe closed their air frontiers just before World War I.

As the debate over space sovereignty wore on, some began to suggest that legal theory would be equally fruitless in space, because no solution could be adopted without the consent of the Great Powers of the space age, the United States and the Soviet Union. "Some of the current proposals for space law seem to assume that decisions will be made directly by the conscience of mankind, or by some presently mythical global court with universal compulsory jurisdiction," noted Myres McDougal and his Yale colleague Leon Lipson. They pointed out that decisions would instead be made by officials of the most powerful nations, who had no incentive to constrain themselves from doing what they perceived to be in their own national interest. Space law, McDougal and Lipson predicted, would be developed not by the formal adoption of rules but by "the slow building of expectations, the continued accretion of repeated instances of tolerated acts, the gradual development of assurance that certain things may be done under promise of reciprocity and that other things must not be done on pain of retaliation." The result would be a customary law of space, a law produced by a series of specific international incidents.[16]

The prospect of resolving the dilemma of space sovereignty in this way was anathema to many of the early space lawyers, who saw it as nothing more than might making right. That powerful nations might simply do whatever they wanted, without any thought to what was best for the world as a whole, was precisely why they were urging the creation of space law before it was too late. "That is one of the reasons why all the lawyers are of the opinion that a worldwide agreement—a truly worldwide one—is necessary," urged Eugène Pépin of McGill's Institute of International Air Law. But if writers like McDougal and Lipson could be criticized for not moving quickly enough to draft rules governing sovereignty in space, lawyers like Pépin were just as easily mocked for their idealism. "The space lawyers have projected themselves into pretty esoteric realms where there appears to be not only no air, but no cold war, and no generals and admirals to define the national interest," chided Philip Quigg, the managing editor of *Foreign Affairs*. Issues "are more likely to be set by precedents as yet unknown than by international agreement." Others agreed that law would follow, not precede, the events the law would regulate.[17]

Such was the prevailing view within the U.S. government all through the 1950s and the early 1960s. Because American officials expected the United States to be unrivaled in space by any other nation except the Soviet Union, they consistently advised against agreeing to any international rules governing space, because any rules would necessarily fetter the United States the most. The U.S. Air Force repeatedly opposed any formal resolution of the sovereignty question. The State Department maintained complete public agnosticism as to where American sovereignty ended or if it even ended at all. "The United States Government has not recognized any top or upper limit to its sovereignty," declared Loftus Becker, the State Department's legal advisor, in 1958. "I do not wish to take, nor has the State Department ever officially taken, a definitive position." On one hand, Becker explained, "it would be perfectly rational for us to maintain that under the Chicago Convention the sovereignty of the United States extends 10,000 miles from the surface of the earth, an area which would comprehend the area in which all of the satellites up to this point have entered." On the other hand, he added, "the United States has already engaged in activities which, it could be asserted, have given to it certain rights as distinguished from those states who have not engaged in such activities. Up to this time the United States has made no claims of sovereignty based upon such activities"—the presence of American satellites orbiting above other countries—but Becker cautioned that this forbearance should not be interpreted as any concession on the government's part that it lacked the right to send satellites wherever it wished. The main thing, Becker concluded, was that the State Department was "inclined to view with great reserve any such suggestions as that the principles of the law of space should be codified now." Rather, "it is the position of our Government that the law of space should be based upon the facts of space and there is very much more that we have to learn about the conditions existing in space before we shall be in a position to say what shall be the legal principles applicable thereto."[18]

This difference in perspective, between lawyers within the government and lawyers on the outside, was starkly revealed when Becker testified alongside John Cobb Cooper before the House Select Committee on Astronautics and Space Exploration. "There are a number of areas in which various nations have taken action, even though their respective legal rights were by no means settled," Becker advised. In Antarctica, for example, "that has been going on for 20 years without any difficulty." Space would be just one more arena in which law would crystallize from customary practice. Cooper objected immediately. "It seems to me, sir," he explained, "if there is not understanding as to the legal status of outer space . . . you may have a fruitful possibility of international misunderstanding when new types of satellites are launched."[19] If one were primarily concerned with preserving world peace, law had to come before practice, but if one were primarily concerned with preserving the U.S. government's freedom of action in space, practice had to come before law.

The U.S. government's refusal to be pinned down to any view of the law exasperated those who favored clarifying the sovereignty question before conflicts arose. "Where does the sovereignty go to when it goes into space?" Representative James Fulton of Pittsburgh asked of Becker. "You are a legal adviser and I want an answer to it." When Becker would not give a direct answer, Fulton pressed him further. "Here is what I get into when I take your practical approach of just wait and see what happens, and then we will make up a rule of law as we go." Back in Pittsburgh, some of Fulton's constituents had plans of their own.

> Mr. Fulton: The 14th Street Boys' Club in my district writes me and says, "We want to put a rocket into space."
>
> You now say, well, let them fire their rocket and see what happens. This brings up this question. First, is a private citizen allowed to go into space? Second, is private industry allowed into space?
>
> Thirdly, can the G.E. Corp. put a rocket up for communications? Fourthly, can an international corporation like the I.T. & T. put a rocket up? Fifthly, can a corporation that is a utility, incorporated either under the laws of the United States or a U.S. agency, put a rocket up? Is there any law against it?
>
> Am I violating the law or should I tell the young kids from the 14th Street Boys' Club, "Go ahead and shoot it up"? . . . The boys want to know. Tell me yes or no. Are they breaking a law?
>
> Mr. Becker: The most practical answer to you is to tell them to hire a lawyer.
>
> Mr. Fulton: I think you are the State Department adviser.
>
> Mr. Becker: I don't give advice to private citizens. I give advice to the Secretary of State.

After a few more rounds like this, Fulton gave up in frustration. "I have not been told where international law takes over in space," he complained, "nor will the witness tell me where his jurisdiction begins." Becker would only repeat the State Department's consistent message, that it was too soon for there to be any rules relating to sovereignty in space. "There has been no determination or position on the part of the United States as to how high in the airspace or beyond the airspace the sovereignty of the United States extends," he concluded. "We have not as yet found it necessary to make that determination."[20]

The Soviet Union, the only other nation with a significant space program, had the same incentive to avoid committing itself to any view of the law that might restrict its own activities in space. Soviet writing on space sovereignty in the 1950s tended to serve Soviet national interests just as strongly as American government statements tracked American national interests.[21] Neither side believed it could give an inch in space, for fear of compromising its defense against the other. Despite all the proposals for the formulation of international law regarding sovereignty in space, therefore, the decade ended without any formal law on the subject at all.

Yet law of a sort *was* created during the period—the customary law envisioned by Myres McDougal and others. Between 1956 and 1960 there was a series of space disputes between the United States and the Soviet Union. The outcomes of these disputes would produce more space law than any code of written rules.

In early 1956 the U.S. government sent hundreds of large plastic balloons equipped with cameras and meteorological instruments high into the air above Turkey and Western Europe. Prevailing winds carried the balloons across the Soviet Union at altitudes ranging from twenty-five thousand to fifty thousand feet, above the flight paths then used by commercial airlines. The gondolas containing the cameras and other equipment were to be recovered by military pilots in the air over the Pacific, after disengaging from the balloons and releasing parachutes. The cameras were ostensibly for taking pictures of cloud formations, but in fact the balloons were part of a complex project, several years in preparation, to spy on the Soviet Union.[22]

The Soviet Union protested immediately that the balloons had "committed a gross violation of Soviet airspace." Within a few days the United States received similar protests from China, Mongolia, and all the countries of Eastern Europe. Soviet lawyers insisted that sovereignty had no upper limit, and that the Soviet Union accordingly had the right to forbid foreign overflights of Soviet territory at any height.[23] The question of sovereignty in space had been debated for a few years, by lawyers and in the popular press, but this was the first event calling for an answer.

Secretary of State John Foster Dulles maintained the government's standard position. Asked at a press conference about the international law governing the balloons and other possible satellites, Dulles—one of the most experienced international lawyers of the era—professed utter ignorance. "I wish I could tell you," he apologized, "but that whole subject, as somebody once said about Russia, 'is a mystery wrapped in an enigma.'" Whether nations were sovereign over their upper airspace "is a disputable question," Dulles explained. "In the main, it is a recognized practice to avoid putting up into the air anything which could interfere with any normal use of the air by anybody else," but beyond that, "the legal position is quite obscure." After insisting that the balloons were simply gathering information about air currents, and that they were not bothering anyone, Dulles returned one more time to the sovereignty question. "What the legal position is," he concluded, "I wouldn't feel in a position to answer, because I do not believe that the legal position has even been codified, you might say."[24]

Yet if Dulles was careful not to admit that the United States had done anything wrong, he was equally careful to avoid making any claim that the United States was in the right. "This studied hesitancy," one law professor remarked shortly afterward, "may perhaps be interpreted as a euphemistic admission that the United States did not have an absolute right to fly these camera-carrying balloons over the territory of another State."[25] The United States called off the balloon program after the Soviet complaint, which further suggests an implicit American concession that nations were sovereign at least to fifty thousand feet, at least with respect to overflights for reconnaissance.

The following year the Soviet Union launched *Sputnik I,* the first artificial satellite. *Sputnik* traveled in an elliptical orbit, inclined 65 degrees to the equator, that took 96 minutes to complete. It passed over the United States several times each day, but at much higher altitudes than any craft the United States had ever sent over the Soviet Union. At its closest point to earth, *Sputnik* was 145 miles away; at its farthest, 560 miles away. The news of *Sputnik* of course raised all sorts of alarms about the ability of the United States to compete with the Soviet Union. It also, inevitably, raised the sovereignty question. Was *Sputnik* infringing other nations' airspace?[26]

The initial Soviet answer was that *Sputnik* could not be violating the sovereignty of any state, "because it does not fly into the space over other states. Instead, the territories of those states, by dint of the earth's rotation, pass so to speak under the satellite's orbit." This statement was roundly ridiculed in the American press. Soon after, it was replaced by a different view, that air sovereignty ended somewhere between twelve and eighteen miles above the earth. By 1958, Soviet writers had shifted to a third position, the same agnosticism maintained by the American government. "There are no definite norms of international law with respect to cosmic space," they insisted. "Both Western international jurists and juridical-science representatives of the people's democracy write frankly about this." In the absence of any prohibition, "any state can freely use interplanetary space and can launch its satellites and rockets therein without requesting permission for this from other states."[27] Legal uncertainty was useful to those with the power to act in space, on either side of the cold war.

As *Sputnik* beeped overhead, some nervous Americans thought it an affront to the sovereignty of the United States. A city councilman in Texas was reported to have introduced a resolution prohibiting Russian satellites from flying over his city. But members of the legal academic and defense communities viewed the legal implications of *Sputnik* more benignly. The Soviet Union had not complained in 1955 when the United States announced its intention to develop a similar satellite, Eugène Pépin noted, so *Sputnik* could be viewed as an explicit confirmation of an earlier tacit agreement between the two nations to orbital overflights. "It is widely agreed by international lawyers," reported two of them, "that the United States, by assuming its present prominent role in the satellite program of the International Geophysical Year, has put the world on notice of its understanding that all space at and beyond the altitude of satellite operation is 'free' space . . . not subject to control in any degree by a single nation." Indeed, while *Sputnik* came as a shock to cold war propagandists and much of the public, it must have come as something of a relief to government lawyers, who had feared that the Soviet Union would protest overflights by the much-anticipated American satellite, and who recognized that by launching *Sputnik* first the Soviets had in effect waived any right to complain.[28]

The United States placed a satellite of its own into orbit a few months after *Sputnik*. By mid-1958 both the Soviet Union and the United States had multiple satellites circling the earth, regularly passing over the territories of several nations, including each other. None of the countries below had protested. Lawyers understood that a new rule of international law had come into existence. "The present satellite flights appear to be sanctioned by an implied international agreement," declared George Feldman, chief counsel to the House Select Committee on Astronautics and Space Exploration. He found this agreement in "the acquiescence of other governments in the announcements by the United States and the U.S.S.R. that satellites would be launched." Oscar Schachter, who had become director of the United Nations legal division, agreed that "these principles are now beginning to be accepted as a practical basis for a new law of space. Five satellites have been placed in orbit, and both the U.S. and the U.S.S.R. have acted on the assumption that their right to place these satellites in orbit for peaceful purposes is not dependent on the consent of any subjacent state—a position which by necessary implication rejects for outer space the concept of territorial sovereignty which applies to the airspace below." In light of the satellites, a committee of the American Bar Association recognized, "wherever the theoretical 'boundary' between airspace and outer space was, it would be below the perigee of existing satellites."[29]

In September 1959, when the Soviet Union landed an unmanned spaceship on the moon, the United States immediately declared that the moon did not thereby come within the sovereignty of the Soviet Union. Characteristically, the State Department would not go so far as to say that a nation could never exercise sovereignty over the moon. The government had "no views on how far you would have to go" to claim the moon, a State Department lawyer explained. All he would concede was that "sovereignty doesn't mean anything without possession," and that the Soviet Union had not succeeded in possessing the moon. But if the State Department was interested in preserving the right to possess the moon at a later date, international opinion seemed to reject the notion of lunar sovereignty. Dag Hammarskjold, secretary general of the United Nations, declared that celestial bodies ought not to be appropriated by any nation. More important, the Soviet Union itself denied any intent to claim sovereignty over the moon.[30] Once again, an international legal regime for outer space was emerging from actual practice, a regime in which national sovereignty did not extend as far from earth as the moon.

Less than a year later, the Soviet Union shot down a U-2 reconnaissance plane flown by the American pilot Francis Gary Powers. The Soviet government claimed Powers was flying 12.5 miles above Soviet territory. According to the American government, Powers was at an altitude of 20 miles. Either way, Powers's capture raised the sovereignty question yet again. "What are the rights of high flight?" asked *Time* magazine. Powers had "entered into an area of international law as unexplored and uncertain as outer space itself." Some argued that Soviet sovereignty had not been infringed because Powers had flown above, not through, Soviet airspace. But most commentators acknowledged that "however high it may have been, there can be no doubt but that the U-2 was in Soviet airspace." Through the long period of U.S.-Soviet squabbling that followed the incident, the United States never contended that Powers had flown above the ceiling of Soviet sovereignty, and, soon after, the United States stopped flying reconnaissance planes over Soviet territory. This conduct was most reasonably interpreted as an implicit American concession that sovereignty extended at least as high as the U-2 had flown. The U.S. government no doubt had an eye toward possible Soviet overflights of its own territory. Both nations, in any event, were able within a short time to do their spying from satellites rather than planes.[31]

By 1960, the U.S.-Soviet rivalry in space had given rise to exactly the sort of customary international law expected by Myres

McDougal and other lawyers a few years before. Airplanes and balloons, even at altitudes as great as twenty miles, were acknowledged as invasions of sovereignty, but satellites, which orbited at altitudes measured in hundreds of miles, were not. Like any body of customary law, the emerging law of space could be criticized for its vagueness and its susceptibility to change at the behest of the powerful. Some wondered where exactly the line could be drawn between the planes and the satellites. Others wondered what would happen if technological change led to very high planes or very low satellites, or even aircraft that combined features of both and flew in the gray area between twenty and a hundred miles. And what if the United States or the Soviet Union changed its policy and began interfering with previously permitted flights of the other?[32]

But Morton Jaffe, an American military lawyer, surely had a clearer view of the matter in his 1962 address to the International Astronautical Congress. "Some years ago," Jaffe recalled, "many lawyer-scholars believed there was an urgent requirement for a definition of outer space." The issue had been debated for years, but "no agreement or formal delimitations of space boundaries resulted. The boundary question was found to be practically and intellectually insoluble." Space exploration had been conducted in a legal vacuum for a decade. And yet, Jaffe concluded, the world was not any poorer for the lack of a formal upper bound to national sovereignty. No one, for example, questioned that spaceships orbiting the earth "operated in space, while even sophisticated high powered and high flying jets, at over 13 miles altitude over land, are within the airspace subject to sovereignty." Flights to the moon or to the planets were universally recognized "as spatial or celestial efforts rather than pertaining to aeronautics and airspace." From years of experience, "we have learned in the

NASA officials show the innards of the TIROS-1 weather satellite to
Senator Lyndon Johnson, who seems to have other things on his mind.
TIROS-1, launched in April 1960, orbited the earth at an altitude of
450 miles, well above what the United States and the Soviet Union
had by then come to view as the upper limit of national sovereignty.
Photograph by Warren K. Leffler, LC-U9-4199-18, Prints and Photographs Division, Library of Congress.

absence of new international agreements what nations mean by
space." Custom alone had drawn the boundary between airspace
and outer space. "I am not sure," Jaffe concluded, "that if, in September 1957, the international lawyers had sat down to write a
comprehensive code of space law they would as effectively have
promoted the efficient progress of the technicians and astronauts
which has been achieved in the absence of such code."[33] In the
three years between *Sputnik* and the U-2 incident, the basic rules

of space had emerged from the cold war rivalry of the United States and the Soviet Union.

From the moment people began to debate the question of sovereignty in space, there had been calls for an international treaty under the auspices of the United Nations. If there was ever an issue that engaged every country in the world, if there was ever a topic that affected the planet as a whole, the control of outer space was it. These calls for an international agreement intensified in the late 1950s, after the launch of *Sputnik*. Several nations—including Sweden, Spain, France, Italy, Chile, and Canada—urged the United Nations to decide the altitude at which state sovereignty would end. Secretary General Dag Hammarskjold pressed for an international agreement clarifying that outer space could not be appropriated by any nation.[34] Yet the UN did very little until the early 1960s. By the time nations formally agreed to rules governing sovereignty in space, their agreements only ratified the practices that the United States and the Soviet Union had already established.

In 1958 the United Nations created an ad hoc Committee on the Peaceful Uses of Outer Space, consisting of eighteen countries, including the United States and the Soviet Union. Before the committee convened, however, the Soviet Union refused to participate, on the ground that not enough socialist countries were members. The Soviet Union's complaint prompted the withdrawal of Poland, Czechoslovakia, India, and Egypt, which left a committee dominated by the United States and its allies. The committee's report the following year to the General Assembly unsurprisingly concluded that "the determination of precise limits for air space and outer space did not present a legal problem calling for priority consideration at this moment." The committee instead reflected the views of the United States in determining that "further experience might lead to the acceptance of precise limits through a rule of customary law."[35]

Once that customary law began to crystallize, the United States and the Soviet Union both became more willing to enter into formal international agreements. By 1962 Secretary of State Dean Rusk declared that "the right time to subject activities in space to international law and supervision is now, before possibly untoward developments occur," and his Soviet counterparts likewise emphasized the importance of formal law. "Custom has had its role in the development of space law," explained Abram Chayes, the State Department's legal advisor. "But custom is slow to accumulate and its teaching cannot always be read with clarity." Sounding nothing like his predecessor from only a few years before, Chayes concluded that it was time "for codification and for explicit formulation in this newest branch of law."[36] Both nations accordingly began to work in earnest on reaching an international agreement regarding sovereignty in space.

The first move in that direction was a December 1961 resolution unanimously adopted by the General Assembly. The resolution provided that "outer space and celestial bodies are free for exploration and use by all States in conformity with international law and are not subject to national appropriation." Two years later, the General Assembly approved a more detailed statement to the same effect: "Outer space and celestial bodies are not subject to national appropriation by claim of sovereignty, by means of use or occupation, or by any other means." These resolutions were supported by the two space powers. By the early 1960s it was clear enough that trying to exert sovereignty in outer space or on the moon was not worth the extraordinary cost and effort. The United States and the Soviet Union were primarily interested in maintaining reconnaissance satellites in orbit. Claims of sovereignty from other nations would only make that task harder.[37]

Ultimately these negotiations resulted in the Outer Space Treaty of 1967, which was signed by almost every nation in the world, including the big two.[38] Modeled on the earlier resolutions of the General Assembly, article 2 of the treaty provided that "outer space, including the moon and other celestial bodies, is not subject to national appropriation by claim of sovereignty, by means of use or occupation, or by any other means." Other provisions required the exploration of outer space to be conducted for the benefit of all countries, mandated freedom of scientific investigation in outer space, and barred nuclear weapons and other weapons of mass destruction from outer space.[39]

Like the customary law it codified, the Outer Space Treaty did not define "outer space," so there was still no clear answer to the question of where the sovereign airspace ended and outer space began. "I think all we can say is that an object in orbit is in outer space," Rusk explained to the Senate Foreign Relations Committee. "If we were to try to find a precise definition, there might be at this point still some very complex issues in knowing where to draw that ceiling, that dividing line, between outer space and national space." Fortunately, in Rusk's view, "there seem to be few actual problems whose actual determination depends on the limits of outer space and sovereign space."[40] Nothing flew in the gray area above planes and below satellites, so there was no need for the treaty to be any more exact.

Satellites have lost their glamour. Now we take them for granted —for communication, for navigation, for defense, and for a host of other tasks that would have seemed astonishing when the

Outer Space Treaty was ratified. Once satellites were on the frontier of science; now they are a routine business.

The question of sovereignty in space has lost its allure as well. Identifying the boundary between airspace and outer space seemed very important in the 1950s and 1960s. It was a cutting-edge legal question, one that was simultaneously fundamental to the law of the entire world and associated with a brand new, thrilling field of endeavor. All the lawyers who rushed to offer their opinions can hardly be blamed. What could be more exciting than space law? Yet forty years after the Outer Space Treaty, as satellites have filled the sky, the boundary question is no closer to being answered. Planes are still trespassers in other countries' airspace, satellites can still orbit the earth freely, and there is still no clear line between the two. Today, though, few worry about the lack of a precise boundary. The near consensus among present-day space lawyers is that the world has gotten along perfectly well without a boundary, that it will continue to do so for the foreseeable future, and that it is hard to imagine what all the fuss was about.[41]

The occasional challenges to the current system have been easily rebuffed. In 1979 the Soviet Union proposed setting a boundary by treaty at an altitude of 100 to 120 kilometers (approximately 62 to 75 miles) above sea level. The idea lingered for years on the agenda of the United Nations without going anywhere. A different sort of challenge arose in 1976, when eight equatorial nations proclaimed sovereignty over segments of the geosynchronous orbit, the corridor of space 22,300 miles above the equator in which a satellite will orbit the earth at the same rate at which the earth rotates and thus appear stationary with respect to the earth. Satellites in geosynchronous orbit are extremely useful, but only so many can fit without interfering with one another. The eight nations who claimed sovereignty over their sections of the geosynchronous orbit (Brazil, Colombia, Congo, Ecuador, Indonesia, Kenya, Uganda, and Zaire) were primarily motivated by the fear that the first countries capable of launching satellites would fill up the orbit before poorer nations could acquire satellites of their own. The concept of national sovereignty at an altitude of 22,300 miles was overwhelmingly rejected by the countries represented in the UN's Committee on the Peaceful Uses of Outer Space, including the United States and the Soviet Union.[42]

Sovereignty in space is thus still governed by the customary law that grew out of the cold war in the late 1950s and was ratified by the Outer Space Treaty in the late 1960s. Fifty years earlier, the question of sovereignty in the air had been resolved in just the same way—by an international treaty that ratified the wartime practice of the most powerful countries. National sovereignty over airspace is a product of sovereign power, but then so too is the absence of national sovereignty over outer space.

TEN

Technological Change and Legal Change

Today the air is full of flying things. Commercial jumbo jets, news helicopters, small private planes, model rockets—they and many more have to share a sky that once seemed infinite. With each new use of the air, the law had to adjust. Our airspace came to be divided both vertically and horizontally into several zones, with different rules governing each.

This book has told the first chapter of that story, the allocation of rights between users of the air and owners of the land. Before the airplane, although there were no cases actually raising the question, lawyers and judges often declared that landowners owned up to the heavens. Once the airplane came along, they gradually began to say instead that landowners owned only the airspace directly above the ground and that the rest of it was free for pilots to fly through. In the earliest years of flight, no one was quite sure whether there was an upper limit to national sovereignty. A few years' experience of military aviation persuaded almost everyone that sovereignty should extend at least as high as airplanes could fly. Many years later, when space flight became possible, there came to be a consensus that sovereignty should stop somewhere below the altitude at which satellites orbited the earth.

The law is constantly changing. Sometimes there are so many plausible reasons for any given legal change that it can be difficult to apportion causal weight to each, but these changes seem pretty clearly to have been caused by the invention of new ways of flying. The story of airspace thus provides a good occasion for reflecting on the relationship between technological change and legal change.

Before the airplane, it was possible to utilize the airspace above someone else's land, but none of the methods of doing so was particularly useful. One could fly in a balloon, for example, but balloons were never a practical way of getting from one place to another. One could string telegraph or telephone wires above other people's land, but there was no need to bother landowners when wires could be strung almost as easily above public streets instead. Whatever benefits might flow from using the airspace above land owned by another were tiny, while the burdens such use would impose on landowners could be quite serious. Property in the space above land was allocated to the landowner, because it was reasonable to assume that landowners collectively valued that space more than potential trespassers did.

That balance of costs and benefits was transformed by the airplane, which made the space above other people's land much more useful than it had been before. Now the gains from overflights exceeded the losses that would be collectively suffered by landowners. The imbalance grew larger over time, as planes were able to fly higher (and thus imposed fewer costs on landowners in terms of noise and other annoyances) and farther (and thus became even more valuable for transportation). The upper airspace accordingly changed from a zone owned, nominally at least, by landowners, to a commons free for pilots to fly through.

The airspace story is thus a nice example of a process first identified, at least in the academic world, by the economist Harold Demsetz, who suggested that new property rights will emerge in response to changes in the relative costs and benefits of establishing them.[1] Demsetz in fact included the evolution of rights to airspace as a possible example of this process, one deserving of further study. Most such changes in property rights have involved the establishment of new property rights in assets that were formerly commons used by many or by all, but airspace was a rare example of a commons emerging from a regime of property rights. The people who wrote about airplanes in their early years certainly shared Demsetz's intuition, if not his vocabulary. They too believed that the airplane had rendered the *cujus est solum* maxim a losing proposition, because airspace had now become much more valuable as a highway for airplanes.

The property story and the sovereignty story began identically, with the invention of the airplane, but they ended differently. The owner of land ended up without the right to exclude aircraft from flying overhead, except at very low altitudes. Nations, by contrast, ended up *with* the right to exclude foreign aircraft from flying overhead, except at extremely high altitudes. In the airspace used most frequently, from a few hundred feet up to several miles, nations have a power that individuals lack. How can we explain this difference?

One kind of explanation would assert that nations and individuals have different interests. Nations, on this account, are concerned with security against military opponents, while individuals are primarily interested in peace and quiet, and national security is simply more important. The error here is the assumption that the interests of nations and individuals differ. A nation is an aggregation of individuals. To say that a nation has an interest in protecting its airspace from enemies is equivalent to saying that the nation's residents collectively have that same interest, and to say that an individual has an interest in being free from overhead annoyances is equivalent, if that concern is shared by everyone else (as it surely is), to saying that such is the national interest. Neither individuals nor nations would like to have bombs dropped from overhead, and neither individuals nor nations would like frequent noisy overflights. Both have an interest—the same interest—in excluding unwanted aircraft from flying overhead.

A better explanation, one based on the work of the economist Ronald Coase, would emphasize the importance of "transaction costs," the costs in time and money of entering into and enforcing agreements.[2] In an imaginary world without transaction costs, giving landowners the right to exclude aircraft would not have affected the quantity of aviation. Each pilot could have negotiated the right to fly over each parcel of land. Most landowners would likely have been happy to sell the right of passage overhead, because the planes were not much of a bother, and most pilots would likely have been willing to pay, because the price of flying over any given parcel of land would almost certainly have been very small. The world's overall gains from air travel far exceeded the losses suffered by landowners. Most of those losses were trivial, except those borne by the people living near airports, but even their losses were far smaller than all the benefits associated with the airplane. Landowners, meanwhile, were simultaneously beneficiaries of aviation as passengers, senders and recipients of mail, and consumers of products that could be flown from a distance, so even the worst-off landowners received some offsetting gains. Everyone was either a net gainer or a net loser from the airplane.

In a world without transaction costs, compensation would have flowed from the winners to the losers, and after the losers were compensated there would have been a lot left over.

This is of course an extremely unrealistic scenario, as many noted in the early twentieth century, because the transaction costs of such a system would have been enormous. It would have been impossible for aviators to stop at each property line and negotiate with the owner of the parcel below. One can imagine various methods of streamlining the process, such as gathering all the landowners and all the aviators and hammering out a collective agreement among them, but even then the costs of reaching such an agreement would have been prohibitive, because the number of landowners was so huge. Even using the government's power of eminent domain to condemn the airspace, a solution that was seriously proposed in the early years of flight, would have been far too costly to implement. Aviation simply would not have worked had landowners been accorded the right to exclude planes from their airspace, because transaction costs would have prevented landowners from selling that right to aviators in large enough numbers. Instead we changed our property law. We stopped saying that landowners owned all the way up to the sky, and we allowed planes to fly over private property.

With sovereignty, the transaction costs were much lower. The number of sovereign nations is very small, much smaller than the number of landowners. In the early twentieth century it was even smaller. It was feasible for nations to negotiate with one another about the types of overflights they would allow or forbid. Giving nations the right to exclude foreign aircraft was thus not the insuperable obstacle to aviation that the corresponding right given to property owners would have been. Had the world been divided into millions of tiny countries, perhaps we would have ended up with a sovereignty rule identical to our current property rule. Had landowners numbered in the tens rather than the millions, perhaps we would have ended up with a property rule identical to our current sovereignty rule.

Thinking about the story this way suggests the importance of transaction costs in driving legal change generally. If markets could operate costlessly, the new balance of gains and losses brought about by technological change could be accommodated entirely through private transactions. There would be no need for the law ever to change in response to technological change. It is the costliness of transacting that prevents people from purchasing the ability to do what new technology permits, which in turn impels them to seek a change in the law transferring that ability to them. The early aviation writers knew this very well, even if they did not express it in precisely this way.

Changes in aviation influenced changes in law, but legal change also influenced the world of aviation. Except in the very earliest years of flight, there was never much doubt that the law would adjust to permit airplanes to fly. Airplanes were simply too useful to let the law stand in the way. But *how* the law would change was a question with many possible answers, and the choice of answers played a role in shaping some familiar aspects of the aviation industry.

Airports, for example, are usually located far from city centers. One reason is to avoid infringing the rights of landowners. Had the judges and legislators of the early twentieth century declared that landowners lacked any property rights in the lower airspace—a view of the law that was pushed by the aviation industry in the 1930s, and one that was not put to rest until the Supreme

Court's 1946 *Causby* decision—airports would have had less fear
of being sued by their neighbors. The neighbors might have based
their suits on the law of nuisance instead, but at the time the law
of aerial nuisance was just as much in the process of creation as
the law of aerial trespass. Had these legal decisions been made
differently at midcentury, airports might be much closer to cities
than they are today. They couldn't be surrounded by tall buildings, like many train stations are, because of the space needed for
takeoffs and landings, but they wouldn't have to be quite so far
away. Landowners exchanged one inconvenience, the noise and
potential danger of low overflights, for another, the difficulty of
getting to and from the airport. Technological change, in the form
of the developing nature of the aviation industry, was driving legal change, but meanwhile that very legal change was one of the
forces causing the industry to develop the way it did.

In deciding where to locate the dividing line between the private airspace near the ground and the public thoroughfare above,
courts and legislatures were in effect allocating the burden of air
travel between air carriers and landowners. The airplane had obvious benefits, but who would pay the costs? Farmers like the
Causby family or operators of airports? People like the Hinmans,
the unfortunate couple who lived next door to Burbank Airport,
or airlines like Pacific Air Transport, which routed its planes directly over the Hinmans' house? The aerial trespass issue was often
debated in terms of whether or not planes would be permitted to
fly, but lurking not far beneath the discourse was an important
distributional question. Who would pay the price? The higher
that courts located the ceiling on the landowner's right to exclude
aircraft, the more the burden would shift from landowners to the
aviation industry, and ultimately to the passengers and shippers
who were the industry's primary customers. Again, while the in-

vention of new ways to fly was giving rise to new law, that new law was in turn helping to shape the nature of aviation. The arrow of causation between legal and technological change pointed in both directions at once.

An arrow may be the wrong metaphor, though, because the path from point A to point B was hardly a straight one. There were any number of routes from the pre-airplane world of *cujus est solum* to the post-airplane world of routine overflights. The lawyers and others who created air law in the twentieth century were not blank slates. They were not calculators toting up the costs and benefits of alternative systems of regulation. They were human beings immersed in their culture, whose minds were full of ideas, some of which long predated the invention of the airplane. These ideas constrained their actions. As legislators, they could not simply declare that planes had a right to fly over private property, for fear that the preexisting ground rules of the legal system would require the government to compensate landowners. As lobbyists, they could not simply urge Congress to pass a law authorizing overflights, because of their doubts as to whether Congress had that power. As theorists, their knowledge of the law governing the ocean predisposed them against sovereignty over the air, and later their knowledge of the law governing the air predisposed them in favor of a sharp dividing line between airspace and outer space. In the terminology of historians of technology, the story is less one of technological determinism, in which legal change was driven by technological change in a simple and direct way, than one of contingency, in which the course of legal change was determined by a host of factors, of which technological change was only one.[3] To get from point A to point B required an extraordinarily convoluted journey that took half a century to complete. Broader trends in legal thought pulled the road this way and that and put up barriers here and there. The finish line may not have been all that far from the start, if the trip could have been taken directly. But it was not taken directly at all.

In the end, every country in the world settled on the same basic rules. Everywhere the government was sovereign over the airspace, and the property rights of landowners ended where planes flew. The earliest writers on the subject, lawyers like Charles C. Moore and Eugene Angert, expected as much. They knew that planes would fly over private property. The difficult question was not *whether* the law would change but *how*.

ABBREVIATIONS

HHL   Herbert Hoover Presidential Library, West Branch, Iowa
LC   Library of Congress, Manuscript Division, Washington, D.C.
NUA   Northwestern University Archives, Evanston, Illinois
YUL   Yale University Library, Manuscripts and Archives, New Haven, Connecticut

ONE: A MOMENTOUS PROBLEM

1. *West Publishing Co. v. Edward Thompson Co.*, 169 F. 833, 858 (E.D.N.Y. 1909); Charles C. Moore, *A Treatise on Facts, or, The Weight and Value of Evidence* (Northport, N.Y.: Edward Thompson Co., 1908); Charles C. Moore, "The Woman Lawyer," *Green Bag* 26 (1914): 525; *New York Times*, 15 Jan. 1931, 23.

2. Charles C. Moore, "Aërial Navigation," *Law Notes* 4 (1900): 87–88.

3. "In Vacation," *Virginia Law Register* 8 (1902): 151.

4. Arthur F. Gotthold, "A New Problem of the Law," *Green Bag* 15 (1903): 290.

5. A very short biography of Angert can be found at *Journal of Air Law* 9 (1938): 460, appended to the reprinting of his 1907 essay.

Angert's unusual death is described in the online finding aid to his papers at the Missouri Historical Society in St. Louis, available at http://www.mohistory.org/content/LibraryAndResearch/DownloadFiles/GuideA_C.pdf.

6. E. H. A. [Eugene H. Angert], "A Closed Chapter in Aeritime Law," *Green Bag* 19 (1907): 708–712.

7. "Current Topics," *Youth's Companion* 77 (1903): 554.

8. W. J. Jackman and Thomas H. Russell, *Flying Machines: Construction and Operation* (Chicago: Charles C. Thompson Co., 1910), 169–171; Henry C. Spurr, "Let the Air Remain Free," *Case and Comment* 18 (1911): 119; "Passing of Air Ship over Property as Trespass," *Case and Comment* 19 (1913): 681–682.

9. Gus C. Edwards, *Legal Laughs: A Joke for Every Jury,* 2nd ed. (Clarkesville, Ga.: Legal Publishing Co., 1915), 46; Philip Ambrose, "Landowner vs. Aviator," *Harper's Weekly,* 25 Dec. 1909, 10.

10. Alfred G. Reeves, *A Treatise on the Law of Real Property* (Boston: Little, Brown, and Co., 1909), 1:113; Melvin L. Severy, *Gillette's Industrial Solution: World Corporation* (Boston: Ball Publishing Co., 1908), 133.

11. George W. Platt, "The Airship—A Trespasser?" *Ohio Law Reporter* 7 (1909): 403.

12. "Aeronauts and the Law of Trespass," *Engineering* 87 (1909): 794.

13. H. G. Meyer, "Trespass by Aeroplane," *Law Magazine and Review,* 5th series, 36 (1910): 20–23.

14. B. Baden-Powell, "Law in the Air: A Momentous Problem for Legislators," *National Review* 53 (1909): 84.

15. "Want Laws to Give the Right to Fly," *New York Times,* 10 Jan. 1909, C3; "The Law of Aviation," *Los Angeles Times,* 18 Oct. 1910, II–4; "Trespass on a Landowner's Air," *Literary Digest,* 3 July 1909, 14.

16. *Penruddock's Case,* 77 Eng. Rep. 210 (1598); *Baten's Case,* 77 Eng. Rep. 810 (1610); Edward Coke, *The First Part of the Institutes of the Laws of England,* 15th ed. (1628; London: E. and R. Brooke, 1794),

1:4a; William Blackstone, *Commentaries on the Laws of England,* 10th ed. (1765–1769; London: A. Strahan, 1787), 2:18.

17. William Cruise, *A Digest of the Laws of England Respecting Real Property* (London: J. Butterworth, 1804–1807), 1:3; Nathan Dane, *A General Abridgment and Digest of American Law* (Boston: Cummings, Hilliard and Co., 1823–1829), 4:500; James Kent, *Commentaries on American Law* (New York: O. Halsted, 1826–1830), 3:321; Joseph Chitty, *The Practice of the Law in All Its Departments,* 2nd ed. (Philadelphia: P. H. Nicklin and T. Johnson, 1835–1839), 1:179; Francis Hilliard, *An Abridgment of the American Law of Real Property* (Boston: C. C. Little and J. Brown, 1838–1839), 1:3; John Bouvier, *Institutes of American Law* (Philadelphia: R. E. Peterson, 1851), 2:156; James T. Hoyt, *Mechanics' Liens* (New York: P. F. McBreen, 1881), 106; Earl P. Hopkins, *Handbook on the Law of Real Property* (St. Paul, Minn.: West Publishing Co., 1896), 4.

18. E. S. M., "Horizontal Divisions of Land," *American Law Register* 10 (1862): 577.

19. *Aiken v. Benedict,* 39 Barb. 400 (N.Y. 1863); *Tillmes v. Marsh,* 67 Pa. 507 (1871); *Smith v. Smith,* 110 Mass. 302 (1872); *Rasch v. Noth,* 74 N.W. 820 (Wis. 1898); *Norwalk Heating and Lighting Co. v. Vernam,* 55 A. 168 (Conn. 1903); *Murphy v. Bolger Brothers,* 15 A. 365, 367 (Vt. 1888); *Reimer's Appeal,* 100 Pa. 182 (1882); *Wilmarth v. Woodcock,* 25 N.W. 475 (Mich. 1885); *Shrago v. Gulley,* 93 S.E. 458 (N.C. 1917); *Corbett v. Hill,* 9 Eq. 671 (1870).

20. *Lemmon v. Webb,* [1891–1894] All ER Rep. 749 (1894); *Lyman v. Hale,* 11 Conn. 177 (1836); *Hoffman v. Armstrong,* 48 N.Y. 201 (1872).

21. "The Law of Trespass," *Game Bag and Gun* 11 (1878): 390; *Herrin v. Sutherland,* 241 P. 328, 332 (Mont. 1925).

22. *Ellis v. Loftus Iron Co.,* 10 C.P. 10 (1874); *Hannabalson v. Sessions,* 90 N.W. 93, 95 (Iowa 1902); "Trespass—Entry above Surface—Firing Projectiles Across Land," *Columbia Law Review* 23 (1923): 402.

23. William L. Scott and Milton P. Jarnagin, *A Treatise upon the Law*

of Telegraphs (Boston: Little, Brown, and Co., 1868), 33–44; Robert Luther Thompson, *Wiring a Continent: The History of the Telegraph Industry in the United States, 1832–1866* (Princeton: Princeton University Press, 1947); *Electric Telegraph Co. v. Overseers of the Poor of the Township of Salford*, 156 Eng. Rep. 795, 797 (1855).

24. *Butler v. Frontier Telephone Co.*, 79 N.E. 716, 718 (N.Y. 1906).

25. Theodore F. C. Demarest, *The Rise and Growth of Elevated Railroad Law* (New York: Baker, Voorhis and Co., 1894), 3; *Metropolitan West Side Elevated Railroad Co. v. Springer*, 49 N.E. 416, 418 (Ill. 1897).

26. *Pickering v. Rudd*, 171 Eng. Rep. 70 (1815).

27. *Saunders v. Smith* (1838), reprinted in *American Jurist and Law Magazine* 21 (1839): 221, 225; *Bagram v. Karformah*, 3 Bengal L. Rep. 18, 43 (1869); "Liability for Acts of Animals," *Albany Law Journal* 11 (1875): 145 (discussing a recent article in the *Solicitors' Journal*); "Unnecessary Exposure to Danger," *Central Law Journal* 27 (1888): 278; H. S. Theobald, *The Law of Land* (London: William Clowes and Sons, 1902), 55.

28. *Aiken v. Benedict*, 39 Barb. 400 (N.Y. 1863); *Tillmes v. Marsh*, 67 Pa. 507, 512 (1871).

29. Chauncey Hackett, "Rights in Air Space and Lord Ellenborough's Dictum," *Virginia Law Review* 10 (1924): 312–316; *Kenyon v. Hart*, 122 Eng. Rep. 1188 (1865); "Trespass by a Balloon in the Air," *American Law Review* 20 (1886): 560 (discussing a recent article in the *Law Journal* of London); "Notes," *Albany Law Journal* 38 (1888): 204 (reprinting a recent article from the *Law Journal* of London); Henry T. Terry, *Some Leading Principles of Anglo-American Law* (Philadelphia: T. and J. W. Johnson and Co., 1884), 379.

30. Frederick Pollock, *The Law of Torts* (London: Stevens and Sons, 1887), 281–282.

31. Francis H. Bohlen, *Cases on the Law of Torts* (Indianapolis: Bobbs-Merrill Co., 1915), 1:40; *Guille v. Swan*, 19 Johns. 381 (N.Y. 1822); "Aeronauts, Attention!" *American Lawyer* 12 (1904): 2; "Humor-

ous Phases of the Law," *Albany Law Journal* 2 (1870): 167; Irving Browne, "The Balloon and the Garden-Sauce," *Green Bag* 1 (1889): 282.

32. Herbert Spencer, *Justice* (London: Williams and Norgate, 1891), 80–81; Henry George, *A Perplexed Philosopher* (New York: Charles L. Webster and Co., 1892), 196–198.

33. Boyd Henry Bode, *An Outline of Logic* (New York: Henry Holt and Co., 1910), 33–36.

34. "The Air Space as Corporeal Realty," *Harvard Law Review* 29 (1916): 525–528.

35. Stuart S. Ball, "Division into Horizontal Strata of the Landspace above the Surface," *Yale Law Journal* 39 (1930): 616–658; Laird Bell, "Air Rights," *Illinois Law Review* 23 (1928): 261; Theodore Schmidt, "Public Utility Air Rights," *Journal of Air Law* 1 (1930): 56; Nathan William MacChesney, "The Developing Law of the Air," *Nebraska Law Bulletin* 8 (1929): 56, 59.

36. Robert Wohl, *A Passion for Wings: Aviation and the Western Imagination, 1908–1918* (New Haven: Yale University Press, 1994); Laurence Goldstein, *The Flying Machine and Modern Literature* (Bloomington: Indiana University Press, 1986); Victor Appleton [pseud.], *Tom Swift and His Great Searchlight* (New York: Grosset and Dunlap, 1912), 127.

37. Herbert Quick, *Virginia of the Air Lanes* (Indianapolis: Bobbs-Merrill Co., 1909), 365–381.

38. John Haffenden, *William Empson: Among the Mandarins* (Oxford: Oxford University Press, 2005), 43–47.

39. Wayne C. Williams, "The Law of the Air," *Case and Comment* 18 (1911): 131.

40. "Airships—A Legal Problem," *Solicitors' Journal and Weekly Reporter* 51 (1907): 771; "The Right to the Atmosphere," *The Bar* 15 (1908): 41.

41. "Rights and Liabilities of Aviators," *Maine Law Review* 4 (1910): 58; "Moot Court: John Seligman v. William Thorpe," *Dickinson Law*

Review 14 (1910): 256–260; *Case and Comment* 18 (Aug. 1911); "Thirty-Five Little Questions for the Aviator," *Literary Digest,* 5 Apr. 1919, 58.

42. "Legal Problems of Aeronautics," *Bench and Bar* 18 (1909): 50; Rollin Lynde Hartt, "The Aerial Age," *Outlook,* 26 Mar. 1919, 520; J. B. Mackenzie, "Aerial Navigation and the Law Which Should Govern It," *Canada Law Journal* 47 (1911): 208–209.

43. Simeon E. Baldwin, "The Law of the Air-Ship," *American Journal of International Law* 4 (1910): 95, 97; Frederick H. Jackson, *Simeon Eben Baldwin: Lawyer, Social Scientist, Statesman* (New York: Columbia University Press, 1955), 75–77.

TWO: AN AERIAL TERRITORY

1. Paul Fauchille, "Le Domaine Aérien et le Régime Juridique des Aérostats," *Révue Générale de Droit International Public* 8 (1901): 414.

2. Norman Bentwich, "Espionage and Scientific Invention," *Journal of the Society of Comparative Legislation* 10 (1909): 249; Lucien Chessex, "Du Domaine Aérien et de sa Réglementation Juridique," *Journal du Droit International Privé* 36 (1909): 685 (translating and summarizing Alexander Meyer, *Die Erschliessung der Luftraumes in ihren Rechtlichen Folgen* [Frankfurt, 1909]); Denys P. Myers, "The Criminal in the Air," *Journal of the American Institute of Criminal Law and Criminology* 4 (1914): 815–816.

3. Harold D. Hazeltine, *The Law of the Air* (London: University of London Press, 1911), 9–41; Johanna F. Lycklama à Nijeholt, *Air Sovereignty* (The Hague: Martinus Nijhoff, 1910), 9–14; Martti Koskenniemi, *The Gentle Civilizer of Nations: The Rise and Fall of International Law, 1870–1960* (Cambridge: Cambridge University Press, 2002), 11–97; Mark Weston Janis, *The American Tradition of International Law: Great Expectations, 1789–1914* (Oxford: Clarendon Press, 2004), 117–154; Blewett Lee, "Sovereignty of the Air," *American Journal of International Law* 7 (1913): 471.

4. S. Jules Enthoven, "The Peace Conference at the Hague," *Law*

Magazine and Review 24 (1899): 458; George B. Davis, "The Launching of Projectiles from Balloons," *American Journal of International Law* 2 (1908): 528.

5. For example, Baron L. de Staël-Holstein, *La Réglementation de la Guerre des Airs* (The Hague: Martinus Nijhoff, 1911); *Armements et Aviation: Compte Rendu de la Conférence de l'Union Interparlementaire Tenue a Genève en 1912* (Paris: Libraire Ch. Delagrave, 1912); Jean Bellenger, *La Guerre Aérienne et le Droit International* (Paris: A. Pedone, 1912).

6. Jonathan Ziskind, "International Law and Ancient Sources: Grotius and Selden," *Review of Politics* 35 (1973): 537–559; David Armitage, *The Ideological Origins of the British Empire* (Cambridge: Cambridge University Press, 2000), 100–124; C. G. Roelofsen, "The Sources of *Mare Liberum:* The Contested Origins of the Doctrine of the Freedom of the Seas," in Wybo P. Heere, ed., *International Law and Its Sources* (Antwerp: Kluwer, 1988), 93–124; Richard Tuck, *Philosophy and Government, 1572–1651* (Cambridge: Cambridge University Press, 1993), 212–214.

7. Hugo Grotius, *The Freedom of the Seas* (originally published in 1608 under the Latin title *Mare Liberum*), trans. Ralph van Deman Magoffin, ed. James Brown Scott (New York: Oxford University Press, 1916), 27, 30, 34, 36–37.

8. John Selden, *Of the Dominion, or, Ownership of the Sea* (originally published in 1635 under the Latin title *Mare Clausum*), trans. Marchamont Nedham (London, 1652) (Clark, N.J.: The Lawbook Exchange, 2004), 27, 130.

9. W. E. Butler, "Grotius and the Law of the Sea," in Hedley Bull et al., eds., *Hugo Grotius and International Relations* (Oxford: Clarendon Press, 1990), 209–220.

10. Paul Fauchille, *Traité de Droit International Public* (Paris: Rousseau et Cie., 1921–1926).

11. Fauchille, "Le Domaine Aérien," 414–416.

12. Ibid., 425.

13. H. Brougham Leech, "The Jurisprudence of the Air," *Fortnightly Review* 92 (1912): 240–243.

14. Henry Wheaton, *Elements of International Law,* 2nd English ed. (London: Stevens and Sons, 1880), 251; Grotius, *Freedom of the Seas,* 28.

15. Édouard d'Hooghe, *Droit Aérien* (Paris: Librairie Administrative Paul Dupont, 1912), 8; Lee, "Sovereignty of the Air," 488; Joseph J. Corn, *The Winged Gospel: America's Romance with Aviation, 1900–1950* (New York: Oxford University Press, 1983), 37–38.

16. Norman Bentwich, "The Law of the Air," *Law Journal* 45 (1910): 402; Arthur K. Kuhn, "The Beginnings of an Aërial Law," *American Journal of International Law* 4 (1910): 113; G. D. Valentine, "The Air—A Realm of Law," *Juridical Review* 22 (1910): 19.

17. *Georgia v. Tennessee Copper Co.,* 206 U.S. 230, 238 (1907); Hazeltine, *Law of the Air,* 47; George Grafton Wilson, "Aerial Jurisdiction," *American Political Science Review* 5 (1911): 178.

18. J. E. G. De Montmorency, "The Control of Air Spaces," *Problems of the War* 3 (1917): 67–68; H. Erle Richards, *Sovereignty over the Air* (Oxford: Clarendon Press, 1912), 8; Valentine, "The Air," 20; Amos S. Hershey, "The International Law of Aerial Space," *American Journal of International Law* 6 (1912): 383; "Command of the Air," *Youth's Companion* 93 (1919): 318; Baden Baden-Powell, "Law in the Air: A Momentous Problem for Legislators," *National Review* 53 (1909): 81.

19. Lassa Oppenheim, *International Law: A Treatise,* 2nd ed. (London: Longmans, Green and Co., 1912), 237; Arthur K. Kuhn, "Aerial Navigation in Its Relation to International Law," *Proceedings of the American Political Science Association* 5 (1908): 87; Denys P. Myers, "The Sovereignty of the Air," *Green Bag* 24 (1912): 233; F. P., "Sovereignty over the Air," *Law Quarterly Review* 29 (1913): 1; Paul Fauchille, "La Circulation Aérienne et les Droits des États en Temps de Paix," *Revue Juridique Internationale de la Locomotion Aérienne* 1 (1910): 15.

20. G. D. Valentine, "Sovereignty or Freedom in the Atmosphere," *Juridical Review* 23 (1912): 336.

21. André Blachère, *L'Air: Voie de Communication et le Droit* (Paris: Librairie de la Société du Recueil Sirey, 1911), 128.

22. Hans Sperl, "The Legal Side of Aviation," *Green Bag* 23 (1912): 398; Myers, "Sovereignty of the Air," 230.

23. Georges Montenot, *La Circulation Aérienne Envisagée au Point de Vue Juridique* (Dijon: Imprimerie Jobard, 1911), 7; Lycklama à Nijeholt, *Air Sovereignty,* 15.

24. Paul Loubeyre, *Les Principes du Droit Aérien* (Paris: A. Pedone, 1911), 165; Berkeley Davids, *The Law of Motor Vehicles* (Northport, N.Y.: Edward Thompson Co., 1911), 287; Hazeltine, *Law of the Air,* 48–49.

25. A. van Hemert Engert, review of J. de Louter, *Het Stellig Volkenrecht, American Journal of International Law* 5 (1911): 837.

26. Alexandre Mérignhac, *Le Domaine Aerien Privé et Public* (Paris: A. Pedone, 1914), 4; Enrico Catellani, *Le Droit Aérien,* trans. Maurice Bouteloup (Paris: Librairie Nouvelle de Droit et de Jurisprudence, 1912), 6.

27. "Le Congrès de Vérone," *Revue Juridique Internationale de la Locomotion Aérienne* 1 (1910): 182.

28. Institut de Droit International, "Le Régime Juridique des Aérostats" (1911), http://www.idi-iil.org/idiF/resolutionsF/1911_mad _02_fr.pdf; *Premier Congrès du Comité Juridique International de l'Aviation* (Paris: A. Pedone, 1912); *Deuxième Congrès du Comité Juridique International de l'Aviation* (Paris: A. Pedone, 1912); *Troisième Congrès International de Législation Aérienne du Comité Juridique Internationale de l'Aviation* (Paris: Édition Aérienne, 1922). On the formation and activities of the Committee, see Joseph Hamel, *Le Droit Privé Aérien dans le Projet de Code International de l'Air* (Paris: Librairie Arthur Rousseau, 1923), 3–7.

29. John Cobb Cooper, "The International Air Navigation Conference, Paris 1910," *Journal of Air Law and Commerce* 19 (1952): 127–143.

30. Wilmot E. Ellis, "Aerial-Land and Aerial-Maritime Warfare," *American Journal of International Law* 8 (1914): 266; William M. Gibson, "The Development of International Air Law to 1919," *Temple Law*

Quarterly 5 (1931): 177–178; "Exchange of Notes between France and Germany concerning Aërial Navigation," *American Journal of International Law Supplement* 8 (1914): 214–217; A. Boutin, "La Liberté de l'Air," *Revue Juridique Internationale de la Locomotion Aérienne* 5 (1914): 28; G. G. P., "Aircraft in War," *Journal of the Society of Comparative Legislation* 15 (1915): 42.

31. A. Bowdoin Van Riper, *Imagining Flight: Aviation and Popular Culture* (College Station: Texas A&M University Press, 2004), 23–26; Alfred Tennyson, *The Poetical Works of Alfred Tennyson* (Boston: Ticknor and Fields, 1857), 192; H. G. Wells, *The War in the Air* (London: George Bell and Sons, 1908); Robert Wohl, *A Passion for Wings: Aviation and the Western Imagination, 1908–1918* (New Haven: Yale University Press, 1994), 69–94; John H. Morrow, Jr., *The Great War in the Air: Military Aviation from 1909 to 1921* (Washington, D.C.: Smithsonian Institution Press, 1993), 11–57.

32. J. M. Spaight, *Aircraft in Peace and the Law* (London: Macmillan and Co., 1919), 8, 10; J. E. G. de Montmorency, "Air-Space above Territorial Waters," *Journal of the Society of Comparative Legislation* 17 (1917): 174–175; Hugh H. L. Bellot, "The Sovereignty of the Air," *International Law Notes* 3 (1918): 138; Alexander McAdie, "The Freedom of the Skies," *Scientific American* 121 (1919): 84; M. W. Royse, "Who Owns the Air?" *Aviation* 10 (1921): 464.

33. Kenneth W. Colegrove, *International Control of Aviation* (Boston: World Peace Foundation, 1930), 59; *Convention for the Regulation of Aerial Navigation* (London: His Majesty's Stationery Office, 1922), 7; Arthur K. Kuhn, "International Aerial Navigation and the Peace Conference," *American Journal of International Law* 14 (1920): 372; William Latey, "The Law of the Air," *Transactions of the Grotius Society* 7 (1921): 73.

34. Blewett Lee, "The International Flying Convention and the Freedom of the Air," *Harvard Law Review* 33 (1919): 23–30 (for the text of the Convention), 38 (for Lee's opinion).

35. John C. Cooper, "United States Participation in Drafting Paris Convention, 1919," *Journal of Air Law and Commerce* 18 (1951): 266–

200, Rowan A. Greer, *International Aerial Regulations*, Air Service Information Circular No. 566 (Washington, D.C.: Government Printing Office, 1926), 7; *Aircraft: Hearing before the President's Aircraft Board* (Washington, D.C.: Government Printing Office, 1925), 1486; *Ninth Annual Report of the National Advisory Committee for Aeronautics* (Washington, D.C.: Government Printing Office, 1923), 14.

36. Edward P. Warner, "International Air Transport," *Foreign Affairs* 4 (1926): 278; Roger F. Williams, "Developments in Aerial Law," *University of Pennsylvania Law Review* 75 (1926): 148; James A. Constantin, "Multilateralism in International Aviation," *Southern Economic Journal* 16 (1949): 202; Peter H. Sand et al., *An Historical Survey of the Law of Flight* (Montreal: McGill University Institute of Air and Space Law, 1961), 24–25.

37. D. H. N. Johnson, *Rights in Air Space* (Manchester: Manchester University Press, 1965), 70–74.

THREE: THE PECULIAR BEAUTIES OF THE COMMON LAW

1. Judson S. West, *Practical Law Made Plain* (Hartford: Edwin Valentine Mitchell, 1921), 71.

2. Henry Randall Webb, "Can I Fly Over Your Land?" *Washington Law Reporter* 48 (1920): 673–674.

3. H. G. Meyer, "Trespass by Aeroplane," *Law Magazine and Review*, 5th Series, 36 (1910): 20–23. This analysis was interesting enough to American lawyers to be reprinted as "Trespass by Aeroplane," *Central Law Journal* 72 (1911): 12–13.

4. "Trespass by Airplane," *Harvard Law Review* 32 (1919): 571; S. Walter Jones, *A Treatise on the Law of Telegraph and Telephone Companies* (Kansas City: Vernon Law Book Co., 1916), 152.

5. Lyttleton Fox, "The Law of Aerial Navigation," *North American Review* 190 (1909): 105–106; Carl Zollman, "Air Space Rights," *American Law Review* 53 (1919): 714.

6. W. J. Jackman and Thomas H. Russell, *Flying Machines: Con-

struction and Operation (Chicago: Charles C. Thompson Co., 1910), 173.

7. John A. Eubank, "Well-Defined Aerial Highways Are Imperative," *Canadian Air Review,* June 1930, 49–52.

8. Edmund F. Trabue, "The Law of Aviation," *American Bar Association Journal* 9 (1923): 777.

9. W. Archibald McClean, "The Evolution of a Legal Sky Pilot," *Green Bag* 16 (1904): 464; "The Law of the Airship," *Virginia Law Register* 16 (1910): 78; E. F. Albertsworth, "The Common Law in a Transitional Era," *American Bar Association Journal* 9 (1923): 519.

10. William Blackstone, *Commentaries on the Laws of England,* 10th ed. (1765–1769; London: A. Strahan, 1787), 1:17; Thomas Wood, *An Institute of the Laws of England,* 3rd ed. (London: Richard Sare, 1724), 4; John Cowell, *The Institutes of the Lawes of England* (London: J. Ridley, 1651), 4.

11. Robert Green McCloskey, ed., *The Works of James Wilson* (Cambridge: Harvard University Press, 1967), 1:353; James Sullivan, *The History of Land Titles in Massachusetts* (Boston: I. Thomas and E. T. Andrews, 1801), 16–17; Joel Prentiss Bishop, *The First Book of the Law* (Boston: Little, Brown, and Co., 1868), 38.

12. McCloskey, *Works of James Wilson,* 1:353; James Kent, *Commentaries on American Law,* 2nd ed. (New York: O. Halsted, 1832), 1:478–479.

13. John Anthon, *The Law Student, or Guides to the Study of the Law in Its Principles* (New York: D. Appleton and Co., 1850), 68; James M. Walker, *The Theory of the Common Law* (Boston: Little, Brown, and Co., 1852), 6.

14. Benjamin N. Cardozo, *The Nature of the Judicial Process* (New Haven: Yale University Press, 1921), 59–62.

15. "Who Owns the Air?" *New York Times,* 6 Aug. 1922, 36; Berkeley Davids, *The Law of Motor Vehicles* (Northport, N.Y.: Edward Thompson Co., 1911), 295–296.

16. William R. McCracken [sic], "Air Law," *American Law Review* 57 (1923): 98.

17. Edgar B. Kinkead, *Jurisprudence: Law and Ethics* (New York: Banks Law Publishing Co., 1905), 200; William S. Pattee, *The Essential Nature of Law* (Chicago: Callaghan and Co., 1909), 224; John Chipman Gray, *The Nature and Sources of the Law* (New York: Columbia University Press, 1909), 280.

18. Edward Coke, *The First Part of the Institutes of the Laws of England*, 15th ed. (1628; London: E. and R. Brooke, 1794), 1:97b; Giles Jacob, *The Student's Companion: or, the Reason of the Laws of England* (London: T. Corbett, 1725), 112; Blackstone, *Commentaries*, 1:70.

19. Blackstone, *Commentaries*, 1:69.

20. Craig Evan Klafter, *Reason Over Precedents: Origins of American Legal Thought* (Westport: Greenwood Press, 1993); Nathaniel Chipman, *Reports and Dissertations* (Rutland: Anthony Haswell, 1793), 128; Zephaniah Swift, *A System of the Laws of the State of Connecticut* (Windham: John Byrne, 1795), 42.

21. Hugh Henry Brackenridge, *Law Miscellanies* (Philadelphia: P. Byrne, 1814), 91; James Coolidge Carter, *Law: Its Origin, Growth and Function* (New York: G. P. Putnam's Sons, 1907), 182, 193; Lewis A. Grossman, "James Coolidge Carter and Mugwump Jurisprudence," *Law and History Review* 20 (2002): 604–614.

22. John Norton Pomeroy, *An Introduction to Municipal Law* (New York: D. Appleton and Co., 1865), 176; Oliver Wendell Holmes, Jr., "Common Carriers and the Common Law," *American Law Review* 13 (1879): 631; Gray, *Nature and Sources of the Law*, 96; William Carey Jones, ed., *Blackstone's Commentaries* (San Francisco: Bancroft-Whitney Co., 1916), 120 n. 6.

23. *James B. Beam Distilling Co. v. Georgia*, 501 U.S. 529, 549 (1991).

24. Jean Brissaud, *A History of French Private Law*, trans. Rapelje Howell (Boston: Little, Brown, and Co., 1912), 283 (the first French edition was published 1898–1900); Luigi Miraglia, *Comparative Legal Philosophy Applied to Legal Institutions*, trans. John Lisle (New York: Macmillan Co., 1921), 474–475 (the Italian edition was published in 1903); Paul Loubeyre, *Les Principes du Droit Aérien* (Paris: Pedone,

1911), 23–28; Raymond Leblanc, *La Navigation Aérienne au Point de Vue du Droit Civil* (Paris: A. Pedone, 1914), 11–15.

25. Henry John Roby, *Roman Private Law in the Times of Cicero and of the Antonines* (Cambridge: Cambridge University Press, 1902), 1:414, 498; Henry Goudy, "Two Ancient Brocards," in Paul Vinogradoff, ed., *Essays in Legal History* (London: Oxford University Press, 1913), 230–232.

26. J. E. G. de Montmorency, "The Control of Air Spaces," *Problems of the War* 3 (1917): 63–65; Eugène Sauze, *Les Questions de Responsabilité en Matière d'Aviation* (Paris: M. Giard & É. Brière, 1916), 23–24.

27. Francesco Lardone, "Airspace Rights in Roman Law," *Air Law Review* 2 (1931): 455–467; John Cobb Cooper, "Roman Law and the Maxim *Cujus est Solum* in International Law," *McGill Law Journal* 1 (1952): 23–65; Herbert David Klein, "Cujus est Solum Ejus est . . . Quousque Tandem?" *Journal of Air Law and Commerce* 26 (1959): 237–254; Yehuda Abramovitch, "The Maxim 'Cujus est Solum Ejus Usque ad Coelum' as Applied to Aviation," *McGill Law Journal* 8 (1962): 247–269; Harold D. Hazeltine, *The Law of the Air* (London: University of London Press, 1911), 58; Simeon E. Baldwin, "The Law of the Air," *Columbia Law Review* 12 (1912): 94.

28. John W. Salmond, *A Summary of the Law of Torts* (London: Stevens and Haynes, 1912), 113–114; "Flight of Aircraft over Land as Trespass on the Land," *Central Law Journal* 99 (1926): 327; "Aviation and Wireless Telegraphy as respects the Maxims and Principles of the Common Law," *Central Law Journal* 71 (1910): 2; Norman Bentwich, *Wanderer between Two Worlds* (London: Kegan Paul, 1941), 37; Norman Bentwich, "The Law of the Air," *Law Journal* 45 (1910): 402. Bentwich would later become a prominent Zionist and the first attorney general of British Palestine.

29. Edwin C. Fischer, "A Discussion of the Law of the Air," *St. Louis Law Review* 10 (1925): 145; Henry C. Spurr, "Let the Air Remain Free," *Case and Comment* 18 (1911): 122.

30. "Aviation and the Law," *Law Times* 143 (1917): 369–370; Zollman, "Air Space Rights," 718–719.

31. Stuart S. Ball, "The Jural Nature of Land," *Illinois Law Review* 45 (1928): 51; G. D. Valentine, "The Air—A Realm of Law," *Juridical Review* 85 (1910): 90.

32. "Editorial Notes," *New Jersey Law Journal* 32 (1909): 325; "The Law of the Air," *American Law Review* 44 (1910): 109.

33. Zollman, "Air Space Rights," 725–729; Valentine, "The Air," 87, 95.

34. "Right of Aviation over Private Property," *Law Notes* 18 (1914): 62; O. M. Biggar, "The Law Relating to the Air," *Canadian Law Times* 41 (1921): 670; Simeon E. Baldwin, "Liability for Accidents in Aerial Navigation," *Michigan Law Review* 9 (1910): 20; Spurr, "Let the Air Remain Free," 125.

35. "The Right to Air Space Superincumbent on Land," *Law Times* 137 (1914): 154; "All Aviators Said to Be Trespassers of the Air," *Literary Digest*, 14 Aug. 1920, 80.

36. Richard J. Mollica, "The Extent of the Right of the Owner of Land to the Space Above," *Bi-Monthly Law Review* 11 (1928): 141–142.

37. David W. Robertson, "The Legal Philosophy of Leon Green," *Texas Law Review* 56 (1978): 393–437; Leon Green, "Landowner v. Intruder; Intruder v. Landowner: Basis of Responsibility in Tort," *Michigan Law Review* 21 (1923): 501; "The Right to the Atmosphere," *The Bar* 15 (1908): 40–41.

38. "Airships—A Legal Problem," *Solicitors' Journal and Weekly Reporter* 51 (1907): 771–772; "The Airship in Court," *Virginia Law Register* 18 (1912): 383–384; "Aviation and Trespass," *American Law Review* 48 (1914): 915–917.

39. Warder Rannells, "Aerial Navigation in the Law of Trespass," *St. Louis Law Review* 4 (1919): 205–208.

40. "The Law of the Air," *Central Law Journal* 70 (1910): 174; Denys P. Myers, "The Air and the Earth Beneath," *Green Bag* 26 (1914): 364–365; George E. Haas, "Law of the Air," *Marquette Law Review* 2 (1918): 114.

41. Henry Woodhouse, "Aeronautical Maps and Aerial Transportation," *Geographical Review* 4 (1917): 343–347; Wayne C. Williams, "The Law of the Air," *Outlook,* 22 Sept. 1920, 144.

42. Thomas H. Marshall, "Some Legal Problems of the Aeronaut," *Illinois Law Quarterly* 6 (1923): 57–58; "Forty-fourth Annual Association Meeting," *American Bar Association Journal* 7 (1921): 480.

43. Martha McLendon, "Aviation and the Law of Trespass," *Kansas City Law Review* 1 (1932): 13; Fox, "Law of Aerial Navigation," 106.

44. McCracken, "Air Law," 99.

45. R. Floyd Clarke to editor of New York Herald, 21 Oct. 1909, Baldwin Family Papers, box 96, file 1008, YUL.

46. Zollman, "Air Space Rights," 735–736.

47. Peter L. Jakab and Rick Young, eds., *The Published Writings of Wilbur and Orville Wright* (Washington, D.C.: Smithsonian Books, 2000), 205; Hubert Work, "Speeding the Mails," *Aerial Age* 16 (1923): 110.

FOUR: A UNIFORM LAW

1. "Legal Problems of Aeronautics," *Bench and Bar* 49 (1909): 51.

2. Laurence La Tourette Driggs, "Can Air Be Too Free?" *The Independent* 104 (1920): 374.

3. Carl Zollman, "Governmental Control of Aircraft," *American Law Review* 53 (1919): 902.

4. Howard Schweber, "The 'Science' of Legal Science: The Model of the Natural Sciences in Nineteenth-Century American Legal Education," *Law and History Review* 17 (1999): 421–466; "Whether Law Is a Science?" *American Jurist* 9 (1833): 349, 355–356.

5. Thomas C. Grey, "Langdell's Orthodoxy," *University of Pittsburgh Law Review* 45 (1983): 1–53; Christopher C. Langdell, *A Selection of Cases on the Law of Contracts,* 2nd ed. (Boston: Little, Brown, and Co., 1879), viii–ix; "The Harvard Law School," *Law Quarterly Review* 3 (1887): 124.

6. Oliver Wendell Holmes, Jr., *The Common Law* (Boston: Little, Brown, and Co., 1881), 1.

7. Francis Bacon James, *Codification of Branches of Commercial Law* (Cincinnati: Gibson and Perin Co., 1902), 3–4; Joseph H. Beale, *The Diversity of Laws* (n.p., 1916), 21.

8. Ovid F. Johnson, *Remarks of Ovid F. Johnson upon Uniformity of State Legislation* (n.p., 1892), 1–2; Lyman D. Brewster, *Uniform State Laws* (n.p., 1898), 19.

9. George B. Rose, *Uniformity or Diversity?* (n.p., 1900), 6–7.

10. Walter P. Armstrong, Jr., *A Century of Service: A Centennial History of the National Conference of Commissioners on Uniform State Laws* (St. Paul, Minn.: West Publishing Co., 1991), 11–28.

11. Amasa M. Eaton, *Uniformity of Legislation* (St. Louis: n.p., 1904), 11.

12. Eaton, *Uniformity of Legislation*, 10; William O. Hart, *Uniformity of Legislation* (n.p., 1910), 9.

13. Eaton, *Uniformity of Legislation*, 10–11.

14. Simeon E. Baldwin, "Liability for Accidents in Aerial Navigation," *Michigan Law Review* 9 (1910): 25.

15. Bryant Barrett, trans., *The Code Napoleon* (London: W. Reed, 1811), 1:116 (sec. 552); J. F. Lycklama à Nijeholt, *Air Sovereignty* (The Hague: Martinus Nijhoff, 1910), 34–35.

16. Charles-Louis Julliot, "De la Propriété du Domaine Aérien," *Revue des Idées* 5 (1908): 510–532; Émile Laude, *Le Droit de l'Air* (Brussels: Veuve Ferdinand Larcier, 1910), 15–25; Henri Guibé, *Essai sur la Navigation Aérienne* (Caen: E. Lanier, 1912), 26; Gaston Bonnefoy, *Le Code de l'Air* (Paris: Marcel Rivière, 1909), 118.

17. Chung Hui Wang, trans., *The German Civil Code* (London: Stevens and Sons, 1907), 202 (sec. 905); Ernest J. Schuster, *The Principles of German Civil Law* (Oxford: Clarendon Press, 1907), 386–387.

18. Ivy Williams, ed., *The Swiss Civil Code* (Oxford: Oxford University Press, 1925), 4:167 (sec. 667); Virgile Rossel and F.-H. Mentha, *Manuel du Droit Civil Suisse* (Lausanne: Librairie Payot, 1922), 2:337.

19. Simeon E. Baldwin, "The Law of the Air-Ship," *American Journal of International Law* 4 (1910): 98; G. D. Valentine, "The Air—A Realm of Law," *Juridical Review* 22 (1910): 96; Denys P. Myers, "The Air and the Earth Beneath," *Green Bag* 26 (1914): 364.

20. Aristide N. Basilesco, *La Propriété de l'Espace Aérien* (Paris: Jouve, 1920), 30; "French Government's Air Bill," *Law Times* 135 (1913): 70; Hiram L. Jome, "Property in the Air as Affected by the Airplane and the Radio," *Journal of Land and Public Utility Economics* 4 (1928): 264; G. D. Valentine, "Aerial Trespassers," *Juridical Review* 24 (1913): 321–322; "Aviation and Trespass," *American Law Review* 48 (1914): 914 n. 1.

21. F. P. Walton, "Civil Codes and Their Revision: Some Suggestions for Revision of the Title 'Of Ownership,'" *Southern Law Quarterly* 1 (1916): 105; Ambroise Colin and H. Capitant, *Cours Élémentaire de Droit Civil Français,* 4th ed. (Paris: Librairie Dalloz, 1923) 1:722; "Right of Aviation over Private Property," *Law Notes* 18 (1914): 62.

22. "Aerial Transport," *Law Times* 146 (1918): 106.

23. Lawrence Arthur Wingfield and Reginald Brabant Sparkes, *The Law in Relation to Aircraft* (London: Longmans, Green and Co., 1928), 107.

24. William Latey, "The Law of Aviation," *Journal of Comparative Legislation and International Law* 7 (1925): 97.

25. "The Connecticut Statute for the Regulation of Aerial Navigation," *Bench and Bar* 26 (1911): 10; George Gleason Bogert, "Problems in Aviation Law," *Cornell Law Quarterly* 6 (1921): 288.

26. 1911 Conn. Public Acts c. 86; 1913 Mass. Acts c. 663.

27. George Gleason Bogert, "Recent Developments in the Law of Aeronautics," *Cornell Law Quarterly* 8 (1922): 31–32; William R. McCracken [sic], "Air Law," *American Law Review* 57 (1923): 104–105; Elza C. Johnson, *Legal Questions Affecting Federal Control of the Air,* Air Service Information Circular No. 181 (Washington, D.C.: Government Printing Office, 1921), 11–14.

28. Earl N. Findley, "Twenty Months of Commercial Aeronautics," *New York Times,* 16 Jan. 1921, BR3.

29. Driggs, "Can Air Be Too Free?" 357; "Trespass in the Air Has Legal Tangles," *New York Times*, 4 Sept. 1927, SM19; "A New Trespass Situation," *Wall Street Journal*, 14 July 1928, 2.

30. *Pittsburgh Sun*, 28 May 1921, in William P. MacCracken, Jr., Papers, box 36, HHL.

31. *Commonwealth v. Nevin*, 2 Pa. D. & C. 241 (1922).

32. "Aerial Trespassers Exonerated," *Aviation* 13 (1922): 155; "Trespass—Aviator Flying Low over Land," *University of Pennsylvania Law Review* 71 (1922): 88.

33. *Johnson v. Curtiss Northwest Airplane Co.* (Minn. Dist. Ct. 1923), *Aviation Cases* (New York: Commerce Clearing House, 1947–), 1:61–63 (erroneously labeled as a federal case).

34. "Air Rights," *American Law Review* 57 (1923): 908–911; "The Freedom of the Air," *Aviation* 16 (1924): 116.

35. *Handbook of the National Conference of Commissioners on Uniform State Laws and Proceedings of the Thirtieth Annual Conference* (n.p., 1920), 120.

36. Bogert, "Problems in Aviation Law."

37. Bogert, "Recent Developments," 34 n. 28; *Reasons for the Enactment of the Uniform State Law for Aeronautics* (n.p.: National Conference of Commissioners on Uniform State Laws, 1922), unpaginated.

38. *Handbook of the National Conference of Commissioners on Uniform State Laws and Proceedings of the Thirty-first Annual Meeting* (n.p., 1921), 291–292.

39. Bogert, "Recent Developments," 26–34; McCracken, "Air Law," 100; Henry G. Hotchkiss, *A Treatise on Aviation Law* (New York: Baker, Voorhis, and Co., 1928), 25; Stuart S. Ball, "The Vertical Extent of Ownership in Land," *University of Pennsylvania Law Review* 76 (1928): 679 n. 152.

40. Nathan William MacChesney, *Uniform State Laws: A Means to Efficiency Consistent with Democracy* (n.p., 1916); Nathan William MacChesney, *Uniform Laws: A Needed Protection to and Stimulus of Interstate Investment* (n.p., 1911); *New York Times*, 26 Nov. 1922, 9.

41. Nathan William MacChesney, "Progress in Passage and Formu-

lation of Uniform State Laws," *American Bar Association Journal* 9 (1923): 657.

42. Roger F. Williams, "Developments in Aerial Law," *University of Pennsylvania Law Review* 139 (1926): 152; *Uniform Laws Annotated* (Brooklyn, N.Y.: Edward Thompson Co., 1922–1966), 11:157.

43. "Joint Meeting of Committee of the Conference of Commissioners on Uniform State Laws, and Committee of the American Bar Association on the Law of Aeronautics" (25 Feb. 1922), 133, 171–172, William P. MacCracken, Jr., Papers, box 36, HHL.

44. "Joint Meeting," 54; T. C. Powell, *"Airplanes and Terminals": Address before the Western Railway Club* (1928), 5, William P. MacCracken, Jr., Papers, box 10, HHL.

45. "Joint Meeting," 5, 42–43, 50–51.

46. Relevant excerpts of the New York bar committee's report are in *Civil Aeronautics: Legislative History of the Air Commerce Act of 1926* (Washington, D.C.: Government Printing Office, 1928), 142–149.

47. *Handbook of the National Conference of Commissioners on Uniform State Laws and Proceedings of the Thirty-fifth Annual Meeting* (n.p., 1925), 913, 164–165, 306–307, 918.

48. Chester W. Cuthell, "Aviation from the Lawyer's Viewpoint," in *International Civil Aeronautics Conference* (Washington, D.C.: Government Printing Office, 1928), 518–519.

FIVE: INTERSTATE COMMERCE IN THE AIR

1. Burdett A. Rich, "Federal Control over Air Navigation," *Case and Comment* 17 (1910): 288; "The Law of the Air," *The Bar* 18 (1911): 41.

2. "The Connecticut Statute for the Regulation of Aerial Navigation," *Bench and Bar* 26 (1911): 10; Berkeley Davids, *The Law of Motor Vehicles* (Northport, N.Y.: Edward Thompson Co., 1911), 302; Wayne C. Williams, "The Law of the Air," *Case and Comment* 18 (1911): 133.

3. Simeon E. Baldwin, "Liability for Accidents in Aerial Navigation," *Michigan Law Review* 9 (1910): 25–27.

4. *Report of the Thirty-Fourth Annual Meeting of the American Bar Association* (Baltimore: Lord Baltimore Press, 1911), 383–384.

5. Charles C. Goetsch, "The Future of Legal Formalism," *American Journal of Legal History* 24 (1980): 240–246.

6. Richard R. John, *Spreading the News: The American Postal System from Franklin to Morse* (Cambridge: Harvard University Press, 1995), 3; Adam S. Grace, "From the Lighthouses: How the First Federal Internal Improvement Projects Created Precedent That Broadened the Commerce Clause, Shrunk the Takings Clause, and Affected Early Nineteenth Century Constitutional Debate," *Albany Law Review* 68 (2004): 97–153; Michele L. Landis, "'Let Me Next Time Be "Tried by Fire"': Disaster Relief and the Origins of the American Welfare State, 1789–1874," *Northwestern University Law Review* 92 (1998): 967–1034; Theda Skocpol, "America's First Social Security System: The Expansion of Benefits for Civil War Veterans," *Political Science Quarterly* 108 (1993): 96.

7. Pamela L. Baker, "The Washington Road Bill and the Struggle to Adopt a Federal System of Internal Improvement," *Journal of the Early Republic* 22 (2002): 437–464.

8. 1 Stat. 55 (1789); 1 Stat. 106 (1790); 1 Stat. 131 (1790); 3 Stat. 2 (1813); 4 Stat. 394 (1830); 5 Stat. 304 (1838); 10 Stat. 61 (1852); John K. Brown, *Limbs on the Levee: Steamboat Explosions and the Origins of Federal Public Welfare Regulation, 1817–1852* (Middlebourne, W. Va.: International Steamboat Society, 1989); John G. Burke, "Bursting Boilers and the Federal Power," *Technology and Culture* 7 (1966): 1–23; 9 Stat. 127 (1847); 9 Stat. 220 (1848); 10 Stat. 715 (1855).

9. David P. Currie, *The Constitution in Congress: Democrats and Whigs, 1829–1861* (Chicago: University of Chicago Press, 2005), 13–20, 123–126; Harry N. Scheiber, "The Transportation Revolution and American Law: Constitutionalism and Public Policy," in *Transportation and the Early Nation* (Indianapolis: Indiana Historical Society, 1982), 1–29.

10. Carl B. Swisher, *History of the Supreme Court of the United States: The Taney Period, 1836–64* (New York: Macmillan, 1974), 403.

11. Paul Starr, *The Creation of the Media: Political Origins of Modern Communications* (New York: Basic Books, 2004), 161–162; 14 Stat. 221 (1866); *Pensacola Telegraph Co. v. Western Union Telegraph Co.*, 96 U.S. 1, 9 (1878).

12. James W. Ely, Jr., *Railroads and American Law* (Lawrence: University Press of Kansas, 2001), 90–93; Morton Keller, *Regulating a New Economy: Public Policy and Economic Change in America, 1900–1933* (Cambridge: Harvard University Press, 1990), 47–51; Charles Warren, *The Supreme Court in United States History* (Boston: Little, Brown, and Co., 1922), 3:451–453.

13. Warren, *The Supreme Court*, 3:458–459; Robert Eugene Cushman, "The National Police Power under the Commerce Clause of the Constitution," *Minnesota Law Review* 3 (1919): 289.

14. *Hammer v. Dagenhart*, 247 U.S. 251 (1918); *Federal Base Ball Club of Baltimore, Inc. v. National League of Professional Base Ball Clubs*, 259 U.S. 200 (1922).

15. Carl Zollman, "Governmental Control of Aircraft," *American Law Review* 53 (1919): 902; "Free as Air," *Scientific American*, 10 May 1919, 484; Laurence La Tourette Driggs, "Can Air Be Too Free?" *Independent* 104 (1920): 374; W. Jefferson Davis, "The Civil Aeronautics Act of 1923," *American Bar Association Journal* 9 (1923): 421.

16. "American Backwardness in Formulating Laws of the Air," *Literary Digest*, 4 Dec. 1920, 66; *Buffalo News*, 21 July 1921; Nick A. Komons, *Bonfires to Beacons: Federal Civil Aviation Policy under the Air Commerce Act, 1926–1938* (Washington, D.C.: Smithsonian Institution Press, 1978), 23.

17. "Notes for Meeting of the Air Craft Men Monday," 16 July 1921, Herbert Hoover Papers, Commerce Period, box 39, folder 739, HHL; "Airplane Traffic Control Imperative," *New York Journal of Commerce*, 20 Sept. 1921; W. L. Brackett (president, Aerial Transport Corporation) to Herbert Hoover, 7 Sept. 1921, Herbert Hoover Papers, Commerce Period, box 122, folder 2161, HHL; Roger J. Adams (president, Adams Aerial Transportation Company) to Herbert Hoover, 12 Dec. 1921,

Herbert Hoover Papers, Commerce Period, box 122, folder 2161, HHL; S. B. Johnston (Huff Daland Aero Corporation) to Herbert Hoover, 9 Aug. 1922, Herbert Hoover Papers, Commerce Period, box 122, folder 2162, HHL; Luther K. Bell, "The Need for Federal Aerial Legislation," *American City* 21 (1919): 415–417; "Wants Aviation Laws Fixed by Congress," *New York Times,* 19 Oct. 1919, 5; "Urges Government Control of Flying," *New York Times,* 20 Sept. 1921, 33.

18. H. P. Stellwagen to Herbert Hoover, 28 Jan. 1924, Herbert Hoover Papers, Commerce Period, box 122, folder 2163, HHL; J. Rowland Bibbins to Senator Wesley L. Jones, 15 Feb. 1922, William P. MacCracken, Jr., Papers, box 50, HHL; Chamber of Commerce of the United States, "Aeronautical Legislation," enclosure in Julius Barnes to Herbert Hoover, 29 May 1924, Herbert Hoover Papers, Commerce Period, box 122, folder 2163, HHL.

19. *Civil Aviation in the Department of Commerce: Hearing before a Subcommittee of the Committee on Commerce, United States Senate, Sixty-Seventh Congress, Second Session, on S. 2815,* 19 Dec. 1921 (Washington, D.C.: Government Printing Office, 1922), 24; *Bureau of Aeronautics in Department of Commerce,* S. Rep. No. 460, 67th Cong., 2nd Sess. (1922), 2.

20. Michael Osborn and Joseph Riggs, *"Mr. Mac": William P. Mac-Cracken, Jr., on Aviation, Law, Optometry* (Memphis: Southern College of Optometry, 1970), 33–48; *New York Times,* 10 Aug. 1926, 21; "Short Sketches of the Aeronautics Branch," *Aviation* 27 (1929): 142; Donald R. Whitnah, *Safer Skyways: Federal Control of Aviation, 1926–1966* (Ames: Iowa State University Press, 1966), 28–29.

21. Alex Roland, *Model Research: The National Advisory Committee for Aeronautics, 1915–1958* (Washington, D.C.: National Aeronautics and Space Administration, 1985), 1:51–71; Roger E. Bilstein, *Orders of Magnitude: A History of the NACA and NASA, 1915–1990* (Washington, D.C.: National Aeronautics and Space Administration, 1989), 1–9; F. Robert van der Linden, *Airlines and Air Mail: The Post Office and the Birth of the Commercial Aviation Industry* (Lexington: University Press of

Kentucky, 2002), 4–16; *Civil Aviation in the Department of Commerce,* 28; Theodore Roosevelt, "A National Aviation Policy," *Outlook,* 15 June 1921, 288; William A. Moffett, "Aviation Progress in America," *Current History* 17 (1923): 775–782.

22. David D. Lee, "Herbert Hoover and the Development of Commercial Aviation, 1921–1926," *Business History Review* 58 (1984): 78–102; "Statement of Secretary Hoover on Commercial Aviation" (24 Sept. 1925), Herbert Hoover Papers, Commerce Period, box 40, folder 741, HHL; *Report of President's Aircraft Board* (Washington, D.C.: Government Printing Office, 1926), 7–10; Thomas Worth Walterman, "Airpower and Private Enterprise: Federal-Industrial Relations in the Aeronautics Field, 1918–1926" (Ph.D. diss., Washington University Department of History, 1970), 288, 301; *The Promotion of Commercial Aviation,* S. Rep. No. 2, 69th Cong., 1st Sess. (1925), 4.

23. Walterman, "Airpower and Private Enterprise," 377–425; W. Jefferson Davis, "Putting Laws over Wings," *American Bar Association Journal* 11 (1925): 531.

24. *Report of the Forty-fourth Annual Meeting of the American Bar Association* (Baltimore: Lord Baltimore Press, 1921), 500–502.

25. American Bar Association Special Committee on the Law of Aviation, *First Preliminary Report to the Executive Committee* (New York: n.p., 1921), 7.

26. "From Judicial Grant to Legislative Power: The Admiralty Clause in the Nineteenth Century," *Harvard Law Review* 67 (1954): 1230–37; *Southern Pacific Co. v. Jensen,* 244 U.S. 205, 215 (1917).

27. *Aircraft: Hearing before the President's Aircraft Board* (Washington, D.C.: Government Printing Office, 1925), 1484; *Civil Aviation in the Department of Commerce,* 12; "Joint Meeting of Committee of the Conference of Commissioners on Uniform State Laws, and Committee of the American Bar Association on the Law of Aeronautics" (25 Feb. 1922), 112, William P. MacCracken, Jr., Papers, box 36, HHL.

28. William Velpeau Rooker, *Letter on the Jurisprudence of the Atmosphere as Applied in the Arts of Aviation and Aerography* (Indianapolis:

n.p., 1920), 1; *Report of the Forty-fourth Annual Meeting,* 84; William Velpeau Rooker to Simeon Baldwin et al., 5 Jan. 1920, Baldwin Family Papers, box 96, file 1008, YUL; Simeon Baldwin to William Velpeau Rooker, 23 Feb. 1920, Baldwin Family Papers, box 96, file 1008, YUL.

29. Arnold W. Knauth, "Aviation and Admiralty," *Air Law Review* 6 (1935): 226; *The Crawford Bros. No. 2,* 215 F. 269, 271 (W.D. Wash. 1914); "Aeroplanes and Admiralty," *Harvard Law Review* 28 (1914): 200; "Admiralty: Aeroplane Not a Subject of Admiralty Jurisdiction," *California Law Review* 3 (1915): 143; *Reinhardt v. Newport Flying Service Corp.,* 232 N.Y. 115, 118 (1921); *Report of the Forty-fourth Annual Meeting,* 93–94; *Law Memoranda upon Civil Aeronautics* (Washington, D.C.: Government Printing Office, 1923), 51.

30. *Missouri v. Holland,* 252 U.S. 416, 433–434 (1920); Alexander M. Bickel and Benno C. Schmidt, Jr., *The Judiciary and Responsible Government, 1910–1921* (New York: Macmillan, 1984), 476–483.

31. *Report of the Forty-fourth Annual Meeting,* 90.

32. New York State Bar Association Committee on Law Reform, "Report to Forty-fourth Annual Meeting, 1921," William P. MacCracken, Jr., Papers, box 53, HHL; *Report of the Forty-fourth Annual Meeting,* 505–506.

33. Elza Johnson to Director of Air Service, n.d. [ca. 1921], William P. MacCracken, Jr., Papers, box 50, HHL.

34. *Report of the Forty-fourth Annual Meeting,* 91; "Joint Meeting," 21–22; *Report of the Forty-fifth Annual Meeting of the American Bar Association* (Baltimore: Lord Baltimore Press, 1922), 415.

35. *Civil Aviation in the Department of Commerce,* 68.

36. Thomas H. Marshall, "Some Legal Problems of the Aeronaut," *Illinois Law Quarterly* 6 (1923): 60; *Bureau of Aeronautics,* 3–4.

37. Barry Cushman, *Rethinking the New Deal Court: The Structure of a Constitutional Revolution* (New York: Oxford University Press, 1998), 144–154; David Gordon, "*Swift & Co. v. United States:* The Beef Trust and the Stream of Commerce Doctrine," *American Journal of Legal History* 28 (1984): 244–279; *Swift & Co. v. United States,* 196 U.S. 375,

398–399 (1905); *Houston, East & West Texas Railway Co. v. United States,* 234 U.S. 342, 351–352 (1914); *Civil Aviation in the Department of Commerce,* 9–10.

38. *Railroad Commission of Wisconsin v. Chicago, Burlington & Quincy Railroad Co.,* 257 U.S. 563, 588 (1922); *Stafford v. Wallace,* 258 U.S. 495, 520–521 (1922); *Board of Trade v. Olsen,* 262 U.S. 1, 36 (1923).

39. William R. McCracken [sic], "Air Law," *American Law Review* 97 (1923): 108; *Bureau of Civil Air Navigation in the Department of Commerce: Hearings before the Committee on Interstate and Foreign Commerce, House of Representatives, Sixty-eighth Congress, Second Session, on H.R. 10522* (Washington, D.C.: Government Printing Office, 1924), 62, 3.

40. *Civil Aviation: A Report by the Joint Committee on Civil Aviation* (New York: McGraw-Hill, 1926), 6.

41. *Report of the Forty-fourth Annual Meeting,* 87, 84, 91; *Law Memoranda,* 54.

42. Laurence LaTourette Driggs to William P. MacCracken, Jr., 23 Mar. 1925, William P. MacCracken, Jr., Papers, box 51, HHL; *Legal Questions Affecting Federal Control of the Air,* Air Service Information Circular No. 181 (Washington, D.C.: Government Printing Office, 1921), 11.

43. *Bureau of Civil Air Navigation,* 60.

44. 44 Stat. 568 (1926); Frederic P. Lee, "The Air Commerce Act of 1926," *American Bar Association Journal* 12 (1926): 374; "Examine Pilot's License before Flying, Says MacCracken," 13 Sept. 1927, Herbert Hoover Papers, Commerce Period, box 40, folder 744, HHL; Frederic P. Lee, "State Adoption and Enforcement of Federal Air Navigation Law," *American Bar Association Journal* 16 (1930): 715–718; "The Air Commerce Act of 1926," *Columbia Law Review* 27 (1927): 990.

45. *Civil Aeronautics: Legislative History of the Air Commerce Act of 1926* (Washington, D.C.: Government Printing Office, 1928), 42–43.

46. M. W. Royse, "An Air Law for America," *Nation* 123 (1926): 659; *New York Times,* 16 Aug. 1926, 14; Charles H. Holland, "Aviation

Insurance," *Annals of the American Academy of Political and Social Science* 131 (1927): 134; W. Jefferson Davis, "Clearing the Air for Commerce," *Annals of the American Academy of Political and Social Science* 131 (1927): 144–145; Carl Solberg, *Conquest of the Skies: A History of Commercial Aviation in America* (Boston: Little, Brown, and Co., 1979), 74–248; Jacob A. Vander Meulen, *The Politics of Aircraft: Building an American Military Industry* (Lawrence: University Press of Kansas, 1991), 90–102; Susan B. Carter et al., eds., *Historical Statistics of the United States,* Millennial Edition On Line (Cambridge University Press, 2006), table Df1112–1125.

47. Henry G. Hotchkiss, *A Treatise on Aviation Law* (New York: Baker, Voorhis and Co., 1928), 251–252; *Neiswonger v. Goodyear Tire & Rubber Co.,* 35 F.2d 761 (N.D. Ohio 1929).

48. I. E. Lambert, "The Law of the Air," *Lincoln Law Review* 2 (1928): 25; John A. Eubank, "Who Owns the Airspace?" *American Law Review* 63 (1929): 23–31; Arthur L. Newman II, "Aviation Law and the Constitution," *Yale Law Journal* 39 (1930): 1127–28; Alonzo H. Tuttle and Dale E. Bennett, "Extent of Power of Congress over Aviation," *University of Cincinnati Law Review* 5 (1931): 267–270; Charles C. Rohlfing, *National Regulation of Aeronautics* (Philadelphia: University of Pennsylvania Press, 1931), 228–248.

SIX: LANDOWNERS AGAINST THE AVIATION INDUSTRY

1. Hiram L. Jome, "Property in the Air as Affected by the Airplane and the Radio," *Journal of Land and Public Utility Economics* 4 (1928): 265–266.

2. *New York Times,* 4 Sept. 1927, SM19; *New York Times,* 20 June 1929, 50; *Chicago Daily Tribune,* 12 July 1930; "Negligence—Liability for Disturbing Fox Farm by Low Flight," *Air Law Review* 3 (1932): 349; *Meloy v. City of Santa Monica,* 12 P.2d 1072, 1073 (Cal. App. 1932); Fred D. Fagg, Jr., "A Survey of State Aeronautical Legislation," *Journal of*

Air Law 1 (1930): 452; Byron K. Elliott, "Law of the Air," *Indiana Law Journal* 6 (1930): 165; Joseph B. Murphy, "The Legal Problems of Aviation," *United States Law Review* 64 (1930): 524.

3. *Smith v. New England Aircraft Company,* 170 N.E. 385 (Mass. 1930); *New York Times,* 6 Apr. 1945, 15.

4. Albert B. Southwick, *Once-Told Tales of Worcester County* (Worcester: Worcester Telegram & Gazette, 1985), 143–144. On the nationwide boom in airport construction in the late 1920s, see Janet R. Daly Bednarek, *America's Airports: Airfield Development, 1918–1947* (College Station: Texas A&M University Press, 2001), 41–66.

5. George B. Logan, "The Case of Smith v. New England Aircraft Company," *Journal of Land and Public Utility Economics* 6 (1930): 316–324; "Aviation—Trespass—Nuisance," *Michigan Law Review* 29 (1930): 242–243; Edward C. Sweeney, "Aircraft—Airport—Trespass—Nuisance: Common Law Doctrine Modified," *Journal of Air Law* 1 (1930): 367; Robert Marvin, "Airplane—Trespass—Nuisance," *Boston University Law Review* 10 (1930): 382–387; "Aviation—Constitutional Law—Property—Right of Flight—Regulation of Aerial Navigation," *Southern California Law Review* 3 (1930): 413–423.

6. *Sysak v. De Lisser Air Service Corporation,* 1 Aviation Cases (CCH) 273 (N.Y. Sup. Ct. 1931).

7. *Swetland v. Curtiss Airports Corporation,* 41 F.2d 929 (N.D. Ohio 1930).

8. "Sky the Limit?" *Time,* 4 Aug. 1930; "Court Rule for Flyers under Fire," *Los Angeles Times,* 12 July 1930, 1.

9. Thompson George Marsh, "Ownership of Space," *Dicta* 8 (1930): 12; "Air Law—Invasion of Air Space above Privately Owned Land as Trespass," *Yale Law Journal* 40 (1930): 131–133; "Trespass Quare Clausum Fregit—Space above Land—What Constitutes Trespass by Airplanes," *Chicago-Kent Law Review* 9 (1930): 48–50; Leo E. Falkin, "Torts: Liability of an Aviator for Trespass to Realty," *Cornell Law Quarterly* 6 (1930): 119–125; Lyman B. Gillet, "Air Law," *Marquette Law Review* 15 (1930): 47; George B. Logan, "Aviation and the Maxim Cujus Est Solum," *St. Louis Law Review* 16 (1931): 303–310; Leo Jaffe,

"Air Law—Trespass by Airplane," *Texas Law Review* 9 (1931): 240–244; "Aircraft—Low Flight over Property Adjoining Airport as Trespass Entitling Owner to Injunctive Relief," *Virginia Law Review* 17 (1930): 77; William H. Smith, "Servitudes—Trespass by Airplane—Invasion of Rights Incidental to Possession of Land—Effective Possession," *Wisconsin Law Review* 6 (1930): 47–49; Edward C. Sweeney, "Aircraft—Airport—Trespass—Nuisance—Constitutional Law—Common Law Doctrine Modified—Effective Possession—Jurisprudence," *Journal of Air Law* 2 (1931): 82–83.

10. *Swetland v. Curtiss Airports Corporation,* 55 F.2d 201 (6th Cir. 1932).

11. Jack C. Burdett, "Injunctions—Airports—Nuisance," *West Virginia Law Quarterly* 38 (1932): 366–368; George Foster, Jr., "Airports—Nuisance—Injunction—Trespass—Flights over Adjoining Property," *Air Law Review* 3 (1932): 151–158; Edward C. Sweeney, "Airport—Nuisance—Trespass—Maxim—Rights of Neighboring Landowners," *Journal of Air Law* 3 (1932): 293–306; R. L. B., "Torts: Aircraft: Trespass by Aeroplane," *California Law Review* 20 (1932): 668.

12. *New York Times,* 12 Dec. 1929, 1, and 1 Mar. 1931, 6.

13. Charles C. Goetsch and Margaret L. Shivers, eds., *The Autobiography of Thomas L. Chadbourne* (New York: Oceana, 1985), 197.

14. Charles Pickett, "The Empire State Building Mooring Mast," *Air Law Review* 2 (1931): 130–152.

15. *New York Times,* 16 Sept. 1931, 6; 30 Sept. 1931, 11; Mark Kingwell, *Nearest Thing to Heaven: The Empire State Building and American Dreams* (New Haven: Yale University Press, 2006), 12.

16. Carl Zollman, "Statutory Changes in Air Law in 1931," *Marquette Law Review* 16 (1932): 202.

17. Brief for the Aviation Corporation as Amicus Curiae, *Swetland v. Curtiss Airports Corporation,* 39; Motion on Behalf of Aeronautical Chamber of Commerce of America, Inc., for Leave to File Brief as Amicus Curiae, and Brief as Amicus Curiae, *Swetland v. Curtiss Airports Corporation,* 4, 12.

18. George B. Logan, *Aircraft Law—Made Plain* (St. Louis: n.p.,

1928), 14–16; Dorothy M. Brown, *Mabel Walker Willebrandt: A Study of Power, Loyalty, and Law* (Knoxville: University of Tennessee Press, 1984), 201–202.

19. *Report of the Fifty-fourth Annual Meeting of the American Bar Association* (Baltimore: Lord Baltimore Press, 1931), 317–319.

20. Ibid., 319, 74–75.

21. Fred D. Fagg, Jr., "Airspace Ownership and the Right of Flight," *Journal of Air Law* 3 (1932): 400–402; Edward C. Sweeney, "Adjusting the Conflicting Interests of Landowner and Aviator in Anglo-American Law," *Journal of Air Law* 3 (1932): 584–585; James J. Hayden, "Objections to the New Uniform Aeronautical Code," *American Bar Association Journal* 18 (1932): 121–124, 136; Henry V. Hubbard, Miller McClintock, and Frank B. Williams, *Airports: Their Location, Administration and Legal Basis* (Cambridge: Harvard University Press, 1930), 115–116.

22. Charles P. Hine to Nathan W. MacChesney, Nathan W. MacChesney Papers, box 21, file 62, HHL; MacChesney to Frederick L. Swetland, 25 May 1932, Nathan W. MacChesney Papers, box 21, file 62, HHL; MacChesney to Swetland, 14 Aug. 1933, Nathan W. MacChesney Papers, box 21, file 63, HHL; MacChesney to Hine, 21 May 1932, Nathan W. MacChesney Papers, box 21, file 62, HHL; Nathan William MacChesney, "In re: Rights of Land Owners with Reference to Operation of Aircraft," *Journal of Air Law* 1 (1930): 211–218.

23. Frederick L. Swetland to Nathan W. MacChesney, 20 May 1932 and 7 June 1932, Nathan W. MacChesney Papers, box 21, file 62, HHL; Swetland to MacChesney, 28 July 1933, Nathan W. MacChesney Papers, box 21, file 63, HHL.

24. *Report of the Fifty-fourth Annual Meeting,* 86–88.

25. Nathan W. MacChesney to Francis H. Bohlen, 25 Apr. 1932, Nathan W. MacChesney Papers, box 21, file 62, HHL; MacChesney to Randolph Barton, Jr., et al., 14 July 1933, Nathan W. MacChesney Papers, box 21, file 63, HHL.

26. N. E. H. Hull, "Restatement and Reform: A New Perspective

on the Origins of the American Law Institute," *Law and History Review* 8 (1990): 55–96; William P. LaPiana, "'A Task of No Common Magnitude': The Founding of the American Law Institute," *Nova Law Review* 11 (1987): 1085–1126; Ellen Condliffe Lagemann, *The Politics of Knowledge: The Carnegie Corporation, Philanthropy, and Public Policy* (Middletown: Wesleyan University Press, 1989), 71–93.

27. *Report of the Committee on the Establishment of a Permanent Organization for Improvement of the Law Proposing the Establishment of an American Law Institute* (Philadelphia: n.p., 1923), 4.

28. *The American Law Institute Seventy-fifth Anniversary, 1923–1998* (Philadelphia: American Law Institute, 1998), 11–12, 47.

29. *The American Law Institute Fiftieth Anniversary* (Philadelphia: American Law Institute, 1973), 132.

30. American Law Institute, *Restatement of the Law of Torts: Tentative Draft No. 7* (Philadelphia: American Law Institute, 1931), 11, 50–51, 53.

31. *Los Angeles Times*, 10 May 1931, 12; American Law Institute, *Restatement of Torts: Tentative Draft No. 11* (Philadelphia: American Law Institute, 1933), 18–20.

32. *Los Angeles Times*, 7 May 1933, 10; *New York Times*, 16 Aug. 1933, 16; Emory H. Niles, "The Present Status of the Ownership of Airspace," *Air Law Review* 5 (1934): 155. Compare Alan Schwartz and Robert E. Scott, "The Political Economy of Private Legislatures," *University of Pennsylvania Law Review* 143 (1995): 595–654.

33. George B. Logan, "Recent Developments in Aeronautical Law (1934)," *Journal of Air Law* 5 (1934): 549. The final version of the *Restatement* provision included an expanded condition (a)—"for the purpose of travel through the air space or for any other legitimate purpose"—and a new condition (d)—"in conformity with such regulations of the State and federal aeronautical authorities as are in force in the particular State." *Restatement of the Law of Torts* sec. 194 (St. Paul: American Law Institute Publishers, 1934), 1:460.

34. William M. Wherry and Cyril Hyde Condon, "Air Travel and

Trespass," *United States Law Review* 68 (1934): 78–81; William M. Wherry and Cyril Hyde Condon, "Aerial Trespass under the Restatement of the Law of Torts," *Air Law Review* 6 (1935): 113.

35. *Gay v. Taylor,* 19 Pa. D. & C. 31 (1932).

36. *Thrasher v. City of Atlanta,* 173 S.E. 817 (Ga. 1934).

37. *Hinman v. Pacific Air Transport,* 84 F.2d 755 (9th Cir. 1936).

38. Clement L. Bouvé, "Private Ownership of Navigable Air Space under the Commerce Clause," *American Bar Association Journal* 21 (1935): 416.

39. *NLRB v. Jones & Laughlin Steel Corp.,* 301 U.S. 1 (1937); *Wickard v. Filburn,* 317 U.S. 111 (1942); 52 Stat. 973 (1938), sec. 3.

40. John M. Hunter, Jr., "The Conflicting Interests of Airport Owner and Nearby Property Owner," *Law and Contemporary Problems* 11 (1946): 548–549; *Burnham v. Beverly Airways,* 42 N.E.2d 575 (Mass. 1942); *Delta Air Corporation v. Kersey,* 20 S.E.2d 245 (Ga. 1942); *Vanderslice v. Shawn,* 27 A.2d 87 (Del. Ch. 1942); *Warren Township School District No. 7 v. City of Detroit,* 14 N.W.2d 134 (Mich. 1944).

41. William M. Allen, "The Right of Flight over Private Property," *Washington Law Review* 7 (1932): 274; Arthur S. Arnold, book review, *Temple Law Quarterly* 6 (1932): 296; James J. Hayden, "The New Deal in Airspace Rights," *Journal of Air Law and Commerce* 10 (1939): 166; John A. Eubank, "The Doctrine of the Airspace Zone of Effective Possession," *American Bar Association Journal* 18 (1932): 817.

42. "Aeronautics—Property Rights in the Air Column—Flight by Aircraft as Constituting Trespass or Nuisance," *Minnesota Law Review* 21 (1937): 584–585.

SEVEN: THE RISE AND FALL OF AIR LAW

1. W. Archibald McClean, "The Evolution of a Legal Sky Pilot," *Green Bag* 16 (1904): 468; *New York Times,* 6 Mar. 1910, SM6.

2. On aviation's shift from frontier-like adventure to routine business, see David T. Courtwright, *Sky as Frontier: Adventure, Aviation, and Empire* (College Station: Texas A&M University Press, 2005).

3. J. F. Lycklama à Nijeholt, *Air Sovereignty* (The Hague: Martinus Nijhoff, 1910); Harold D. Hazeltine, *The Law of the Air* (London: University of London Press, 1911); book review, *Harvard Law Review* 25 (1912): 486; book review, *American Journal of International Law* 6 (1912): 251; book review, *Columbia Law Review* 12 (1912): 94; Henry Woodhouse, *Textbook of Aerial Laws* (New York: Frederick A. Stokes Co., 1920); Rowland W. Fixel, *The Law of Aviation* (Albany: Matthew Bender, 1927); Carl Zollman, *Law of the Air* (Milwaukee: Bruce Publishing Co., 1927); Henry G. Hotchkiss, *A Treatise on Aviation Law* (New York: Baker, Voorhis and Co., 1928); W. Jefferson Davis, *Aeronautical Law* (Los Angeles: Parker, Stone and Baird, 1930), xv; Chester W. Cuthell, "Development of Aviation Laws in the United States," *Air Law Review* 1 (1930): 93.

4. W. Jefferson Davis, "Air Law—The New Field," *American Bar Association Journal* 15 (1929): 108; Edward A. Harriman to John H. Wigmore, 19 July 1929, Records of the Air Law Institute, box 1, folder 1, NUA; Rudolf Hirschberg, "The Liability of the Aviator to Third Persons," *Southern California Law Review* 2 (1929): 405; Raymond W. Clifford, "The Beginnings of a Law for the Air," *Washington Law Review* 7 (1932): 216.

5. John H. Wigmore, "The Value of an Air Law Institute," *Journal of Air Law* 1 (1930): 92.

6. *Air Law Institute Syllabus on Aeronautical Law* (Chicago: Air Law Institute, 1934).

7. *New York Times,* 2 June 1929, N3, and 10 Feb. 1930, 18.

8. *Los Angeles Times,* 1 Feb. 1930, A4.

9. Laura Kalman, *Legal Realism at Yale, 1927–1960* (Chapel Hill: University of North Carolina Press, 1986), 3–44; Herman Oliphant, "A Return to Stare Decisis," *American Bar Association Journal* 14 (1928): 160; Karl N. Llewellyn, "Some Realism about Realism—Responding to Dean Pound," *Harvard Law Review* 44 (1931): 1237, 1240.

10. Leon Green, *The Judicial Process in Tort Cases* (St. Paul: West Publishing Co., 1931); Harold Canfield Havighurst, *A Selection of Contract Cases and Related Quasi-Contract Cases* (Rochester: Lawyers Co-

operative Publishing Co., 1934); Myres S. McDougal, Harold D. Lasswell, and Ivan A. Vlasic, *Law and Public Order in Space* (New Haven: Yale University Press, 1963).

11. G. G. Depew, book review, *Yale Law Journal* 30 (1921): 315. Spad was a French aircraft manufacturer that produced biplanes used extensively in World War I.

12. Harold F. Mook, book review, *University of Pennsylvania Law Review* 78 (1930): 447.

13. Sayre MacNeil, book review, *Harvard Law Review* 43 (1930): 981–982.

14. Hazleton Mirkil, "A Summary, in the Light of the Cases, of the Law in Relation to Aeronautics," *Temple Law Quarterly* 4 (1930): 254; J. Byron McCormick, "Air Law," *Rocky Mountain Law Review* 1 (1929): 241.

15. Justin Miller to Fred Fagg, 23 Apr. 1930, Records of the Air Law Institute, box 1, folder 2, NUA; Louis Caldwell to Fred Fagg, 25 Apr. 1930, Records of the Air Law Institute, box 1, folder 2, NUA; Fred Fagg to George Mason, 1 July 1930, Records of the Air Law Institute, box 1, folder 2, NUA; Frederic Crossley to Fred Fagg, 9 July 1930, John Henry Wigmore Papers, box 19, folder 1, NUA; Fred Fagg to Alison Reppy, 24 July 1930, Records of the Air Law Institute, box 1, folder 2, NUA; Alison Reppy, "Announcement," *Air Law Review* 12 (1941): 371–372.

16. List of subscriptions, 30 Aug. 1929, John Henry Wigmore Papers, box 19, folder 1, NUA; Leon Green to Walter Dill Scott and William A. Dyche, 11 Oct. 1932, Leon Green Papers, box 16, folder 3, NUA; Budgets, ca. 1937–1938, Leon Green Papers, box 16, folder 4, NUA; Edward C. Sweeney, "Air Law, Research and the University," *Journal of Air Law and Commerce* 16 (1949): 326; John H. Wigmore to Mrs. Stuart G. Tipton, 29 Apr. 1938, John Henry Wigmore Papers, box 19, folder 2, NUA; Leon Green to Franklyn B. Snyder, 1 Aug. 1939, Leon Green Papers, box 16, folder 3, NUA; Leon Green to Ralph K. Ball, 11 Nov. 1939, Leon Green Papers, box 16, folder 3, NUA; John Wigmore to Fred Fagg, 16 Jan. 1941, John Henry Wigmore Papers, box 19, folder 2, NUA.

17. J. H. Wigmore, "The Journal of Air Law and Commerce," *Journal of Air Law and Commerce* 10 (1939): 74; Fred Fagg to Franklyn B. Snyder, 5 Aug. 1938, Leon Green Papers, box 16, folder 3, NUA; Fred Fagg to Franklyn B. Snyder, 8 Nov. 1938, Leon Green Papers, box 16, folder 3, NUA; Franklin M. Kreml, "Publisher's Announcement," *Journal of Air Law and Commerce* 27 (1960): 331.

18. John C. Cooper, "Aviation Law Comes Home to the Main Street Lawyer," *Law and Contemporary Problems* 11 (1946): 556.

19. Stephen E. Doyle, "An American Aerospace Law Institute," *American Journal of International Law* 59 (1965): 913.

20. John A. Eubank, "Judicial Determination of Rights in Airspace," *Dickinson Law Review* 51 (1947): 161n; http://www.abanet.org/forums/airspace/home.html.

21. Richard J. Lazarus, *The Making of Environmental Law* (Chicago: University of Chicago Press, 2004).

22. Alan Heinrich, Karl Manheim, and David J. Steele, "At the Crossroads of Law and Technology," *Loyola of Los Angeles Law Review* 33 (2000): 1048; Lawrence Lessig, "The Law of the Horse: What Cyberlaw Might Teach," *Harvard Law Review* 113 (1999): 502.

23. Frank H. Easterbrook, "Cyberspace and the Law of the Horse," *University of Chicago Legal Forum* (1996): 207–216; Joan S. Howland, "Let's Not 'Spit the Bit': In Defense of 'The Law of the Horse'—The Historical and Legal Development of American Thoroughbred Racing," *Marquette Sports Law Review* 14 (2004): 475.

EIGHT: WILLIAM DOUGLAS HAS THE LAST WORD

1. Information about the *Causby* case comes from the Transcript of Record filed in the Supreme Court, which is in the electronic database *U.S. Supreme Court Records and Briefs, 1832–1978,* available at www.gale.com.

2. *Army Air Forces Statistical Digest* (n.p.: Office of Statistical Control, 1945), 311.

3. Morton J. Horwitz, *The Transformation of American Law, 1780–*

1860 (Cambridge: Harvard University Press, 1977), 63–66; William Michael Treanor, "The Origins and Original Significance of the Just Compensation Clause of the Fifth Amendment," *Yale Law Journal* 94 (1985): 694–716; James W. Ely, "'That Due Satisfaction May Be Made': The Fifth Amendment and the Origins of the Compensation Principle," *American Journal of Legal History* 36 (1992): 1–18; *Pumpelly v. Green Bay Co.,* 80 U.S. 166, 177–178 (1871); *Jacobs v. United States,* 290 U.S. 13 (1933); *Hurley v. Kincaid,* 285 U.S. 267 (1932).

4. *Peabody v. United States,* 46 Ct. Cl. 39 (1911).

5. *Peabody v. United States,* 231 U.S. 530 (1913); *Portsmouth Harbor Land & Hotel Co. v. United States,* 250 U.S. 1 (1919); *Portsmouth Harbor Land & Hotel Co. v. United States,* 260 U.S. 327 (1922). Back in the Court of Claims, the owner of the hotel could not prove that the government had fired very many missiles across the land or intended to fire any more, so the petition was dismissed. 64 Ct. Cl. 572 (1928).

6. Brief for Appellants, *Portsmouth Harbor Land & Hotel Co. v. United States,* 260 U.S. 327 (1922), 1, 7.

7. *Causby v. United States,* 104 Ct. Cl. 342 (1945).

8. Petition for a Writ of Certiorari, *United States v. Causby,* 328 U.S. 256 (1946).

9. Notes on certiorari petition, *United States v. Causby,* William O. Douglas Papers, box 136, LC; notes on certiorari petition, *United States v. Causby,* Wiley Rutledge Papers, box 140, LC.

10. *Northwest Airlines, Inc. v. Minnesota,* 322 U.S. 292, 302–303 (1944).

11. Bruce Allen Murphy, *Wild Bill: The Legend and Life of William O. Douglas* (New York: Random House, 2003), 32–33, 508–510.

12. Then again, the most comprehensive study of the effect of war on Supreme Court decisions suggests that the existence of war has had no effect on war-related cases like *Causby.* Lee Epstein, Daniel E. Ho, Gary King, and Jeffrey A. Segal, "The Supreme Court during Crisis: How War Affects Only Non-War Cases," *New York University Law Review* 80 (2005): 1–116.

13. Brief for the United States, *United States v. Causby,* 328 U.S. 256 (1946).

14. Jeremy Bentham, *Principles of the Civil Code* (Edinburgh: W. Tait, 1843), 308–309.

15. Frédéric Bastiat, "Property and Law" (1848), in Frédéric Bastiat, *Selected Essays on Political Economy,* trans. Seymour Cain, ed. George B. de Huszar (Irvington-on-Hudson, N.Y.: Foundation for Economic Education, 1964), 97–99.

16. Thomas W. Merrill, "The Landscape of Constitutional Property," *Virginia Law Review* 86 (2000): 885–999; *United States v. Powelson,* 319 U.S. 266, 279 (1943); *Webb's Fabulous Pharmacies v. Beckwith,* 449 U.S. 155, 164 (1980); Bruce A. Ackerman, *Private Property and the Constitution* (New Haven: Yale University Press, 1977), 113–167.

17. My account of the conference is drawn from the notes taken by Douglas and Rutledge. William O. Douglas Papers, box 136, LC; Wiley Rutledge Papers, box 140, LC. In some of the quotations I have expanded abbreviations and inserted missing words to form complete sentences.

18. James F. Simon, *Independent Journey: The Life of William O. Douglas* (New York: Harper and Row, 1980), 353–354.

19. *United States v. Causby,* 328 U.S. 256 (1946).

20. Because this part of the opinion firmly rejects the *cujus est solum* maxim, *Causby* is sometimes misunderstood as a victory for aviators over landowners. See, for example, Lawrence Lessig, *Free Culture* (New York: Penguin, 2004), 2–3. Aviators had already won that battle by the 1940s, however. The only dispute left was whether landowners had *any* property rights in the lower airspace, and on that question, *Causby* was a victory for landowners.

21. *Griggs v. County of Allegheny,* 369 U.S. 84 (1962).

22. *Smith v. New England Aircraft Company,* 170 N.E. 385 (Mass. 1930); *Swetland v. Curtiss Airports Corporation,* 55 F.2d 201 (6th Cir. 1932); *Gay v. Taylor,* 19 Pa. D. & C. 31 (1932).

23. Lee Epstein, Jeffrey A. Segal, Harold J. Spaeth, and Thomas G.

Walker, *The Supreme Court Compendium: Data, Decisions, and Developments,* 3rd ed. (Washington, D.C.: CQ Press, 2003), 216–220; Thomas G. Walker, Lee Epstein, and William J. Dixon, "On the Mysterious Demise of Consensual Norms in the United States Supreme Court," *Journal of Politics* 50 (1988): 361–389.

24. *New York Times,* 28 May 1946, 35; *Causby v. United States,* 75 F. Supp. 262 (Ct. Cl. 1948).

25. Dix W. Noel, "Airports and Their Neighbors," *Tennessee Law Review* 19 (1946): 563; "Airspace Rights of the Subjacent Landowner," *Arkansas Law Review* 2 (1948): 453; Richard H. Munsterman, "Air Law—Continued Low Flights by Aircraft Constitutes Taking of Property," *Nebraska Law Review* 26 (1946): 123; "A New Theory for the Protection of the Landowner against Injury by the Aviator," *Illinois Law Review* 41 (1946): 564; Robert A. Mace, "Ownership of Airspace," *University of Cincinnati Law Review* 17 (1948): 366; John A. Eubank, "Judicial Determination of Rights in Airspace," *Dickinson Law Review* 51 (1947): 167; Lowell White, "Trespass and Nuisance as Related to Future Development of Aviation," *Insurance Counsel Journal* 15 (1948): 53.

26. James D. Hill, "Liability for Aircraft Noise—The Aftermath of *Causby* and *Griggs,*" *University of Miami Law Review* 19 (1964): 19–20; Terrence J. Benshoof, "Air Law—The Memory Lingers On: *Ad Coelum* in the 1970's—Some New Approaches," *DePaul Law Review* 20 (1971): 534–541; Gerald L. Hallworth, "Judicial Legislation in Airport Litigation—A Blessing or Danger?" *Notre Dame Lawyer* 39 (1964): 418; Federal Aviation Act of 1958, 72 Stat. 731, 739 (1958); *Griggs v. County of Allegheny,* 369 U.S. 84 (1962).

27. William B. Harvey, "Landowners' Rights in the Air Age: The Airport Dilemma," *Michigan Law Review* 56 (1958): 1313–32; Roderick B. Anderson, "Some Aspects of Airspace Trespass," *Journal of Air Law and Commerce* 27 (1960): 341–359; Richard A. Repp, "Wrongs and Rights in the Superterraneous Airspace: *Causby* and the Courts," *William and Mary Law Review* 9 (1967): 460–475; Robert R. Wright, *The Law of Airspace* (Indianapolis: Bobbs-Merrill, 1968), 207; Colin

Cahoon, "Low Altitude Airspace: A Property Rights No-Man's Land," *Journal of Air Law and Commerce* 56 (1990): 197.

NINE: SOVEREIGNTY IN SPACE

1. Ivan A. Vlasic, foreword, in John Cobb Cooper, *Explorations in Aerospace Law* (Montreal: McGill University Press, 1968), ix–xi.

2. John C. Cooper, "High Altitude Flight and National Sovereignty," *International Law Quarterly* 4 (1951): 411–418.

3. Walter A. McDougall, . . *The Heavens and the Earth: A Political History of the Space Age* (1985; Baltimore: Johns Hopkins University Press, 1997), 108–110.

4. Oscar Schachter, "Who Owns the Universe?" *Collier's*, 22 Mar. 1952, 36; *New York Times*, 30 July 1955, 9; "Sovereignty in Space," *Newsweek*, 19 Dec. 1955, 82; "Who Owns the Unknown?" *Economist*, 1 Sept. 1956, 727; "What Flags for Space?" *Manchester Guardian Weekly*, 20 Sept. 1956, 9; Willy Ley, "Who'll Own the Planets?" *Galaxy*, May 1957, 51; "Who Owns the Moon?" *Saturday Review*, 7 Dec. 1957, 32; Sir Leslie Munro, "Law for the 'Heav'n's Pathless Way,'" *New York Times*, 16 Feb. 1958, SM82; Donald Cox and Michael Stoiko, *Spacepower: What It Means to You* (Philadelphia: John C. Winston, 1958), 154.

5. William R. Sheeley, "Remarks on Space Law," *Alabama Lawyer* 17 (1956): 370–375; John C. Hogan, "Legal Terminology for the Upper Regions of the Atmosphere and for the Space beyond the Atmosphere," *American Journal of International Law* 51 (1957): 362–375; Frank Simpson III, *Space Law and the Practicing Attorney* (n.p., 1958), 1–2; Michael Aaronson, "Earth Satellites and the Law," *Law Times* 220 (1955): 116.

6. Ming-Min Peng, "Le Vol à Haute Altitude et l'Article 1 de la Convention de Chicago, 1944," *Revue du Barreau* 12 (1952): 285; R. C. Hingorani, "An Attempt to Determine Sovereignty in Upper Space," *University of Kansas City Law Review* 26 (1957): 11; Arnold W. Knauth, *Legal Problems of Outer Space in Relation to the United Nations* (New York: Hecla Press, 1958), 7–8; *New York Times*, 24 Feb. 1958, 18.

7. Andrew E. Haley, "Space Law—Basic Concepts," *Tennessee Law Review* 24 (1956): 643–657; D. Broward Craig, "National Sovereignty at High Altitudes," *Journal of Air Law and Commerce* 24 (1957): 384–397; Stephen Gorove, "On the Threshold of Space: Toward a Cosmic Law," *New York Law Forum* 4 (1958): 305–328; Stephen Latchford, "The Bearing of International Air Navigation Conventions on the Use of Outer Space," *American Journal of International Law* 53 (1959): 407–408; C. E. S. Horford, "The Law of Space" (1955), in *Legal Problems of Space Exploration*, S. Doc. No. 26, 87th Cong., 1st Sess. (1961), 21–22; Oscar Svarlien, "Legal Problems in the Extra-Terrestrial Age," *University of Florida Law Review* 12 (1959): 14; H. B. Jacobini, "Problems of High Altitude or Space Jurisdiction," *Western Political Quarterly* 6 (1953): 682; H. B. Jacobini, "Effective Control as Related to the Extension of Sovereignty in Space," *Journal of Public Law* 7 (1958): 115.

8. Alex Meyer, "Legal Problems of Flight into the Outer Space" (1952), in *Legal Problems of Space Exploration*, 13; Welf Heinrich, "Air Law and Space," *St. Louis University Law Journal* 5 (1958): 59.

9. C. Wilfred Jenks, "International Law and Activities in Space," *International and Comparative Law Quarterly* 5 (1956): 103–104; "International Air Law," *American Society of International Law Proceedings* 50 (1956): 96; G. Vernon Leopold and Allison L. Scafuri, "Orbital and Super-Orbital Space Flight Trajectories—Jurisdictional Touchstones for a United Nations Space Authority," *University of Detroit Law Journal* 36 (1959): 519; Karl. W. Deutsch, "On Outer Space and International Politics," in *International Political Implications of Activities in Outer Space* (Santa Monica, Calif.: RAND Corporation, 1960), 173; Chester Ward, "Projecting the Law of the Sea into the Law of Space," *JAG Journal*, Mar. 1957, 5.

10. Oscar Schachter, "Legal Aspects of Space Travel," *Journal of the British Interplanetary Society*, 11 (1952): 14.

11. Eugène Pépin, "The Legal Status of the Airspace in the Light of Progress in Aviation and Astronautics," *McGill Law Journal* 3 (1956): 72; "Where Does Space Begin?" *Science Digest*, Jan. 1958, 97; Michael

Aaronson, "Space Law," *International Relations* 1 (1958): 420; Albert I. Moon, Jr., "A Look at Airspace Sovereignty," *Journal of Air Law and Commerce* 29 (1963): 344; *Draft Code of Rules on the Exploration and Uses of Outer Space* (London: David Davies Memorial Institute of International Studies, 1962), 7; D. H. N. Johnson, *Rights in Air Space* (Manchester: Manchester University Press, 1965), 61; *Wall Street Journal*, 20 Jan. 1958, 1; Andrew G. Haley, *Space Law and Government* (New York: Appleton-Century-Crofts, 1963), 78; Martin Menter, *Astronautical Law* (Washington, D.C.: Industrial College of the Armed Forces, 1959), 27.

12. Hal H. Bookout, "Conflicting Sovereignty Interests in Outer Space: Proposed Solutions Remain in Orbit!" *Military Law Review* 7 (1960): 37; Leon Lipson and Nicholas deB. Katzenbach, *Report to the National Aeronautics and Space Administration on the Law of Outer Space* (Chicago: American Bar Foundation, 1961), 14; Joe C. Savage, "Legal Control of Outer Space," *Kentucky Law Journal* 52 (1964): 409–410; Nicholas Katzenbach, "Law and Lawyers in Space," *Bulletin of the Atomic Scientists* 14 (1958): 220; William Hildred and Frederick Tymms, "The Case against National Sovereignty in Space," *The Aeroplane*, 23 May 1958, 712–714.

13. Philip C. Jessup and Howard J. Taubenfeld, *Controls for Outer Space and the Antarctic Analogy* (New York: Columbia University Press, 1959), 208; Nicolas Mateesco Matte, *Aerospace Law* (London: Sweet and Maxwell, 1969), 62; Robert D. Crane, *Planning for Space Legal Policy* (New York: American Rocket Society, 1961), 9.

14. Felix S. Cohen, "Transcendental Nonsense and the Functional Approach," *Columbia Law Review* 35 (1935): 809; Myres S. McDougal, "The Prospects for a Regime in Outer Space," in Maxwell Cohen, ed., *Law and Politics in Space* (Montreal: McGill University Press, 1964), 117–118; Spencer M. Beresford, "The Future of National Sovereignty," in Andrew G. Haley and Welf Heinrich, eds., *Second Colloquium on the Law of Outer Space* (Vienna: Springer-Verlag, 1960), 8–9; F. B. Shick, "Space Law and Space Politics," *International and Comparative Law Quarterly* 10 (1961): 693; Modesto Seara Vázquez, *Cosmic International*

Law, trans. Elaine Malley (Detroit: Wayne State University Press, 1965), 41; J. E. S. Fawcett, *International Law and the Uses of Outer Space* (Manchester: Manchester University Press, 1968), 20–21.

15. J. F. McMahon, "The Legal Aspects of Outer Space: The Problem of Sovereignty," *World Today* 18 (1962): 329; John A. Johnson, "Freedom and Control in Outer Space," in Mortimer D. Schwartz, ed., *Proceedings of the Conference on Space Science and Space Law* (South Hackensack, N.J.: Fred B. Rothman, 1964), 141.

16. Matt Bille and Erika Lishock, *The First Space Race: Launching the World's First Satellites* (College Station: Texas A&M University Press, 2004); Myres S. McDougal and Leon Lipson, "Perspectives for a Law of Outer Space," *American Journal of International Law* 52 (1958): 417–421; Myres S. McDougal, Harold Lasswell, and Ivan A. Vlasic, *Law and Public Order in Space* (New Haven: Yale University Press, 1963), 281.

17. Eugène Pépin, "Space Penetration," *American Society of International Law Proceedings* 52 (1958): 232; Philip W. Quigg, "Open Skies and Open Space," *Foreign Affairs* 37 (1958): 96–97; Richard T. Murphy, Jr., "Air Sovereignty Considerations in Terms of Outer Space," *Alabama Lawyer* 19 (1958): 11; Morton S. Jaffe, "Some Considerations in the International Law and Politics of Space," *St. Louis University Law Journal* 5 (1959): 379.

18. Delbert R. Terrill, Jr., *The Air Force Role in Developing International Outer Space Law* (Maxwell Air Force Base, Ala.: Air University Press, 1999), 19–62; Loftus Becker, "Major Aspects of the Problem of Outer Space," *Department of State Bulletin* 38 (1958): 966–967.

19. *Astronautics and Space Exploration: Hearings before the Select Committee on Astronautics and Space Exploration* (Washington, D.C.: Government Printing Office, 1958), 1286.

20. *International Control of Outer Space: Hearings before the Committee on Science and Astronautics* (Washington, D.C.: Government Printing Office, 1959), 90–92.

21. Robert D. Crane, "Soviet Attitude toward International Space Law," *American Journal of International Law* 56 (1962): 686–692; Sam-

uel Kucherov, "Legal Problems of Outer Space: U.S.A. and Soviet Viewpoints," in Haley and Heinrich, *Second Colloquium,* 66–68.

22. Curtis Peebles, *The Moby Dick Project: Reconnaissance Balloons over Russia* (Washington, D.C.: Smithsonian Institution Press, 1991).

23. *New York Times,* 6 Feb. 1956, 1; A. Kislov and S. Krylov, "State Sovereignty in Airspace" (1956), in *Legal Problems of Space Exploration,* 1040–41, 1045.

24. *New York Times,* 8 Feb. 1956, 10.

25. Bin Cheng, "International Law and High Altitude Flights: Balloons, Rockets and Man-Made Satellites," *International and Comparative Law Quarterly* 6 (1957): 489.

26. "Outer Space: Dividing Nothing by Ninety," *Economist,* 26 Oct. 1957, 293; "Space: Who Owns It, Anyway?" *Maclean's,* 18 Jan. 1958, 13.

27. G. Zadorozhnyi, "The Artificial Satellite and International Law" (1957), in *Legal Problems of Space Exploration,* 1049; Michael Aaronson, "Aspects of the Law of Space," *Law Times* 224 (1957): 220; F. J. Krieger and J. R. Thomas, *Translations of Two Soviet Articles on Law and Order in Outer Space* (Santa Monica, Calif.: RAND Corporation, 1958), 5–6.

28. *Los Angeles Times,* 20 Nov. 1957, 17; Andrew G. Haley, "Law of Outer Space—A Problem for International Agreement," *American University Law Review* 7 (1958): 75; C. G. Fenwick, "How High Is the Sky?" *American Journal of International Law* 52 (1958): 98; Eugène Pépin, "Legal Problems Created by the Sputnik," *McGill Law Journal* 4 (1957): 67; Philip B. Yeager and John R. Stark, "Decatur's 'Doctrine'—A Code for Outer Space?" *U.S. Naval Institute Proceedings* 83 (1957): 936; McDougall, *Heavens and the Earth,* 120.

29. George J. Feldman, "An American View of Jurisdiction in Outer Space," in *Legal Problems of Space Exploration,* 457–458; Oscar Schachter, "Warning: Early Unilateral Positions," *New York County Lawyers Association Bar Bulletin* 16 (1958): 33; "Report of the Committee on Law of Outer Space—Recommendations: 1959," in *Legal Problems of Space Exploration,* 581.

30. *New York Times,* 14 Sept. 1959, 1, and 15 Sept. 1959, 20.

31. "What Are the Rights of High Flight?" *Time,* 23 May 1960; Jerome Morenoff, *World Peace through Space Law* (Charlottesville, Va.: Michie, 1967), 127–128; Quincy Wright, "Legal Aspects of the U-2 Incident," *American Journal of International Law* 54 (1960): 847; "Legal Aspects of Reconnaissance in Airspace and Outer Space," *Columbia Law Review* 61 (1961): 1085–86; David Christopher Arnold, *Spying from Space: Constructing America's Satellite Command and Control Systems* (College Station: Texas A&M University Press, 2005).

32. "National Sovereignty of Outer Space," *Harvard Law Review* 74 (1961): 1167–68; Gyula Gál, *Space Law* (Leyden: A. W. Sijthoff, 1969), 98–104.

33. Morton S. Jaffe, "Reliance upon International Custom and General Principles in the Growth of Space Law," *St. Louis University Law Journal* 7 (1962): 130–133.

34. S. Houston Lay and Howard J. Taubenfield, *The Law Relating to the Activities of Man in Space* (Chicago: University of Chicago Press, 1970), 40; Dag Hammarskjold, "The United Nations and Outer Space" (1958), in *Legal Problems of Space Exploration,* 263.

35. *Legal Problems of Space Exploration,* 1270.

36. C. Wilfred Jenks, *Space Law* (New York: Frederick A. Praeger, 1965), 7; Abram Chayes, "International Organization and Space," in *Proceedings of the Conference on the Law of Space and of Satellite Communications* (Washington, D.C.: National Aeronautics and Space Administration, 1964), 60.

37. Rita Taubenfeld and Howard J. Taubenfeld, *Man and Space: Politics, Law, Organization* (Dallas: Arnold Foundation, 1964), 17–18; Nicolas Mateesco Matte, ed., *Space Activities and Emerging International Law* (Montreal: McGill University Center for Research of Air and Space Law, 1984), 224–226.

38. Paul G. Dembling and Daniel M. Arons, "The Evolution of the Outer Space Treaty," *Journal of Air Law and Commerce* 33 (1967): 419–456.

39. The treaty can be found at, among other places, www.state.gov/t

/ac/trt/5181.htm. Treaties have the status of international law, but resolutions of the General Assembly do not.

40. Imre Anthony Csabafi, *The Concept of State Jurisdiction in International Space Law* (The Hague: Martinus Nijhoff, 1971), 117; *Treaty on Outer Space: Hearings before the Committee on Foreign Relations, United States Senate* (Washington, D.C.: Government Printing Office, 1967), 17.

41. Katrin Nyman Metcalf, *Activities in Space—Appropriation or Use?* (Uppsala: Iustus Förlag, 1999), 67; S. Neil Hosenball and Jefferson S. Hofgard, "Delimitation of Air Space and Outer Space: Is a Boundary Needed Now?" *University of Colorado Law Review* 57 (1986): 892; E. R. C. van Bogaert, *Aspects of Space Law* (Antwerp: Kluwer Law and Taxation, 1986), 11; J. E. S. Fawcett, *Outer Space: New Challenges to Law and Policy* (Oxford: Clarendon Press, 1984), 17; Manfred Lachs, *The Law of Outer Space: An Experience in Contemporary Law-Making* (Leiden: Sijthoff, 1972), 58; Irvin L. White, *Decision-Making for Space: Law and Politics in Air, Sea, and Outer Space* (West Lafayette, Ind.: Purdue University Studies, 1970), 193.

42. P. P. C. Haanappel, *The Law and Policy of Air Space and Outer Space: A Comparative Approach* (The Hague: Kluwer Law International, 2003), 27; Stephen Gorove, "The Geostationary Orbit: Issues of Law and Policy," *American Journal of International Law* 73 (1979): 444–461.

TEN: TECHNOLOGICAL CHANGE AND LEGAL CHANGE

1. Harold Demsetz, "Toward a Theory of Property Rights," *American Economic Review Papers and Proceedings* 57 (1967): 347–359.

2. R. H. Coase, "The Problem of Social Cost," *Journal of Law and Economics* 3 (1960): 1–44.

3. Merritt Roe Smith and Leo Marx, eds., *Does Technology Drive History? The Dilemma of Technological Determinism* (Cambridge: MIT Press, 1994).

I'd like to thank the librarians at UCLA, Yale, Northwestern, the Library of Congress, and the Herbert Hoover Presidential Library for help with the research. Thanks also to Joyce Seltzer, Wendy Nelson, John Witt, and an anonymous referee for some very helpful suggestions. For advice on drafts of chapters, thanks to Rick Abel, Barry Cushman, Gary Rowe, Rick Sander, Clyde Spillenger, and participants in workshops at UCLA, Tel Aviv University, and the annual meeting of the Law and Society Association. For research funding I am grateful to Mike Schill and the UCLA Academic Senate.